Yale Agrarian Studies Series
James C. Scott, series editor

TOIL AND PLENTY

*Images of the
Agricultural Landscape
in England, 1780–1890*

Christiana Payne

Yale Center for British Art

Yale University Press
New Haven and London

Published in conjunction with the exhibition
*Toil and Plenty: Images of the Agricultural Landscape
in England, 1780–1890*, organized by the
Nottingham University Art Gallery and the
Yale Center for British Art.

Nottingham University Art Gallery
7 October–14 November 1993

Yale Center for British Art
15 January–13 March 1994

The exhibition at Nottingham is made possible
by grants from Booker Countryside and from
Heygate and Sons Ltd., Northampton. The exhibition at Yale is made possible by the generous
support of the National Endowment for the Humanities, a Federal agency.

Published with assistance from the foundation
established in memory of Philip Hamilton
McMillan of the Class of 1894, Yale College.

Set in Janson type by The Composing Room of
Michigan, Grand Rapids, Michigan.

Printed in the United States of America by
Thomson-Shore, Inc., Dexter, Michigan.

Library of Congress Cataloging-in-Publication
Data

Payne, Christiana.
Toil and plenty : images of the agricultural landscape in England, 1780–1890 / Christiana Payne.
p.   cm. — (Yale agrarian studies)
"Nottingham University Art Gallery, 7 October–
14 November 1993;
Yale Center for British Art, 15 January–13 March
1994"—T.p. verso. Includes bibliographical references and index.
ISBN 0-300-05773-3
1. Landscape painting, English—Exhibitions.
2. Landscape painting—18th century—England—
Exhibitions.   3. Landscape painting—19th
century—England—Exhibitions.   4. Agriculture
in art—Exhibitions.   I. Nottingham University
Art Gallery.   II. Yale Center for British Art.
III. Title.   IV. Series.
ND1354.4.P39   1993
758′.142′09420747468—dc20   93-13885 CIP

A catalogue record for this book is available from
the British Library.

The paper in this book meets the guidelines for
permanence and durability of the Committee on
Production Guidelines for Book Longevity of the
Council on Library Resources.

10 9 8 7 6 5 4 3 2 1

Contents

Directors' Foreword

In 1830 William Cobbett wrote of the Suffolk landscape that "you can, in no direction, go . . . a quarter of a mile without finding views a painter might crave and . . . the country round about it so well cultivated . . . the ploughman so expert." He referred, of course, to the landscape of Gainsborough and Constable, already rich in pictorial associations which have continued to resonate, to the point of cliché, down to the present. It is only in the last few years, however, that art historians have turned their attention from the cravings of painters to the expertise of ploughmen— only to discover that Constable, for one, was possessed of a far more intimate knowledge of what he painted than the urban reporter Cobbett could pick up in the course of his *Rural Rides*. From this company of recent scholars we are fortunate to have enlisted Christiana Payne, whose interest is in both sides of the coin: the painted landscape and what it contains of agriculture and its social implications. She focuses upon a period of profound change in the later eighteenth and early nineteenth centuries, when improvements in farming methods coincided with the growth of an urban population detached from the land. Her thesis is demonstrated by means of this extraordinary exhibition, which she has selected and catalogued.

For his encouragement of the project in its initial stages we are grateful to Nicholas Alfrey of Nottingham University. Dr. Payne's own acknowledgments follow; we would like to endorse these and to reinforce her thanks to our colleagues in Nottingham and New Haven. We take great satisfaction in this exhibition, which pools the skills and resources available to our two university art museums. It emerges from research encouraged by both, and it is designed to engage an array of scholars on both sides of the Atlantic in debate. At Yale we welcome especially the involvement of the Program in Agrarian Studies and its director, James C. Scott. We are also grateful to Yale University Press for undertaking to publish the catalogue.

No exhibition on this scale is possible without the generous support of lenders, both public and private. Of the latter, many prefer to remain anonymous, but even so, credits in the catalogue entries make plain our dependence upon a large number of individuals and institutions. The exhibition at Nottingham is made possible by grants from Booker Countryside and from Heygate and Sons Ltd., Northampton. At Yale, both the exhibition and its related programs are dependent upon the generous support of the National Endowment for the Humanities. To all of the above, we express sincere thanks.

Duncan Robinson, Director
Yale Center for British Art

Joanne Wright, Director
Nottingham University Art Gallery

Acknowledgments

While researching this book and selecting and cataloguing the works in this exhibition, I have received generous help from a great many individuals and institutions. Professor Michael Kitson, who supervised my thesis at the Courtauld Institute of Art, London University, has been a continuing source of inspiration and practical advice. Nicholas Alfrey of the University of Nottingham recognised the theme's potential for an exhibition and, with Joanne Wright, Director of the University Art Gallery, was the first to give it firm backing. The enthusiasm of Duncan Robinson, Director of the Yale Center for British Art, ensured the project's expansion and eventual realisation.

I am grateful to all the staff at both galleries, who have worked so hard on the practical details of the exhibition: Tracey Isgar at Nottingham, and Barbara Allen, Elizabeth Anscombe, Suzanne Beebe, Richard Caspole, Susan Casteras, Cecie Clement, Theresa Fairbanks, Chris Foster, Timothy Goodhue, Marilyn Hunt, Richard Johnson, Julie Lavorgna, David Mills, Patrick Noon, Sammy Redd, Maria Rossi and Lorelei Watson at Yale. Particular mention should be made of Liz Reintjes at Nottingham and Elisabeth Fairman, Beth Miller, and Scott Wilcox at Yale, for their exceptional commitment and dedication.

Special thanks are due to all the lenders who have generously agreed to part with their pictures for several months to make the exhibition possible. I would also like to thank, for their help with my research, Reginald Alton, Chris Beetles, Judith Bronkhurst, Joan Linnell Burton, Jane Cunningham, Robert Dimsdale, Martyn Gregory, Christopher Gridley, Robin Hamlyn, Michael Hickox, Anne Lyles, Eunice Martin, Bernadette Nelson, Christopher Newall, Felicity Owen, Leslie Parris, Francis Russell, Susan Sloman, Sam Smiles, Julian Treuherz, Henry Wemyss, Catherine Whistler, and Linda Whiteley. My colleagues at Oxford Brookes University and the Open University (especially Lizzie Howe) have given me valuable support and encouragement.

Nicholas Alfrey, Matthew Cragoe, Duncan Robinson, Michael Rosenthal, Professor James Scott, Sadie Ward, and Scott Wilcox kindly read drafts of the book and provided much useful advice. Judy Metro and Richard Miller at Yale University Press edited it efficiently and sympathetically.

My greatest debt is to my family, and particularly to my husband Giles and my daughter Charlotte. Their enthusiasm for *Toil and Plenty* has never failed, even under the pressure of lengthy transatlantic telephone calls at bedtime.

Lenders to the Exhibition

The Visitors of the Ashmolean Museum, Oxford

The Lord Barnard, Raby Castle

Birmingham Museums and Art Gallery

Bristol Museums and Art Gallery

Trustees of the British Museum, London

Government Art Collection of the United Kingdom

Hereford City Library

Holburne Museum and Crafts Study Centre, Bath

Hulton Deutsch Collection, London

Ipswich Borough Council Museums and Galleries

Leicestershire Museums and Art Gallery

Lincolnshire County Council, Usher Gallery, Lincoln

Maidstone Museum and Art Gallery

Trustees of the National Museums and Galleries on Merseyside. Lady Lever
Art Gallery, Port Sunlight, and Walker Art Gallery, Liverpool

Christopher and Jenny Newall

His Grace the Duke of Norfolk

Norfolk Museums Service (Norwich Castle Museum)

Norwich Central Library

Oxford City Library

Private collections

Richmond Gallery, Cork Street, London

Rural History Centre, University of Reading

Suffolk Record Office

Tate Gallery, London

Tullie House, City Museum and Art Gallery, Carlisle

The Board of Trustees of the Victoria and Albert Museum, London

Victoria Art Gallery, Bath City Council

Virginia Museum of Fine Arts, Richmond

Whitworth Art Gallery, University of Manchester

Yale Center for British Art, New Haven

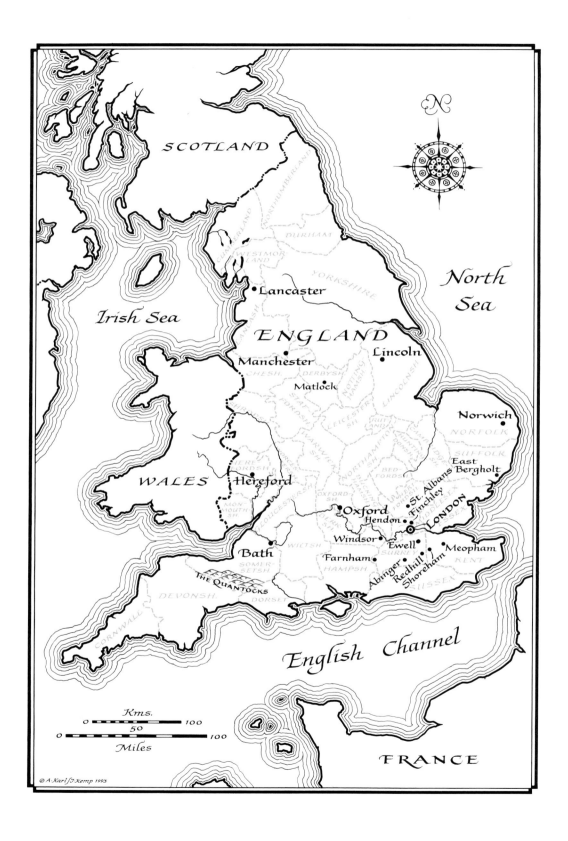

SCOTLAND

North
Sea

Irish Sea

•Lancaster

ENGLAND

Lincoln•

•Manchester

Matlock•

Norwich•

WALES

Hereford•

East
Bergholt•

Oxford•
Hendon•

St. Albans•
•Finchley

LONDON

Windsor•

Ewell•

•Meopham

Bath•

Farnham•

Abinger•

Redhill•

Shoreham•

THE QUANTOCKS

English Channel

Kms.
0 —•—•—•—•— 100
50
0 —•—•—•—•— 100
Miles

FRANCE

© A.Karl/J.Kemp 1993

Introduction

Artistic renderings of nineteenth-century agricultural life in Britain are both appealing and
fascinating to the modern viewer: fascinating
because the traditional agricultural processes
they represent are so remote from our experience; appealing because so many of them con-
vey a vision of a peaceful, bountiful, unchang-
ing landscape possessing aesthetic advantages
that are unmatched by modern agriculture.
The crowded fields of nineteenth-century
harvests and the participation of women, children and horses provided a degree of variety,
and references to artistic precedents, with
which the solitary farmworker driving a large
machine can hardly compete. In comparison
with the stook-studded fields and the hay-
stacks and cornricks of the past, even the modern agricultural landscape itself is relatively
monotonous.

Aesthetic considerations, however, can
easily become entangled with moral ones. Today, as in the nineteenth century, scenes of
traditional agriculture may appeal to nostalgic
regrets for a preindustrial, unpolluted world,
perhaps even for a world of social harmony
and stability associated with childhood, holidays, and escapist retreat from the stresses of
urban life. An element of myth pervaded
nineteenth-century attitudes to the country-

side, and our own attitudes are undoubtedly affected by similar myths. It is important to remember the background of poverty, distress, hard labour and class conflict that lay behind these apparently idyllic scenes, and to be aware that, beautiful as they undoubtedly are, they are not a simple reflection of some lost golden age of rural happiness.

Despite the apparent continuity in the look of the countryside, the period from 1780 to 1890 was one of deep social, political and economic change. It was in this era that Britain was transformed from an agricultural to an industrial nation. Its population shifted decisively from the country to the towns, and important political battles were fought, and lost, by the landed interest over the Great Reform Act and the repeal of the Corn Laws.[1] By the end of the nineteenth century the agricultural labourer had won the right to vote, and his children were now entitled to primary education. Throughout the period the farm labourer was widely recognised as the victim, not only of poverty, but also of injustice, particularly as a result of enclosure, the Game Laws and the new Poor Law. Discontent, whether expressed through arson or, later on, through union activity, was a constant feature of rural life. The appearance of stability and harmony in the paintings, then, should not be taken at face value.

The period spans the interval between two important contributions to the genre of agricultural landscape painting: the first versions of George Stubbs's *Haymakers* and *Reapers* in the early 1780s and the paintings done by George Clausen in the early 1880s. An additional reason for choosing 1890 as the cutoff point is that it was at about this time that the traditional agricultural processes became outdated (although it was only many years later that they died out altogether). Nowadays artists produce paintings of horse ploughing, for example, that bear no relation to what is actually going on in the countryside. The artists working from 1780 to 1890 did not do this, and did not need to. However much they may have exaggerated the elegance or contentment of agricultural workers, they did depict the current agricultural practice of their times. Mechanisation affected English agriculture slowly and sporadically, and, except towards the end of the nineteenth century, artists did not have to travel far to find wheat being reaped by hand or hay being tedded with pitchforks.

Since 1890 the appearance of English agriculture has been radically transformed. One reason for the appeal of these earlier images today is that they show a traditional agriculture that has been almost totally superseded in the developed world. It is a cliché to say that the old rural world of England has disappeared (as Raymond Williams pointed out, people have been saying that for many generations),[2] yet the scenes depicted in these paintings would be difficult to find in the modern English countryside, except in agricultural museums. This is even more the case in the United States, where in the nineteenth century mechanisation advanced more rapidly than it did in England.

The term *agricultural landscape* means primarily images of agricultural labourers at work in the fields. This type of painting combines two accepted artistic categories: landscape and genre (that is, paintings of everyday life). It has attracted much academic interest in recent years, for several reasons. Firstly, well-known British artists produced memorable examples of agricultural landscape. Secondly, the subject matter of these paintings is connected with issues of great importance: the representation of the poor in art, the use of the countryside and attitudes to rural life. Hence art historians, specialists in English literature, social and agricultural historians, geographers and landscape historians have all investigated this theme from a variety of viewpoints. From the perspective of art history, significant contributions have been made by John Barrell, David Solkin, Michael Rosenthal and Ann Bermingham.[3] These writers have aroused much controversy, partly because they have attacked, implicitly or explicitly, some of the comfortable myths about the countryside and partly because they challenge established art-historical methods.

My aim is to combine the traditional discipline of art history with some of the insights offered by the "new" art historians, and I am indebted to the work of the aforementioned scholars, without, however, endorsing their judgments completely. In particular, John Barrell's stress on the paintings as representations of the "desirable" virtues of the poor, created for the benefit of the rich, and Michael Rosenthal's interest in the practical details of agriculture have provided the starting points for two of my major themes: the agricultural processes depicted and the myths and values propagated by these paintings. I have tried to adopt a truly "interdisciplinary" approach by grounding my discussion of the paintings in a social and political analysis of the English countryside and an awareness of the specifically artistic precedents, conventions and practices affecting the artists.

The artistic response to the agricultural landscape is a huge subject. A large number of eighteenth- and nineteenth-century British paintings include some reference to agriculture, even if it is only a sheep, a labourer or a hedged field. The word *agriculture*, however, also has a more limited, more specific meaning: the cultivation of the fields (*ager*), the farming of arable land, and it is this meaning that is adopted here. For geographical and historical reasons, this type of farming has been concentrated in the lowland areas of southeast England, which also happens to be the area closest to London, where most artists were based in this period. Thus the fields were easily accessible for sketching trips, and many pictures were painted in, or based on studies made in, the counties near London, such as Suffolk, Berkshire, Surrey, Kent, Middlesex and Hertfordshire. Scotland and Wales have generally been excluded from this book, because these were areas of mixed and pastoral farming and because the social and economic conditions of the labourer were so different, particularly in Scotland, where the predominance of Scottish-born artists, such as David Wilkie, Thomas Faed, and James Guthrie, makes Scottish agricultural landscape worthy of a separate study. Owing to these regional variations, social and agricultural histories often concentrate on England, rather than Britain, and I have followed their example.[4]

The main text of the book is divided into three chapters. Chapter 1 deals with the historical background to paintings of agricultural landscape: the social and economic circumstances of the agricultural labourer's life, political issues that affected attitudes to the countryside, the major traditional agricultural processes and the impact of mechanisation. In Chapter 2 the emphasis shifts from fact to myth, from history to ideology (although recent developments in methodology have shown how difficult it is to keep the two distinct from each other, and readers may well feel that some of my "history" is really myth, and vice versa).[5] This chapter investigates the main elements in the prevailing rural myths, drawing on the evidence of paintings, literature and exhibition reviews. It shows how nineteenth-century artists, writers and patrons liked to believe, despite many indications to the contrary, that the countryside was a refuge for "traditional" values such as deference, paternalism, piety and family affection. It also suggests some reasons for the persistence of these myths, including middle-class fears of revolution and opposition to the new values of the rising "manufacturing civilisation." In the final chapter I consider the conditions under which agricultural landscape paintings were exhibited, sold and assessed, and give a chronological survey of the main developments within the genre related to the historical events of the era.

Chapter One
The English Countryside

The types of farming practised in England, and the systems of land tenure, varied greatly from one area to another. There was more mixed farming in the north than in the south. In his survey of English agriculture in 1850–1851, James Caird found that the counties to the north and west were chiefly pasture; the corn-growing districts were concentrated in the east and the south, from Lincolnshire to Dorset. In the north, wages were much higher, thanks to the competition of manufacturing industry.[1] Writing at about the same time, William Howitt, who had moved south to Esher, Surrey, after living for fourteen years in Nottingham, noticed a corresponding variation in the demeanour of the labourer. In the counties around London he was "a dull fellow," aware of belonging to "a neglected, despised caste"; in the Midlands and the northern counties the labourer was "a happier and wiser man" who would look "his rich neighbour full in the face, with a fearless, but respectful gaze."[2] A great many agricultural landscape paintings represent the southern corn-growing counties—within easy reach of London, where most artists lived—but also the area where, according to contemporary sources, the labourer's condition was at its worst. The typical farming system in these areas was three-tiered. The landowner was paid rent by a tenant farmer, who in turn employed labourers to do most of the work. G. E. Mingay estimates that at least three-quarters of all the land in England, in the Victorian period, was in the hands of affluent proprietors who rented it out to tenants.[3]

Land was of enormous political significance. Rents provided an important part—in many cases, the whole—of the incomes of the landed aristocracy and gentry, the so-called landed interest that dominated British politics. In addition, the possession of an estate conferred social prestige and was eagerly sought by the newly enriched merchants, manufacturers and other self-made men. At a local level, the squire exercised many of the administrative functions that were to be taken over by county councils after 1888. As a justice of the peace, he adjudicated cases of petty crime, regulated alehouses, supervised jails, and organised repairs to roads and bridges; he might also have the power to appoint the local clergyman, since a large proportion of Anglican livings were in the gift of landowners. The possession of land carried with it political power at a national level as well, since tenants normally voted in accordance with the wishes of their landlord. Before the Great Reform Act of 1832, the counties were overrepresented at the expense of the boroughs, and great landowners could, in many cases, virtually nominate their own representative in Parliament. Both directly and indirectly, then, land ownership was an important source of political power.

The period from 1780 to 1890 saw increasing industrialisation and urbanisation, which affected the political balance, reducing, though not ending, the domination of the landed interest. In 1800 one-third of all workers were engaged in agriculture; by the mid-nineteenth century this proportion had fallen to one-fifth, and in 1900 it was down to one-tenth.[4] After 1851 the population of the towns exceeded that of the countryside, the first time this had happened anywhere in the world. It would be wrong to conclude from these statistics, however, that agriculture ceased to be economically significant. As Alun Howkins has pointed out, agriculture was the largest single employer in England at every census until 1901, and in 1851 "England was far from an industrial nation . . . there were nearly twice as many people employed in agriculture as in the mills and factories of the industrial revolution."[5] It was the improved agriculture of the eighteenth century that made the industrial revolution possible; and in the nineteenth century home-grown wheat provided much of the food needed to feed the growing working class in the cities, bread being the staple item in the working-class diet. Even in the 1850s, after the repeal of the Corn Laws, about three-quarters of the bread eaten in the United Kingdom was made from home-produced wheat.[6] In this period bread really was the staff of life, and this economic fact underlies the significance of that popular subject for artists, the harvest scene.

The typical working figure in the agricultural scenes of this period is the farmworker or agricultural labourer (although at harvest time he might be joined by temporary workers from other occupational groups). In contemporary sources he is often described as a "peasant" or "husbandman," but this is rather misleading, since it implies that he had some stake in the land. Owner occupiers who worked their own land were, however, very much in the minority in late eighteenth-century and nineteenth-century England, especially in the southern counties. The yeoman was more of a fiction (an important one, as we shall see) than a reality.[7] In some paintings there may be a figure whose dress and bearing are different from those of the rest: he may wear leather boots, ride a horse and appear to be directing operations. It is difficult to say whether these men are meant to be farmers or merely bailiffs or overseers: they generally appear in paintings in the late eighteenth and early nineteenth centuries. Later agricultural scenes show workers unsupervised, perhaps in an attempt to appeal to those who questioned the traditional hierarchies of the countryside. John Linnell, for example, who was himself a Radical and painted mainly for merchants and manufacturers, never includes farmers, landowners or overseers in his paintings. The farmworkers were very definitely at the bottom of these hierarchies: they possessed no land, had little security either of housing or of employment (hence the term *day labourer*) and were desperately poor.

Agricultural wages were low everywhere, but particularly low in the southern counties. Caird found that the regular wages ranged from 15s. per week in Lancashire in 1851 to 6s. per week in Wiltshire, although they were much higher during the few weeks of harvest, when there was a greatly increased demand for labour.[8] Family budgets recorded in Suffolk in the 1850s show that the whole of a man's wage might be only just sufficient to buy bread for his family; other items, such as rent for the cottage, candles, bacon, cheese and clothing, would have to come out of the wages of his wife and children.[9] Children worked in the fields as soon as they were able to: from nine or ten years of age, perhaps even from seven; and farmworkers' wives also earned what they could, taking on jobs like weeding and often leaving small children in charge of the babies, with consequences that could be disastrous.[10] In arable districts in the winter, when work was scarce, workers were laid off and their families suffered extreme hardship. Cottages—although often picturesque—were small and unsanitary. William Cobbett, in 1830, described them as "miserable sheds" and "hovels"; reformers of the 1850s, concerned about the spread of cholera, were shocked to find that nearly half of all labourers' cottages had only one bedroom, a cause for scandal at a time when large families of eight or ten children were fairly common.[11] There are many graphic accounts of the inadequate diet and squalid living conditions of nineteenth-century agricultural labourers. Nevertheless, when compared to their counterparts in the cities they might have seemed to be relatively fortunate. In 1842 Edwin Chadwick calculated that the average age at death among the working classes in Manchester was less than half that of the agricultural labourers of Rutland; infant mortality rates were also much lower in the countryside than in the towns—but then conditions were so appalling in the towns of early industrial England that this differential is not very significant, except when looking at contemporary attitudes to farmworkers.[12]

Traditional agriculture involved grindingly hard work. Many labourers had to walk several miles to work before beginning their day, which might involve another sixteen miles walking behind the plough. In the days before rubber boots and waterproofs, clothes gave little protection from wind and rain, and many agricultural workers suffered from rheumatism in later life as a result. Harvesting took place in better weather conditions, but the hours were long and all the operations required constant bending—reaping, binding, setting up sheaves and gleaning. There were the additional dangers of sunstroke and exhaustion, and harvest was generally piecework, so the labourers were under pressure to work as rapidly as possible.[13] In photographs of labourers the effects of hard labour in all weathers are often apparent, and they are stressed also in descriptions such as those of Richard Jefferies. Women field workers, he claimed, had lost all their charms by the age of 25: the effects of labour were "visible in the thin frame, the bony wrist, the skinny arm showing the sinews, the rounded shoulders and stoop, the wrinkles and lines upon the sunburnt faces."[14] Artists of this period only occasionally produced images to match such a description: James Ward's *Wiltshire Peasant* (cat. 54) is a rare example of a convincing portrayal of an exhausted and weather-beaten male farm labourer. Depictions of women workers were even less likely to show wrinkles and deformities: the paintings of George Clausen, a contemporary of Jefferies, are exceptional in this respect (cat. 38).

It comes as no surprise to discover that rural unrest was widespread in this period, especially in the first half of the nineteenth century. There were recurrent outbreaks of machine breaking and rick burning, most notably in 1816, 1822 and 1830. The worst outbreaks were those of the so-called Swing riots of 1830–1832, which affected counties all over southern England. A total of 387 threshing machines and 26 other agricultural machines are recorded as having been destroyed in these years, and the true numbers are probably much higher.[15] Arson attacks and the anonymous letters signed "Captain Swing" raised fears of revolutionary bloodshed, although there was actually very little violence against people as opposed to property. In all, 1,976 persons were tried for offences connected with the Swing riots: 19 were executed (although 252 were originally sentenced to death) and 481 were transported to Australia.[16] In East Anglia there had been similar disturbances in 1816 and 1822. In the latter year John Constable noted their effects, telling his friend John Fisher that his brother had said that Suffolk was "as bad as Ireland—'never a night without seeing fires near or at a distance.'"[17]

Trouble continued after 1832. There were protests against the new Poor Law, and attempts were made to start unions: the famous "Tolpuddle Martyrs" were farm-workers from a Dorset village who were transported to Australia because of their union activities. Rick burning continued to be a problem. In 1844 in Suffolk "fires were of almost nightly occurrence" in the summer and "the corn stacks were placed in fields, a distance from each other, so that if one should be fired the others might escape."[18] The 1850s appear to have been more peaceful, helped by a rise in wages but also by the establishment of an effective rural police force, and perhaps by two decades of repression after the disturbances of 1830.[19] In the late 1860s, however, more organised attempts were made to improve conditions through the establishment of farmworkers' unions. In the early 1870s a national union, under the leadership of Joseph Arch, grew rapidly, and labourers even went on strike at harvest time, necessitating the drafting of soldiers to gather the harvest in some districts. The union's membership reached a peak of 86,000 in 1874 but declined steadily after employers responded to strike action with lockouts. Arch himself, however, went on to become a Liberal M.P. in 1885—the first farmworker ever to enter Parliament.[20]

Contemporary sources often speak of "distress and discontent" in one breath. They were evidently constant features in the life of the agricultural labourer and, indeed, British society generally in the early nineteenth century. As a result, the response to their condition from other, more fortunate members of society was a complicated mixture: distress elicited pity, but discontent brought fear. Even William Cobbett, who was sympathetic to the labourers' grievances, wrote in 1825 that "the manners and principles of the working class are so changed, that a sort of self-preservation bids the farmer (especially in some counties) to keep them from beneath his roof."[21] Cobbett gave this as one reason for the decline in the living-in system, whereby unmarried labourers lodged in the farmhouse; the other reason was that the farmers "cannot keep them *upon so little* as they give them in wages." These mixed reactions affected legislation. The need to improve conditions, for humanitarian reasons, was nearly always allied to the need to keep order, and many politicians believed that prosperity or charity were the best ways to avoid revolutionary upheaval.[22] Similar considerations affected painting. On the one hand, paintings of ragged farmworkers could inspire pity; on the other hand, images of contented, hardworking labourers could help assuage fears of social disorder and counteract the reports of arson, machine breaking, and poaching that would have been well known to readers of newspapers.

Poaching was a chronic problem in nineteenth-century England. Between 1827 and 1830, for example, one-seventh of all criminal convictions in the country were for offences against the Game Laws,[23] which existed to ensure that the landowner retained exclusive rights to hunt and shoot wild animals and birds on his estate. They were generally resented by the farmer, who had to put up with damage to his crops caused both by game and by the hunt coming through his fields. The real victims, however, were the labourers, on whom severe penalties were inflicted for poaching—a crime usually motivated by hunger. The Game Laws were actually made more severe in the early nineteenth century: from 1816, poaching could be punished by seven years' transportation, although in 1828 this was reserved for the third offence. They were bitterly resented by labourers and became a popular target for middle-class reformers, who regarded them as part of the system that maintained the power of the landed gentry. John Bright, one of the founders of the Anti-Corn Law League, was equally zealous in his attacks on the Game Laws. Poaching, with its potentially dramatic consequences (including fights between poachers and gamekeepers), was a fairly popular subject for artists in this period, who sometimes used the poacher as a contrast to the industrious and contented worker, but also showed some sympathy for poachers as victims of unjust laws.[24] Most labourers do not seem to have thought poaching to be intrinsically wrong—why should wild animals be seen as anyone's private property?—and their attitude was shared by many in the middle classes.

With wages so low and agricultural employment so erratic, most farm labourers could not have survived without the help of poor relief. In the 1790s the Speenhamland system allowed outdoor relief to be given, in the form of allowances calculated on the basis of the price of bread and the size of the labourer's family. In 1834, however, the Poor Law Amendment Act was designed to end this system (which was thought to encourage idleness, early marriage and large families) by making entry into the workhouse obligatory before relief could be granted. The conditions that prevailed in nineteenth-century workhouses are well known: families were split up, rations were meagre and the work monotonous—breaking stones to make roads, for example. It is not surprising that the labourers regarded the workhouse as a kind of prison. In 1858 Henry Wallis exhibited *The Stonebreaker*, which showed a labourer who had died while engaged in this work (fig. 1). It was viewed by at least one reviewer as "a protest against the Poor Law—against a social system that makes the workhouse or stone-breaking the end of the model peasant."[25] He was not the first artist to make such a protest. In 1841 Cope had exhibited *The Board of Guardians—the Widow's Application for Bread*, a picture that highlighted the indifference of certain elements in the rural hierarchy to the plight of the agricultural poor (fig. 2).[26]

The changes in the Poor Law were stimulated by increasing poor rates (the rates levied on the better-off inhabitants of a parish and used to support the poor), which in turn reflected increasing rural poverty. Between 1776 and 1820 the amount spent annually on poor relief in England and Wales rose from just over £1.5 million to over £7 million.[27] Modern historians attribute this rise largely to a sudden increase in the population in the late eighteenth century, the causes of which are still rather mysterious. Many contemporary observers, however, put much of the blame on the enclosure of open fields and commons. About one-quarter of the cultivated acreage was enclosed by Acts of Parliament between 1761 and 1845, a large proportion of them falling within the period of the wars with France, from 1793 to 1815.[28] Small hedged fields replaced the open fields of medieval strip farming (about three-quarters of the enclosures were of open fields) and commons and wastes on which the labourer had been allowed to pasture animals and gather fuel. Twentieth-century historians dispute the severity of the effects of enclosure.[29] Most agree, however, that it must have increased the number of landless labourers, men entirely dependent on employment by farmers for their livelihood. K. D. M. Snell has shown that seasonal unemployment invariably rose when parishes were enclosed. Previously, labourers might have used slack periods in the agricultural year to collect fuel or tend their own animals on the common, even if they had no holdings in the open fields.[30] The owners of small strips, or of common rights, were allotted land in enclosure awards, but often they could not afford the cost of hedging the plots and so sold them to larger landowners. The loss of fuel and pasture from the commons had unfortunate effects on diet. In enclosed

1. HENRY WALLIS
The Stonebreaker, 1857–58. Oil on canvas, 25¾ × 31 in. (65.4 × 78.7 cm.).
Birmingham Museums and Art Gallery.

2. CHARLES WEST COPE
The Board of Guardians — the Widow's Application for Bread, 1841. Oil on canvas. Present location unknown.
Photograph courtesy A. C. Cooper Ltd., London.

parishes in arable areas labourers' children rarely drank milk (since they could no longer keep their own cow), and the shortage of fuel meant that labourers ceased to bake their own bread—as well as affecting their ability to keep their cottages warm during the winter.[31] Enclosure affected some areas much more radically than others (which strongly suggests that it was not the only reason for the increasing poverty of rural England as a whole), but in many villages it must have transformed the rural economy, reducing the labourer's formerly varied sources of food and fuel to just two—wages and poor relief.

Certainly, contemporary observers believed that enclosure had important social consequences. Robert Southey claimed in 1816 that it had resulted in the extinction of the yeoman, "a numerous, most useful, and most respectable class, who, from the rank of small farmers, have been degraded to that of day-labourers." As a result, Southey argued, a source of faithful domestic servants, good churchmen and village schoolmasters was no more; and day labourers had lost their respectability, their incentive to save and their respect for the law.[32] Southey's complaints are echoed in the comments of exhibition reviewers in the early and mid-nineteenth century, who often regarded paintings of prosperous-looking peasants as nostalgic representations of the extinct class of yeomen. As for the effect of enclosure on the poor, one of the most famous and most telling assessments was that of Arthur Young. Young had previously championed the enclosure movement because of the stimulus it provided to improvements in agriculture. But in 1801 he wrote, "By nineteen out of twenty Enclosure Acts the poor are injured, in some grossly injured. . . . The poor in these parishes may say, and with truth, 'Parliament may be tender of property; all I know is, I had a cow, and an Act of Parliament has taken it from me.'"[33] Throughout the nineteenth century many of the schemes to improve the condition of the agricultural poor involved providing allotments or garden ground, to give them a stake in the land and to offset the economic consequences of the loss of common rights.

In the debates over enclosure, different sections of the landowning class took different positions. The traditional paternalistic regard for the poor was set against the new economic demands of progressive agriculture. In a sense, the conflict was between feudalism—or at least a system of rights and obligations that derived from feudalism— and capitalism. In other political battles of the early nineteenth century, the new classes thrown up by capitalism—middle-class merchants and manufacturers— clashed with the aristocracy and gentry. Broadly speaking, the Tory party, usually supported by the Church of England, was on one side, the Whigs and Radicals on the other. The Tories opposed the Great Reform Bill, which finally became law in 1832, because it gave more representation to the boroughs and reduced the direct connection between land ownership and political power. On the other hand, they favoured factory reform, which was resisted by the manufacturers. The dreadful conditions suffered by children in mines and factories received much publicity, especially in the 1830s and 1840s, and must have made rural children seem fortunate by comparison.

It was the debate over the Corn Laws, however, that brought the countryside most dramatically into the political arena. When corn prices fell in 1815, at the end of the Napoleonic Wars, a Corn Law was introduced, prohibiting the duty-free import of foreign corn until the home price of wheat had reached 80s. a quarter; this was subsequently modified by the introduction of a sliding scale of duties. The purpose of the Corn Laws was to protect British agriculture against foreign competition and prevent any future dependence on foreign corn, which could be dangerous in wartime. Low corn prices could bring ruin to farmers, increasing the poverty and distress of the labourers, but they also threatened to reduce rents, thus reducing the income (and ultimately the power) of the landowners. On the other side, the Anti-Corn Law League, founded by Cobden and Bright in the 1839, argued that the Corn Laws kept bread prices high and thus increased poverty both in the towns and in the countryside. Tories and landowners defended the Corn Laws; Whigs, Radicals and manufacturers attacked them. In actual fact, when the statistics are studied, the Corn Laws do not seem to have had a great effect on the price of bread. The real issue seems to have been one of principle—not so much the protection of agriculture but the protection of the power of the landed interest.[34] The Anti-Corn Law League openly attacked "feudal tyranny," and Bright wrote, after repeal, "We have not seen the last of the Barons, but we have taught them which way the world is turning."[35]

After seven years of agitation by the Anti-Corn Law League, at a time of bad harvests and economic depression, the Corn Laws were repealed by the Conservative government of Sir Robert Peel in 1846, a measure that was widely regarded as a betrayal of his party. Peel was the politician who transformed the old Tory party into the Conservative party, and one of his underlying aims was to widen the party's social foundations and strengthen the old institutions of the country by means of controlled reform, rather than risking outright revolution by resisting all change. He claimed that he was repealing the Corn Laws to "secure the continuance in the just influence of the landed interest of this country."[36] One of his arguments against the Corn Laws was that they had not produced "a prosperous and contented class of agricultural labourers throughout the country."[37] In an article on William Holman Hunt's *Hireling Shepherd* (fig. 3), Kay Dian Kriz has shown how the Corn Law debates continued to exert an influence on painters and critics in the early 1850s.[38] Because the Anti-Corn Law League claimed that repeal would improve the living standards of farm labourers, paintings of rural poverty could take on a political meaning. Before repeal, they were potential arguments in its favour; but after repeal, pictures of rural prosperity could have the same charge, demonstrating that the removal of the Corn Laws had led to cheaper bread for all.

Underlying much of the legislation and political debates of the early nineteenth century was an acceptance of the reality of the distress and discontent of farm labourers. As Peel stressed, they were neither prosperous nor contented. Churchmen, like politicians, favoured different remedies for this state of affairs. The Church of England, like the Tory party, put its trust in paternalism, personal charity and a resident squirearchy that would help poor neighbours with gifts of alms or of food,

3. WILLIAM HOLMAN HUNT
The Hireling Shepherd, 1851–52. Oil on canvas, 30 × 43 in. (76.2 × 109.2 cm.). Manchester City Art Galleries.

blankets and medicine. Dissenters, however, agreed with the Radicals, and to some extent the Whigs, in believing that this kind of charity led to overdependence and pauperisation: they supported legislation that would encourage the labourer to be self-reliant, such as the new Poor Law. Many of the established clergy did their best to relieve distress through personal charity, but they were closely connected with the hierarchical social system of rural life (many served as clerical magistrates or were appointed by the squire of their parish), and this made labourers suspicious of their motives. A book written in the 1850s, *The Duties of the Parish Priest*, underlines the connection between the clergy and the social hierarchy. The author advocated the foundation of village schools, but the benefits cited were related to the maintenance of the social system. In a village without a school, "the common courtesies of life, usually thought due to rank and station [are] disregarded," but a school would encourage "frugal, regular and *industrious habits* in the labouring class, which, if not religion in themselves, are generally akin to it, conduce to it, and rarely, indeed, are long separated from it."[39] A more genuinely humanitarian stance was taken by clergymen such as Edward Girdlestone, who in the 1860s helped many farm labourers to move to the north of England, where conditions were better than in the south, and assisted in the formation of labourers' unions.[40] Other clergymen helped labourers emigrate to the colonies and to the United States, where they could apply their farming skills as independent tenants or proprietors. However, the clergy risked the disapproval of landowners and farmers in their parishes if they were too sympathetic to the labourers' grievances.

In the second half of the nineteenth century a series of political reforms helped to improve conditions in the countryside and also, ultimately, to raise the status of the agricultural labourer. In the 1860s and 1870s legislation limited child labour on the land and established the nucleus of the state education system. The 1873 Agricultural Children's Act prohibited the employment of any child under eight, except on the farm of a parent or guardian. The 1870 Education Act set up local school boards and empowered them to pass bylaws to make education compulsory between the ages of five and twelve. Meanwhile, the progressive widening of the franchise admitted the labourer, by the end of our period, to a share in the democratic process. It is significant, however, that in the Reform Act of 1867 only working-class voters in the boroughs were enfranchised. The £12 property qualifications in the counties meant that agricultural labourers had to wait until the Reform Act of 1884 before they were entitled to vote—and even then the Tories opposed their enfranchisement, fearing that they would all vote Liberal.[41] In the 1860s, 1870s and 1880s the publicity given to the labourers' grievances as a result of reforms (as well as union activity) affected both painting and critical discourse, and several artists chose to dwell on the plight of country children.

Until the very end of this period of political ferment, the agricultural processes that occupied much of the labourer's daily life continued with little major change. Wheat, the subject of so much bitter political debate, was also the crop that was most consistently studied by artists. It was sown in the autumn, either by seed drill or by being broadcast from a seedlip (as in J. M. W. Turner's watercolour of 1796; cat. 42). The ground was ploughed before sowing and harrowed afterwards, and perhaps rolled as well. All three implements—plough, harrow and rolls—are shown in paintings by Turner and J. F. Herring (cat. 8 and 28). The same procedure was used for sowing barley. The wheat ripened in the summer and was harvested in late July, August and early September. It was cut by sickle, reap hook or bagging hook (or, later in the nineteenth century, by scythe). The sickle, reap hook and bagging hook are all hand-held crescent-shaped tools. The sickle, the smallest of the three, has a serrated cutting edge; the reap hook is larger and heavier than the sickle, and smooth-bladed; the bagging hook was used in conjunction with a crooked stick to hold the stalks together while they were cut. Both men and women used the sickle, although the scythe appears to have been used exclusively by men.[42] When using the sickle, the labourer had to bend down, seize a bundle of stalks in his or her left hand and cut them about halfway up. The stubble left from wheat could thus be more than a foot in height, although artists often depict it as much shorter, perhaps for aesthetic reasons. To the modern eye the wheat sheaves and standing corn in paintings look exaggeratedly high, but today's crops are treated with growth regulators to make mechanical harvesting easier, and it is likely that those of the past did indeed grow to a much greater height.

After the reaper had cut the wheat, it was bound into sheaves tied with a straw rope. Binding was often done by women working behind the reapers. In *Tess of the d'Urbervilles* Thomas Hardy gives a memorable description of Tess binding sheaves, "holding the corn in an embrace like that of a lover." The wheat was left in stooks or shocks to dry before being carted and stacked, ready for threshing by flail or machine. Carting might take place several days after cutting, although the two operations are often depicted as simultaneous in paintings of harvest. With wheat harvesting, the crop was valuable and each operation was urgent. Once cut, wheat could not be left unsheaved and unshocked overnight; shocked wheat could not be left uncarted, once ripe, for fear that it would shed its ears.[43] The carrying of the corn, therefore, could go on far into the night, although the actual cutting usually ceased at dusk. In the autumn, however, if bad weather was forecast, labourers might reap by moonlight, as depicted by Samuel Palmer in the early 1830s (cat. 20) and described by Hardy in *The Mayor of Casterbridge*.[44]

Barley harvest would have presented a fundamentally different appearance from the harvesting of wheat, because barley, like hay, was mown—that is, cut with a scythe, close to the ground—and then left in swathes to dry. The stalks were not bound into sheaves, and a barley rick had a rounded appearance, like a hay rick. It is easy, therefore, for twentieth-century art historians to confuse barley harvest with haymaking, a much more common subject. Haymaking—the process of cutting and drying grass to produce hay—took place earlier than corn harvest, in June or early July. The grass was cut by male labourers with the scythe, falling into swathes, which were turned or "tedded" by haymakers—usually women—with pitchforks. It was then drawn with rakes into windrows or haycocks. When it had dried it was pitched, again by fork, onto a cart or waggon, ready for stacking. Any loose hay remaining on the ground was then raked up, and this job, too, was usually done by women. The actual mowing of the grass was extremely hard work, but the other operations were relatively light. Haymaking was a favourite occupation of the better-off who wanted to play at farm work. The Wells family invited J. M. W. Turner to join them for haymaking (and a harvest home) in 1820; and Leigh Hunt, in 1821, suggested that "the ladies may practise haymaking on a small scale upon lawns and paddocks; and if they are not afraid of giving their fair skins a still finer tinge of the sunny, nothing makes them look better."[45] Haymaking is often treated by artists in a light-hearted way, with much emphasis on the elegance of female haymakers.

Wheat harvesting, however, was easily the most popular agricultural subject for artists, especially in the early nineteenth century and in the 1850s and 1860s. There were a number of reasons for this. Agricultural workers were relatively well off during harvest: their wages were much higher than usual and they were well supplied with food and drink. Many of the workers involved in the harvest were not the regular, desperately poor day labourers: because many hands were needed to gather in the harvest, they were joined by workers from the towns and gangs of itinerant contract workers, who were more independent than the day labourers. It is difficult to assess the status of workers in individual painted harvest scenes, but the knowledge of the mixed composition of the harvest workforce may have reassured artists (and patrons), who would have found rural poverty distressing but were able to see harvest as a cheerful time. The end product of the wheat harvest, the grain, was of great national significance as the source of bread and hence was attractive for its symbolic·value in art. And wheat harvest provided a wide variety of activities for the painter to study. As well as reaping, binding and carrying, there was the vital activity of gleaning, which brought women and children into the harvest fields.

When wheat is harvested by hand there is inevitably some wastage, and it was an age-old custom for the poor to be allowed to pick up the stray stalks and ears left behind after the harvest had been gathered. There was biblical authority for gleaning in the Book of Leviticus and in the story of Ruth and Boaz (a popular subject amongst artists). Gleaning was also of great economic importance to the labourer, providing up to an eighth of a family's annual income, according to a recent estimate.[46] Progressive farmers were not, however, always well disposed towards gleaning, because of the danger that the gleaner would steal from the sheaves and that the labourer would "gather in his employer's corn in a careless and slovenly manner" so that more would be left for the gleaners, who probably included his wife and children.[47] In 1788 a court case established that gleaning was a permissive custom and not a legal right.

Artists were certainly aware of the controversies surrounding gleaning. In 1806 C. Gray's commentary to W. H. Pyne's *Microcosm·*(a source that was probably read by many artists) criticized the "selfishness" of those farmers who put restrictions on gleaning:

> In some parts of the island twenty years ago (and perhaps it is so still) it was customary with our farmers, like Boaz and the farmers of his time, to admit the gleaners into the same field with the reapers. . . . In most parts, however, it must be confessed, that the repulsive selfishness of our luxurious and expensive times is now visible in this, as in other cases. If our modern farmer, who, like the tradesman of town, thinks only of making the most money by his bargain, admits the *fatherless*, the *widow*, and the *stranger*; it is only after the corn is carried, and the field perhaps well raked: and he generally takes care to let loose his pigs to glean along with the less fortunate *partners of his kind*.[48]

This passage suggests a distinction between the old and new values—paternalism versus commercialism—and a sympathy with the old, feudal values, with which several artists seem to have agreed. In paintings of the 1810s and 1820s Peter DeWint depicted gleaners stealing from the stooks or holding meagre gleanings in a field that had been raked; and Constable's decision to show gleaners working alongside reapers in his *Wheatfield* of 1815–16 (fig. 4), accompanied by lines from the poet Bloomfield, can be seen as an affirmation of the survival of the old paternalism, at least in Suffolk. In 1865 an article in the *Cornhill Magazine* confirmed that gleaners were "a class of people dearer to the artist, be he poet or painter, than they are to the farmer or

4. John Constable
The Wheatfield, 1815–16. Oil on canvas, 21 × 30 in. (53.7 × 77.2 cm.). Private collection.

sportsman."[49] (The sportsman—that is, the landowner—would presumably dislike gleaning because the gleaners picked up grain that would otherwise feed pheasants and partridges.)

At the end of the corn harvest, it was traditional for the farmers to give their workers a harvest feast—the "horkey" or harvest home. In the early nineteenth century, contemporary observers complained that this custom was dying out: the farmers were becoming too genteel to sit down with their workers on a basis of temporary equality. Cobbett said in 1825 that the farmers had been "transmuted into a species of mock gentlefolks" while their labourers had been "ground down into real slaves."[50] Both Robert Bloomfield and John Clare, two poets who themselves worked as farm labourers, wrote wistfully of the harvest homes of the past and blamed their decline on the increasing gap between the classes.[51] In the later nineteenth century, the harvest festival in church (first celebrated in the 1840s), followed by a teetotal tea or supper in the village hall, generally replaced the rowdy horkey. Depictions of harvest homes are rather rare considering the aesthetic potential of the subject; Turner's unfinished *Harvest Home* of c. 1809 (fig. 5) is an isolated example. More common were depictions of the end of harvest—the "last load"—which emphasized the relief felt by workers as they came to the end of a period of intense hard work and left open the question of how they would celebrate it.

18   *The English Countryside*

5. J. M. W. TURNER
Harvest Home, c. 1809. Oil on panel, 35½ × 47½ in. (90 × 121 cm.). Tate Gallery, London.

Other crops, such as oats, field beans, turnips and hops, were painted much less often than wheat, although they were a common sight in the countryside. Turnips were an important break crop, introduced to increase the fertility of the land as part of a new system of crop rotation in the eighteenth century. They were grown in between two cereal crops and used to feed cattle, as demonstrated by the cows in the foreground of Turner's *Ploughing Up Turnips* of 1809 (cat. 8). In the 1850s Ford Madox Brown noticed the beautiful and unusual colour of turnip leaves, and chose to make the contrast between the deep green of turnips and the golden yellow of corn the basis of his small landscape *Carrying Corn* (cat. 26).[52] Madox Brown indeed had an eye for crops rarely depicted by other artists. *Walton-on-the-Naze* (fig. 6) features field beans, which were cut and stooked like wheat and left to dry for several months in the field—a very rare subject in this period. Later in the century, crops like turnips were attractive to those artists who wished to stress the rigours of winter work on the land, such as George Clausen and John Robertson Reid.

Hops—used to make beer—were grown in Kent and the adjoining counties, where they were harvested by temporary workers, usually women and children from the East End of London. Hop growing appears in art mainly in the early nineteenth century,

6. Ford Madox Brown
Walton-on-the-Naze, 1859–60. Oil on canvas, 12½ × 16½ in. (31.7 × 42 cm.). Birmingham Museums and Art Gallery.

when artists, including Joshua Cristall and Thomas Uwins, were making excursions to Kent and Surrey in search of subject matter for rural genre paintings. Hops also appear in Samuel Palmer's work, usually combined with his more favoured subjects of ripe corn or sheepfolds. In 1811 Uwins wrote very enthusiastically of the aesthetic merits of hop picking: it was "a most delightful scene, and . . . full of picture. . . . That it has never been made more use of by artists is altogether a mystery to me, it is so much superior to any other harvest that we in England have to boast." It had, however, a major disadvantage as a subject for artists: "There is one thing to be said to it—hop-picking is partial, but hay-making, reaping, &c, are general, and known to everybody, and this is against it [i.e., hop growing] as an exhibition scene. Thousands of Cockneys never saw a hop growing in all their lives."[53] Scenes of hop picking generally look idyllic. The hops were grown on tall poles, which provided shade for the pickers, and the workers could sit down to strip the hops off the poles. On the other hand, the hop pickers were often very poor, unhealthy town dwellers, and this circumstance was noticed by reviewers later in the century.[54]

In the nineteenth century the traditional processes of farming were all under threat from mechanisation—especially those involved in wheat harvesting. The first machines to become common on farms were threshing machines, which began to be used in the 1760s and were widespread by the early decades of the nineteenth century. The early threshing machines were kept in barns and worked by horse gearing; from the 1840s they were superseded by portable threshers powered by steam engines. Both types replaced threshing by flail, which would otherwise occupy farm labourers through much of the winter; they thus increased seasonal unemployment in arable districts (which adversely affected farmers, as well as labourers, through increasing the poor rate). Large numbers were destroyed during the Swing riots, and their use may have declined for a time after 1830.[55] Threshing was a fairly rare subject for artists, but nevertheless it is interesting to note that threshing by machine was hardly ever depicted. Even Pyne's *Microcosm* illustrates threshing by flail, although the accompanying text mentions several kinds of threshing machine.[56]

Other processes involved in wheat growing changed much less radically than threshing. Ploughing with horses was standard practice in 1890, as it had been in 1780: steam ploughs and cultivators were introduced in the 1850s but made little impact, partly because they were very expensive.[57] Ploughs became lighter—cast-iron replacing heavy wooden ploughs—and as they became lighter, fewer draught animals were needed to pull them and the ploughman could work unassisted, as he does in Constable's *Ploughing Scene* of 1825 (cat. 16). Mechanical reapers, and then reaper-binders, were introduced from the 1850s onwards, but as late as 1870 it is estimated that three-quarters of the corn harvest was still being cut by hand.[58] In this period in the United States, where fields were larger and labour scarce, mechanisation advanced rapidly, but in England the old methods persisted for much longer. Even when corn was cut by the mechanical reaper, it still needed to be bound in sheaves and set up in stooks. A study of harvesting in Britain in the nineteenth century concluded that "it was not until the early years of the twentieth century that reaping by hand became an anachronism."[59] As with ploughing, the actual implements changed. From the 1850s the use of the sickle to cut wheat gradually gave way to the scythe, which was more efficient;[60] artists, however, continued to depict reaping by sickle (just as they continued to paint heavy wooden ploughs), partly because of its biblical associations. On the whole, artists with a preference for old-fashioned practices only had to be selective rather than downright mendacious, since the pace of change varied greatly from one part of the country to another: practices died out in some areas decades before they became obsolete in others. The use of oxen as draught animals, for example, ended in East Anglia before the beginning of the nineteenth century, but there were still a dozen or more bullock teams working in Sussex in 1914.[61] In the 1820s Samuel Palmer could have observed oxen working in the Weald of Kent, although not in Shoreham itself.[62]

In general, artists ignored new machinery when they could, preferring to depict the traditional, picturesque agricultural processes, with their biblical and poetic associations. By the 1860s and 1870s the discrepancy between artistic representations and the true state of agricultural technology was beginning to be noticeable. The 1865 *Cornhill*

Magazine article emphasized that gleaning could not go on much longer: "The practice of mowing wheat [i.e., cutting it with the scythe] . . . which is rapidly on the increase, to say nothing of the reaping machine which makes still cleaner work of it, is, we fear, tending to destroy this good old custom. But few ears of corn are left on the ground under either of these two processes, and when they become universal, the gleaner will scarce find her labour pay."[63] In the 1880s Richard Jefferies urged artists to paint the agricultural practices of their time. He gave vivid descriptions of the threshing machine, reaping machine, mowing machine and steam plough, and complained that "so many pictures seem to proceed upon the assumption that steam-plough and reaping-machine do not exist, that the landscape contains nothing but what it did a hundred years ago."[64] The inevitability of change perhaps increased the urgency to record features of agricultural life that would soon disappear, and not many people agreed with Jefferies in finding the new machinery aesthetically appealing. In fact, more would have agreed with the attitude expressed by Hardy in *Tess of the d'Urbervilles*, in which the threshing machine is personified as a despotic tyrant, which, like its engineman, was "in the agricultural world, but not of it."[65]

The nineteenth-century English countryside was marked far more deeply by invisible changes than by visible changes in agricultural practice. Behind the depictions of agriculture and the agricultural labourer lie issues of the widest significance—the distribution of power between the landed and commercial classes, the relationship between rich and poor, the rights of the working class and the change from an agricultural to an industrial economy. Artists, their patrons and their public were aware of these issues and were themselves involved in them. It is impossible to understand what was written about the paintings without a knowledge of this background, and it is also necessary to bear the social and political circumstances in mind when considering, as we shall in the next chapter, the myths and values that are worked into the pictures.

Chapter Two
Rural Myths and Values

Even a cursory glance at images of the nineteenth-century English agricultural landscape shows them to be at odds with the evidence of the social, political and economic circumstances of the agricultural labourer. To read contemporary accounts, or the many twentieth-century histories based on them, one would think that agricultural labourers were not a promising subject for art. All too often they were half-starved, prematurely aged, exploited and despised by their superiors, whom they in turn hated and feared; they lived in squalid cottages, with little opportunity for a happy family life; their inclinations to poaching or arson revealed little respect for the law of the land and the social hierarchy. And yet paintings of the agricultural landscape are attractive, and the figures contribute to their mood: they are almost invariably soothing and optimistic, not threatening or depressing. Such paintings exaggerate the pleasures of agricultural work, the health and contentment of the male agricultural worker, and the happiness of his wife and children. It is evident that, in most cases, they are vehicles for myth rather than accurate reflections of reality. The aim of this chapter is to elucidate some of the myths and values enshrined in these images, and to explain why these were so important to the artists, picture buyers and exhibition visitors of eighteenth- and nineteenth-century England.

There are three pervasive myths about the countryside that are not peculiar to this period but have had a profound influence on Western European culture since classical times or earlier. Briefly, these are the myths that people are happier in the countryside, that country people are more virtuous, and that country people were more virtuous and happy in the past than they are now. The countryside is thus seen as a lost paradise, Eden or Arcadia, and contrasted favourably with the tainted or restricted world of the city or the court. In nineteenth-century England these ancient myths took on specific characteristics. The countryside was contrasted, not just with the corrupt city, but also with the new industrial towns, with their horrific living and working conditions and their irreligious and riotous populations. There was a particular emphasis on the virtues that would maintain social stability and avert revolution, and these virtues were considered to survive in rural England: industriousness, sobriety, piety, domestic affection and deference to rank on the part of the workers, paternalism and charity on the part of their social superiors. The theme of the moral superiority of rural life was adapted to validate the power of the aristocracy and gentry at a time when it was threatened by the newly powerful middle class, the merchants, manufacturers and industrialists, many of whom were based in the northern cities. The myth of the better rural past, similarly, provided support for those who defended "Old England" against a variety of threats: industrialisation and political reform for some observers, enclosure and the unfair treatment of the rural labourer for others. It provided political ammunition, therefore, both for conservatives and for radicals.

The pastoral myth—the idea that simple shepherds and shepherdesses lead blissfully happy lives, with plenty of opportunity for flirtation and festivities—has been an important theme in Western European art, music and literature, from the poetry of Theocritus and Virgil in classical Italy to the paintings of Boucher in eighteenth-century France (fig. 7). Pastorals are usually set in nonagricultural countryside, often in a golden age in which people do not need to till the soil. The pastoral tended to be a courtly, highly artificial art form, which appealed to aristocrats longing for freedom from social restraints. By definition, agricultural landscapes are not true pastorals, and yet the pastoral myth did influence attitudes to agricultural scenes. James Thomson's poem *The Seasons* (1730) belongs to the tradition of English Georgic poetry, which, following the classical prototype of Virgil's *Georgics*, took an interest in the practical details of agriculture. His descriptions of haymaking and harvesting, which continued to be read by artists throughout the nineteenth century, are strongly influenced, however, by pastoral attitudes. He stresses the opportunities for courtship and merriment: at haymaking, the "rustic youth" and the "ruddy maid" work side by side, the maid "half naked" with "all / Her kindled graces burning o'er her cheek." The valleys resound with "the blended voice / Of happy labour, love, and social glee." At harvest time, again, the love interest is strong: "Before the ripened fields the reapers stand / In fair array, each by the lass he loves."[1] In the eighteenth century artists like

7. FRANÇOIS BOUCHER
Shepherd Piping to a Shepherdess, c. 1745. Oil on canvas, 37 × 56 in. (94 × 142 cm.).
Reproduced by permission of the Trustees of the Wallace Collection.

Rowlandson produced pictures that emphasize the fun of agricultural labour. Toward the end of that century the mood becomes more serious and more domestic; but well into the next, artists still quoted from Thomson in the lines they included in exhibition catalogues.

Closely linked with the pastoral myth is the idea that people are better, as well as happier, in the countryside rather than the town. This was given its classic statement in William Cowper's poem *The Task*: "God made the country, and man made the town." The countryside, then, is a place of moral and physical health, free from the corruption of city and court.[2] Whereas the pastoral myth contrasted the rich and the poor, the myth of the moral superiority of rural to urban life could also be applied to opposing sections amongst the better-off, or to the contrast between the rural and the urban working class. It goes back at least to the Roman poet Horace and his image of the contented farmer, who is free of the temptations of city life, a theme that was taken up by members of the English gentry who chose "rural retirement"—life on their country estates—in the seventeenth and eighteenth centuries, withdrawing from politics and court intrigues. In the nineteenth century it could be extended to support the idea that the aristocracy and gentry were morally superior to merchants and manufacturers—and hence more deserving of political power.

If the city was the source of corruption, it was inevitable that the rural paradise would be constantly under threat of "infection": from luxury, trade and commerce in the eighteenth century, from industrialisation and revolutionary ideas in the nineteenth. Perhaps the very impossibility of maintaining that rural life was an idyll tempted poets to place the idyll in the past; and Raymond Williams has shown that, from the sixteenth to the twentieth centuries, writers continually claim that rural England was once happier and more harmonious. Further, Ann Bermingham has demonstrated how apparent nostalgia for the old order could, paradoxically, be combined with the propagation of values that endorsed and accommodated change.[3] Often, the Old England is set in the childhood of the author. Cowper, elsewhere in the *Task*, laments the loss of the old rural virtues in terms similar to those of Wordsworth in *The Excursion* some thirty years later.[4] Cowper blames the rich, who have deserted their traditional paternalistic duties to pursue pleasure in London; Wordsworth blames the factories, which have depopulated the countryside. One of the most powerful statements of the myth of the better rural past was made by Oliver Goldsmith in *The Deserted Village* (1770)—a poem which, like Thomson's *Seasons*, is often quoted in nineteenth-century exhibition catalogues. Goldsmith creates an idyllic vision of rural life but sets it in the past, before enclosure, landscape improvement and the sale of estates to the nouveau riche had taken over the countryside and dispossessed the peasantry:

> Sweet Auburn! Loveliest village of the plain,
> Where health and plenty cheer'd the labouring swain . . .
> But times are alter'd; trade's unfeeling train
> Usurp the land and dispossess the swain . . .
> And rural mirth and manners are no more.[5]

Similarly, in the early nineteenth century the two "peasant poets," Robert Bloomfield and John Clare, lamented the loss of past happiness in the countryside. Bloomfield's explanation was a fairly conventional one: "refinement" and "Pride" were to blame. Clare, however, wrote bitterly about the effects of enclosure, usually in poems that were too politically sensitive to be published in his lifetime.[6] Bloomfield's poem *The Farmer's Boy* (1800) was widely read by artists (including Constable and Fred Walker),[7] but Clare's poetry seems to have had less influence, except perhaps on his friend Peter DeWint.

Most of the poetry of rural life in this period was influenced, to some extent, by the myth that poor rural labourers were happier or more virtuous than the rich and the town dweller (George Crabbe's poetry is an important exception.) Even Wordsworth, whose *Lyrical Ballads* (1800) are far removed from the artificial genre of pastoral, stated in his preface that he had chosen to depict "low and rustic life" because it was there that "the essential passions of the heart find a better soil in which they can attain their maturity."[8] Artists habitually read poetry for inspiration and as a source of subject matter, and so it is hardly surprising that they were inclined to see only the idyllic side of rural life and labour, and to accept the notion that, however poor and overworked the labourers were, there was something inherently poetic and morally invigorating about the agricultural landscape. Indeed, George Eliot complained about this in an influential article in 1856, when she wrote, "The painter is still under the influence of idyllic literature, which has always expressed the imagination of the cultivated and town-bred, rather than the truth of rustic life."[9]

An instructive literary parallel to the paintings is to be found in prose descriptions of the seasons and their occupations, published under such titles as "The Months" or "The Calendar of Nature." These provide a bridge between the poetry and the images: they are evidently influenced by the poets (often they quote from them or use similar words and phrases), but they also describe harvest and other occupations in very visual terms, strongly suggesting that they were influenced by the paintings, and vice versa. Such descriptions help reveal the attitudes underlying the paintings, the emotions they were meant to evoke and the ways in which they were "read" by contemporary observers. A typical example is a piece by John Wilson, published under the pseudonym Christopher North and included in Mary Howitt's *Pictorial Calendar of the Seasons* (1854). It describes harvest:

> At this season of nature's abundance, we might almost persuade ourselves that human want was a fiction; see yonder that line of lusty mowers sweeping down the abundant crop of pale barley, how vigorous, how cheerful their appearance. Those are not the sons of misery and starvation; they have made acquaintance with barley long before this, and in a form quite as congenial to them, whether in the brown loaf or the foaming tankard; and now turn to the wheat-field, which is a still more attractive scene. What a pleasant picture it presents us with. There is the jolly farmer, the king of the field, and there are all his people, stout men and women, young and old, laughing and working together. The broad cornfield with its groups of people; its sunny ears falling below the sickle, and its piled up shocks lying beneath the clear, cloudless sky, which bathes the whole as it were in a flood of calm sunshine, is a splendid picture; but look into it in more detail, and what a number of lesser, but equally interesting pictures it presents; here a group of labourers in their picturesque attire, which spite of our English want of costume, seldom fails of effect on such occasions, resting and refreshing themselves from the basket and the wooden bottle; there a group of children, who having followed their mothers to the field, are yet too young to labour, but find infinite occupation in the hedges or among the shocks; here sleeps a baby pillowed among sheaves; watched perhaps by a little brother or sister, or it may be a dog, more watchful and patient of his confinement than any little human guardian would be on a day and in a scene like this. Yes truly, corn-fields are full of pictures, and they suggest to us many wonderful and lovely passages of life from the remotest times.

Wilson goes on to describe the biblical scenes that are set in cornfields, including the story of Ruth and Boaz, and of Christ and his disciples walking through cornfields on the Sabbath. "All is beautiful," the passage concludes, "all is tender and touching; and as we walk in the cornfields even now, these glorious old scenes live again, and will continue to do so, as long as corn grows."[10]

This passage illustrates many of the features that made the harvest scene appealing to contemporary observers: the social harmony within the rural hierarchy (the "jolly" farmer is like a king, and "his people" are laughing as they work), the biblical associations of the subject, the variety of occupations to be observed, the presence of all ages and both sexes, and particularly children, the opportunities for refreshment and play. Wilson glosses over the fact that even very young children would probably have been gleaning rather than playing. In his discussion of barley harvest, however, he adopts a defensive tone that suggests an awareness that his rapturous account is more myth than reality: "We might almost persuade ourselves that human want was a fiction"; the mowers are "not the sons of misery and starvation."

William Howitt, Mary's husband, gave a similar description of harvest in his *Book of the Seasons* (1830): "It is in the wheat-field that all the jollity, and gladness, and picturesqueness of harvest are concentrated. . . . Wheat is everywhere the 'staff of life.' To reap and gather it in, every creature in the hamlet is assembled. The farmer is in his field, like a rural king among his people." But once again a defensive note creeps in:

> Let no-one say it is not a season of happiness to the toiling peasantry; I know that it is. In the days of boyhood I have partaken of their harvest labours, and listened to the overflowings of their hearts as they sate amid the sheaves beneath the fine blue sky. . . . I know that the poor harvesters are among the most thankful contemplators of the bounty of Providence, though so little of it falls to their share. To them harvest comes as an annual festivity. To their healthful frames, the heat of the open fields, which would oppress the languid and relaxed, is but an exhilarating and pleasant glow.[11]

Both Howitt and Wilson seem to be aware that harvest was, at best, a temporary interruption in the misery of rural life, and yet their descriptions of it are blissfully idyllic. Howitt's account is particularly interesting. He was the son of a yeoman farmer, who had helped on the farm in his youth but then moved to the town to pursue a career as a writer. He was thus typical of many members of the urban bourgeoisie of this period, who associated the countryside with their own childhood, and his memories were clearly coloured by nostalgia. His comments on the heat of the open fields are difficult to reconcile with what we know from other sources about the exhausting and back-breaking nature of harvest work, and his assertions that the harvesters are "thankful" and "healthful" are extraordinary, written as they were at the time of the Swing riots.

An anonymous article entitled "Harvest," published in the *Cornhill Magazine* in 1865, is more explicit about the darker side of rural life. Harvest is "certainly the most cheerful period of the rural year," but this is because "it is out of the corn-gathering that the labourer makes his annual crop, in the shape of wages, which sets him on his legs again—as far, poor fellow, as he can ever be said to be on his legs at all—for the ensuing year." Agricultural wages were not sufficient to support a family; labourers got into debt; the harvest earnings would just wipe out the debt but do no more than that. Harvest provided a temporary illusion of rural happiness:

> Few sights are more pleasing and exhilarating than the groups of reapers and mowers who are now to be met with in all the lanes and roads around a country village . . . returning merrily, if wearily home, after their long day's work. Their sunburnt faces . . . wear a happy and good-humoured look at this season, which is not always to be found on them. They wish you good night as they pass, in a franker and more friendly tone than usual. And these signs of human joy, combined with all the evidence of plenty lying round about one, enable a man, for the moment, to cheat himself into a real belief in the superiority of rural felicity.[12]

Here, then, the consciousness of the reality underlying the myth is stronger: the labourers are not usually so "happy and good-humoured," nor are they usually so frank and friendly (implicitly, towards their social superiors). This writer is evidently aware of the distress and discontent of the countryside, and implies that the old "belief in the superiority of rural felicity" is actually a delusion, though it is an attractive and poetic one.

The specific social and political circumstances of late eighteenth-century and nineteenth-century England made the old myths particularly compelling. People evidently liked to believe in the social hierarchy of the countryside, to see it as a site of stable social relationships: both Howitt and Wilson compare the farmer to a king amongst his people. Fears of revolution made this vision all the more appealing. In his study of Victorian attitudes, *The Victorian Frame of Mind* (1957), W. E. Houghton described British society in the period from 1790 to 1850 as "shot through, from top to bottom, with the dread of some wild outbreak by the masses that would overthrow the established order and confiscate personal property."[13] Despite the evidence of rick burning and machine breaking in the countryside, it was the towns that seemed to offer the greatest threat of revolutionary unrest: the Reform Bill riots of 1831–1832 took place in the towns (Nottingham, Derby and Bristol), and revolutions in Paris in 1830, and again in 1848, suggested a similar lesson. Even in 1833, not long after the Swing riots, William Howitt (who had watched Nottingham Castle being burnt down by rioters in 1831) could write: "Overgrown towns and manufactories may have changed, for the worse, the spirit and feelings of their population; in them 'evil communications may have corrupted good manners'; but in the country at large, there never was a more simple-minded, healthful-hearted and happy race of people than our British peasantry."[14] Observers liked to think that even the Swing riots were fomented by agitators from the towns, although evidence examined by Eric Hobsbawm and George Rudé shows that this was not in fact the case.[15]

A few paintings from this period emphasize the social harmony of the countryside directly and unambiguously. William Collins's *Rustic Civility* (fig. 8) shows a boy

8. William Collins
Rustic Civility, 1832. Oil on canvas, 28 × 36 in. (71.1 × 91.4 cm.). Devonshire Collection, Chatsworth.
Reproduced by permission of the Chatsworth Settlement Trustees.

opening a gate for a rider on horseback. The critic of *The Athenaeum* found it "much to our liking in all things. Three peasant children . . . are come to a gate, towards which, a rider of rank approaches. . . . The eldest, with a singular mixture of bashfulness and awe in his face, puts his hand to where his hat should be, and makes an obeisance with his looks."[16] This was written in 1832, the year the Reform Bill was passed, and it is significant that the writer uses the archaic, feudal word *obeisance*, as if recognising that the painting is a tribute to the paternalistic system threatened by reform. Significantly, the artist himself was worried that revolution might lead to the confiscation of property at the very time he was working on the picture, and the first version of it was sold to a member of the traditional aristocracy, the Duke of Devonshire.[17] William Maw Egley's *Hullo! Largesse* (fig. 9) of thirty years later also presents an approving comment on a hierarchical social structure. The workers he depicts are well dressed and healthy in appearance, young and old alike; rich and poor look benevolently at one another while the little girl feels in her pocket for a coin—a "largesse"—to give to her counterpart. Behind them all is the church, symbol of continuity and of God's blessing on the

9. WILLIAM MAW EGLEY

Hullo! Largesse: A Scene in Norfolk, 1862. Oil on canvas, 48 × 72 in. (121.9 × 182.9 cm.). Private collection.

social order. In other paintings, there is no direct portrayal of deference to rank, but the depiction of a contented, industrious workforce acts as a reassuring indicator that the social structure was safe in the countryside, however much it seemed threatened in the towns.

In 1871, the year when agricultural labourers were going on strike for higher wages, the critic of the *Art Journal* made a comment on Thomas Faed's works that neatly sums up the characteristics of the Victorian view of country life while cynically implying that it was just a myth:

> The pictures of Thomas Faed, R.A., usually speak of a life tranquil and content, of a conscience at ease, of a home made happy, of a peasantry industrious, honest, dutiful, true to the domestic affections, simple cottagers who never break into ambitious rebellion against the lot assigned to them by Providence.[18]

Evidently, contentment was seen as the natural accompaniment to a set of other virtues that would help to avert revolution: piety, industriousness, and family affection. In *The Dark Side of the Landscape* John Barrell has forcefully demonstrated how the demands of politically motivated moralists were reflected in the painting of the late eighteenth and early nineteenth centuries. He argues that the increasing insistence on work in paintings of rural life was not merely descriptive, but prescriptive: "The poor must be shown at work, not only because that is what they do, but because that is what they *ought* to do."[19] In this light the whole genre of agricultural landscape could be seen as didactic, aimed at encouraging industriousness in the working classes, although it should be remembered that the audience for such paintings was made up largely of the urban middle and working classes rather than the rural labourers themselves. There were, once again, a few paintings that were explicitly didactic, although they are generally known only from written records. For example, in 1837 a painter called Edward Prentis showed a pair of paintings: "*Fruits of Idleness*—a wounded poacher with his terrified family—and *Fruits of Industry*, a cottage dinner."[20] Paintings of industrious labourers would be comforting as well as didactic, not only because they showed rural workers as industrious, but also because they implied that the workers were "honest, dutiful"—otherwise they might be tempted to poach or steal instead of supporting their family with their wages.

A happy family life was seen as another characteristic of the rural, as opposed to the urban, working class. Written descriptions of harvest stress the participation of all ages, from the elderly to small children, the implication being that all members of an extended family can work together. In *Hullo! Largesse*, similarly, an old couple sit on one side while a baby lies amongst the sheaves. The family was of overriding importance to Victorian moralists: men who were "true to the domestic affections" would not indulge in drunkenness, crime or sedition, and their children would be brought up to become respectable citizens. For this reason, cosy cottage scenes were immensely popular and, in landscape paintings, family groups replace the flirting couples of the pastoral tradition. If the wives and children are not assisting in the work (for example, binding sheaves or gleaning), then they are shown bringing meals to the field at midday, as in Francis Wheatley's *Noon* (1799; cat. 6).

Central to the Victorian ideal of family life was the ideal wife and mother: modest, neat, frugal, gentle, submissive. Women in agricultural scenes usually conform to this ideal. They are decorously clothed, with high necklines, covered arms and bonnets. Often, they look too delicate and well dressed for a day of hard labour in the open air. Contemporary written accounts describe women field labourers as either very masculine or very promiscuous, inclined to foul language and willing to ignore the conventions of modesty, stripping to their bodices in the heat or tucking up their long skirts between their legs.[21] Such accounts may be exaggerated by middle-class fears of female sexuality, but they do present an interesting contrast to the image of agricultural women in the paintings. From the mid-nineteenth century, writers on the countryside tended to regard field work as "degrading to the female character" and tried to persuade young girls to go into domestic service instead, so that they could be trained as good housewives.[22] Paintings such as W. Holman Hunt's *Hireling Shepherd* (see fig. 3) with its brazen, flirtatious shepherdess, obviously shocked middle-class sensibilities in this area, as Kay Dian Kriz has pointed out.[23]

Amongst the list of peasant virtues cited by the reviewer in 1871—in addition to "a home made happy" and truth "to the domestic affections"—is "a conscience at ease."

10. WILLIAM COLLINS
Sunday Morning, 1836. Oil on canvas, 32 × 42 in. (81.3 × 106.7 cm.). Tate Gallery, London.

The Victorians liked to believe that rural labourers were pious, if only because this meant that they would obey the laws, respect the social hierarchy and avoid the temptations of revolution. Charles Kingsley said, with some justice, that his generation had "used the Bible as if it were a mere special constable's handbook—an opium-dose for keeping beasts of burden patient while they were being over-loaded."[24] Godlessness was associated with revolution: funds were poured into the building of new city churches in the early nineteenth century when it was noticed that the working class stopped attending church once they moved from the country to the town.[25] Several observers, including Hazlitt and Cobbett, pointed out that the rural working class was not, in fact, very pious; nevertheless, the sight of "a village congregation, pouring out from their old grey church on a summer day" was comforting.[26] So, too, was the idea that country people read the Bible (the only book they might possess). Many pictures exhibited in the mid-nineteenth century took titles like *Sunday Morning* (the walk to, or from, the village church; fig. 10) or *Sunday Evening* (cottage interiors, with families reading the Bible or saying prayers).

11. RICHARD REDGRAVE
Sunday Morning: The Walk from Church, 1846. Oil on canvas, 38 × 43⅝ in. (71.1 × 110.8 cm.). Private collection.

A reviewer's reaction to two examples of this type of painting, both shown in 1846, provides evidence of the pleasing associations that such scenes evoked, and of the subtle linkage between rural piety and social stability. Richard Redgrave's *Sunday Morning* (fig. 11) was described as treating "the happiness which surrounds the group of villagers, who, on the Sunday morning, in the quiet retirement of the country, quietly saunter home from church. . . . The selection of the landscape is in excellent keeping with the main topic,—embracing, as it does, the mansion of the squire and the lowly church." Redgrave's picture shows villagers of different social status, suggesting a world of hierarchical harmony supported by church and mansion. In the same review Thomas Webster's *Good Night* (fig. 12) was described in terms that show approval of the family affection, contentment, industriousness and piety of the rural labourer (or perhaps the small farmer, since this cottage looks too prosperous to be that of a day labourer):

> The smoking dish is on its way to the board; but even those whose appetites have been whetted by the day's labour, can pause with delight at the contemplation of the merry children. The expectant look of the hoary veteran, and the affection that beams through the cheerful countenance of the father, are felicitous touches of Nature. See, also, the quiet devotion with which the grandmother listens to the

Rural Myths and Values

12. Thomas Webster
Good Night, 1846. Oil on panel, 28⅛ × 46⅝ in. (71.4 × 118.7 cm.). Bristol Museums and Art Gallery.

prayer that she has taught. The last rays of the evening sun gild the recess of the window, and brighten the picturesque interior of one of those rustic homes where 'blest contentment' is joined with honest labour, and 'good night' is the harbinger of a well-earned rest.[27]

Rural life, then, could offer a didactic illustration of social and domestic virtues closely connected to religion, as well as a comforting statement that these virtues survived in the countryside, at a time when their absence in the city was a source of concern.

The didactic element in these paintings was hardly aimed directly at rural labourers, who, needless to say, did not visit exhibitions, although they might have been able to see prints of the paintings. Large numbers of people, however, attended the annual exhibitions at the Royal Academy and other venues in the mid-nineteenth century, so it is possible that members of the urban working class were exposed to these "lessons" in virtue—and perhaps reminded of the virtues they had left behind when they moved from the country to the town. Their main public, nevertheless, consisted of the upper and middle classes—the picture buyers—and for this group, too, they could be didactic as well as comforting. The reviewer of Webster's *Good Night* asserts that "the strong power of Art, as the evoker of the better feelings of our nature, works ever securely upon our emotions when wielded by the possessor of skill guided by benevolence."[28] The mention of benevolence suggests that the better feelings referred

13. GEORGE MORLAND
The Squire's Door, c. 1790. Oil on canvas, 15⁵⁄₁₆ × 12⁷⁄₈ in. (39.0 ×
32.7 cm.). Yale Center for British Art, Paul Mellon Collection.

to are those of charity—an essential part of a paternalistic social system. In the late
eighteenth century, awareness of distress and fears of revolution stimulated many
members of the governing classes to take a philanthropic interest in the rural poor, in
an attempt to foster the "mutual good will and connexion, which *ought* to subsist
between the rich and the poor."[29] Nigel Everett has described the theories of "improvement" that flourished in the late eighteenth and early nineteenth centuries,
encouraging the rich, especially landowners, to assist their poor neighbours and de-
pendents by building model cottages, providing gardens and generally exercising a
beneficial influence on village life. Stephen Daniels has demonstrated their influence
on the landscape gardening of Humphrey Repton, particularly in his plans for Abbot
Upcher's estate at Sheringham in 1812.[30] In the same period, the literature of "sensibility" emphasized the pleasures to be gained from acts of charity. Paintings that can be
regarded as direct illustrations of charity are fairly common in the late eighteenth
century.[31] In George Morland's *The Squire's Door* (fig. 13) for example, a lady gives
money to a ragged child. Other images are more obliquely related to the theme: the
object of charity is portrayed, but not the giver—his or her place is taken by the viewer
of the painting. Many of Gainsborough's "fancy pictures" are best understood in this

light; and paintings of the poor in general had the function of stimulating the benevolence of the viewer, as well as evoking the pleasurable emotions associated with the practice of charity.

Personal charity was a virtue easier to practise in the countryside than in the towns in the nineteenth century, and one that was becoming associated with a particular class and political viewpoint—that of the Tory landowner. Utilitarians warned of the dangers of indiscriminate almsgiving and derided it as motivated by selfishness and vanity. An article in 1824 in the *Westminster Review*, founded by Jeremy Bentham, argued that almsgiving could cause poverty and presented "sensibility" as a hypocritical aristocratic refinement: "There is something so flattering, so soothing to the vanity of a petty provincial aristocrat to be the object of reverence and gratitude to a set of half-starved peasants."[32] In the towns, strenuous efforts were made to round up beggars and discourage personal almsgiving. In London in 1818, for example, the Mendicity Society employed eight constables to arrest vagrants, and sold tickets for the rich to give to beggars instead of alms so that their cases could be investigated and help rendered only to the "deserving."[33] Paintings, therefore, could—in a sense—keep alive the virtue of personal charity without involving any of its undesirable social consequences.

The theme of charity is closely connected to religion (indeed, Utilitarians complained that charity sermons were to be heard weekly in the churches). The agricultural landscape, in an age of religious revival, was full of religious symbolism and associations—especially the wheat harvest. John Aikin's *Calendar of Nature* (1785) described the harvest scene as "a prospect equally delightful to the eye and the heart, . . . which ought to inspire every sentiment of benevolence to our fellow creatures, and gratitude to our creator."[34] Here, charity goes hand-in-hand with religion: the element of "toil" in the harvest field evokes benevolence, that of "plenty" evokes gratitude to God; and the relationship between God and man is a model for the relationship between the rich and the poor, with benevolence on the one side answered by gratitude on the other. Writers and artists of the late-eighteenth and nineteenth centuries were well aware of the biblical associations of agriculture, especially of the agricultural imagery used in the Psalms and in Christ's parables. Psalm 65 was particularly likely to come to mind in this period at the sight of a harvest field. In 1795 an anonymous pamphlet cited Psalm 65 as appropriate to the harvest of that year: "How naturally ought the season of harvest to send our thoughts to the *great author* of it! . . . The vallies are again covered over with corn, again they shout, for joy they also sing."[35] Samuel Palmer inscribed the words of Psalm 65 on the original mount of *The Valley Thick with Corn* (fig. 14), one of his six sepia landscapes of 1825, now in the Ashmolean Museum, Oxford. The imagery of the psalm is used in several of the hymns written for the Harvest Festival that was instituted in the 1840s; William Howitt begins his chapter on August with it in his *Year Book of the Country* (1850);[36] and Richard Redgrave alluded to it in the title of his harvest landscape of 1864, *The Valleys Also Stand Thick with Corn* (cat. 35).

14. SAMUEL PALMER
The Valley Thick with Corn, 1825. Sepia, mixed with gum and varnished, 7⅛ × 10⅞ in. (18.3 × 27.7 cm.). The Visitors of the Ashmolean Museum, Oxford.

15. JOHN LINNELL
Wheat, 1860. Oil on canvas, 37 × 55 in. (94.2 × 140.6 cm.). Reproduced by permission of the National Gallery of Victoria, Melbourne.

The religious associations of harvest were also important to Peter DeWint and John Linnell, two painters who specialised in the genre. DeWint, said to have been so religious that he never started work without a prayer, often includes churches in the background of his harvest scenes. A critic wrote of these scenes in 1824: "The cornfield is rich and begets reflection. It is the consummation of the farmer's hopes and toil, and excites a whole people to acknowledge the goodness of a bountiful Creator."[37] The terminology here is very similar to Aikin's, although it is interesting to note that the "toil" is attributed to the farmer, not the labourer. John Linnell, who painted many harvest scenes, mostly after 1850 (fig. 15), rarely includes church spires (being a Nonconformist in religion), but religion was a major motivation behind his choice of subject matter. In 1828 he wrote to Samuel Palmer that he was looking forward to seeing the harvest, "that glorious type of the everlasting Harvest of spirits, the gathering of the saints"; and in a poem written in the 1860s he declares:

I'll paint the reapers in the harvest field,
At work or rest, for both will yield
Pictures of happiness and bounteous love,
Bestowed on just and unjust from above.[38]

To a large extent, then, agricultural landscape painting can be seen as an expression of religious feeling, a substitute for the religious painting that it was difficult to produce in Protestant England. Many other artists included churches in the background of agricultural, and especially harvest, scenes, and it is likely that their choice of this motif was not dictated by purely aesthetic considerations.

The biblical associations of harvest were, of course, strongest when traditional methods were used. As William Howitt observed in 1830: "there is something . . . about wheat harvest which carries back the mind and feasts it with the pleasures of antiquity. The sickle is almost the only implement which has descended from the olden times in its pristine simplicity. . . . It is the same now as it was in those scenes of rural beauty which the scripture history . . . presents so livingly to the imagination."[39] Even in 1885, when the mechanisation of harvest was far advanced, P. G. Hamerton wrote that the sight of a poor girl gleaning always made him think of Ruth (partly as a result of the reference to Ruth in Keats's "Ode to a Nightingale"). Although he disliked modern agriculture, Hamerton declared that "almost everything that the peasant does is lifted far above vulgarity by ancient and often sacred associations."[40] The religious meaning of agricultural scenes helps explain why so many artists avoided depicting new methods, and also why certain subjects with strong religious associations, such as harvest and gleaning (an illustration of charity to the poor) were so popular. In an age of technological advance, harvest was a reminder of man's dependence on God; and in an age of revolutions, usually brought on by urban distress, a good harvest could contribute to social stability. In 1842 a national thanksgiving was announced as a result of the good harvest. The *Christian Observer* welcomed the news and commented: "The benefits of an abundant harvest at the present time of distress and discontent, are of incalculable moment; and there is no blessing of Divine Providence which seems more directly to appeal to the eye and the heart as being the gift of God; for whatever man may boast of achieving, he cannot command sunshine, or shower, or genial seasons."[41] It was during the 1840s, too, that the annual harvest festival began to be celebrated in English churches.

A painting of a good harvest was not only an illustration of the goodness of God; it could also be a symbol of peace, prosperity, social harmony and good government, and thus an expression of patriotic pride. The association of harvest scenes with peace has a long history. In 1640 Inigo Jones, designing a background for a masque, used corn-fields, trees, vines and villages to "expresse a country in peace, rich, and fruitful."[42] Thomson, in *The Seasons*, stressed that agricultural scenes were the basis for the greatness of "Happy Britannia": ". . . thy country teems with wealth; / And Property assures it to the Swain."[43] In 1794 William Hodges produced a pair of paintings to illustrate "Peace" and "War": "Peace" included "a rich cornfield."[44] Harvest scenes flourished in British art in the 1810s and again in the 1850s—both periods of war—as if indicating a longing for peace and a recognition of the contribution of agriculture to the war effort. In the late 1840s and 1850s harvest scenes seem to have expressed a pride in the internal peace of Britain, as one of the few European countries to escape revolutionary disorder in 1848. In this period harvest landscapes were often entitled simply *England* (T. Creswick, 1847), *English Landscape* (J. Dearle, 1856) or *English Valley* (J. Jutsum, 1859).[45] The last of these was described by a reviewer as "another cereal poem: he devotes himself in a manner most exemplary to the agricultural prosperity of his country."[46] In 1865 the *Art Journal* revealed the self-confident atti-tude that lay behind such paintings:

> British Art is like the island that gave it birth. . . . Its range . . . is as varied as our inland valleys, our woodland streams, and our sea-girt coasts, peopled by a peaceful peasantry and girded by the gallant mariner. . . . Happy the land that finds in nature a benignant providence; and blessed the people that makes its truth-seeking Art the expression of the joys of domestic life and the reflection of a nation's greatness.[47]

This passage includes many of the elements of the rural myth—the "peasantry" (not labourers) are "peaceful"—that is, contented and docile—providence is "benignant" and art expresses "the joys of domestic life" as well as "a nation's greatness."

Although Thomson had written of Britannia and the *Art Journal* refers to British art, the titles of agricultural landscape paintings often specify *England*—and this usu-ally means southern England, particularly the Home Counties. In this period, the idea that this landscape represents England as a whole had strong political overtones, setting agricultural England against the "manufacturing civilisation" of the growing northern cities and implying that the south was somehow more authentic, the "real" England (despite the fact that industrialisation was an indigenous product). Martin Wiener and Alun Howkins have demonstrated how, in the second half of the nineteenth century, a concept of Englishness was emerging that excluded the industrial north. Wiener writes that the true English character was seen as based in the countryside: "Rural life was the repository of the moral character of the nation. It could *not* change, or England herself would be in mortal danger."[48] In Wiener's analysis, the aristocracy and gentry asserted their cultural superiority over the manufacturers in the wake of their political defeats over the Reform Bill and the Corn Laws; as a result, "preindustrial aristocratic and religious values" were adopted by leaders of commerce and industry.[49] Howkins has emphasized the dominance of the "South country" in this new idea of Englishness.[50]

The history of agricultural landscape painting lends weight to their arguments and suggests that the process began even before 1851, described by Wiener as the "high-water mark of industrial values."[51] Paintings helped establish the cultivated counties of the south as the setting for demonstrations of rural virtue; and already in the 1840s they were seen as symbolic of England as a whole. Wiener has pointed out that newly enriched manufacturers and merchants emulated the traditional gentry, buying country houses and acting out the role of the paternalistic squire, thus adopting the values of the class they had displaced. A similar process can be observed in the purchase by northern industrialists of harvest scenes set in Surrey, such as those of John Linnell. The adoption of "rural" values thus tended to confirm the social prestige of the aristocracy and gentry despite their apparent defeat by the new classes in the 1830s and 1840s. Richard Cobden, co-founder of the Anti-Corn Law League, complained to a friend in 1863: "Feudalism is everyday more and more in the ascendant in political and social life. So great is its power and prestige that it draws to it the support and homage of even those who are the natural leaders of the newer and better civilisation" (by which Cobden meant industrial civilisation).[52]

There was a radical as well as a conservative side to the opposition to "manufacturing civilisation." The myth of a prosperous preindustrial past—the "Merrie England" in which all lived on roast beef and plum pudding—was a potent force in radical and socialist circles of the early and mid-nineteenth century. It was reflected in Feargus O'Connor's Chartist Land Plan, which aimed to restore peasant proprietorship, and also in the writings of Friedrich Engels. The early socialist Robert Owen based his cooperative schemes on the idea of the village; and William Morris, much later in the century, imagined in *News from Nowhere* (1890) a postindustrial socialist paradise in which the population had moved back from the towns to the countryside.[53] William Cobbett railed against the "Great Wen" of London, and repeatedly declared his belief that rural England had once supported a much larger and more prosperous population than it did in the early nineteenth century. Robert Southey, who lamented the demise of the yeoman, advocated paternalistic state intervention in opposition to the laissez-faire principles of the Political Economists and wanted the land to be returned to labourers dispossessed by enclosure.[54]

Both Southey and Cobbett, however, changed their political allegiance in mid-career. Southey began as a Radical but became a Tory; Cobbett moved in the opposite direction, from old-style Toryism to Radical championship of the rights of the working class. In this they were not untypical of their generation. Nigel Everett has pointed out that radical and conservative positions often became indistinguishable, as a result of their common identification of a "liberal" enemy—manufacturing civilisation and political economy.[55] In the socialism of men like Robert Owen and William Morris (and also in the diatribes of Cobbett) there was a strong element of admiration for the feudal past. The charity dispensed by the monasteries before the Reformation, for example, would be compared favourably to the callousness of the new Poor Law and the workhouses. Reacting against the horrifying conditions in the new industrial towns and against the hard, utilitarian values of the industrialists, many would-be radicals were drawn into an idealisation of the rural past which has obvious affinities with its representation in art and literature—and thus into a reactionary, Tory set of values. An inclination to accept rural myths did not necessarily imply a Tory, feudal, pro-aristocracy world view, but, on the whole, rural mythology did help bolster the cultural hegemony of the class that owned, or had owned, the land.

Idyllic rural scenes could appeal to all shades of political opinion in the nineteenth century, too, simply as a contrast to the noise and claustrophobia of the city, the pace of modern urban life and the intellectual threats to traditional belief. Agricultural landscapes, like all rural scenes, were symbols of continuity in a rapidly changing world. As a reviewer wrote of F. R. Lee's *Holm Mill* in 1846: "Such spots speak to the mind of ages of undisturbed quietude, and from among the soot and bricks of London, the eye rests upon their duplicates . . . with a sense of grateful refreshment."[56] The alienated urban intellectual could derive comfort from the apparent peace, companionship and unifying belief of village life. J. A. Froude wrote in 1849 of having "flown to and fro upon the ocean of speculation, finding no place for his soul to rest" and turning back "in thought, at least, to that old time of peace—that village church—that child-faith—which, once lost, is never gained again."[57] In the newly industrialised, recently urbanised society of early Victorian England, the countryside and its traditional occupations were associated with childhood or with holidays, with innocence and refreshment—and this could apply to the urban working class as well as to the middle class. In this sense, rural imagery had an almost universal appeal. This appeal—to all town dwellers, radical or conservative—may explain the fact, noted by Andrew Hemingway, that even the bourgeois radicals closest to utilitarianism failed to produce any critique of "the celebratory mythology of the rural" in the early nineteenth century, despite attacking the aristocratic privileges that were supported by this mythology.[58]

As we have seen, many of the myths enshrined in the paintings were only half believed in. They were contradicted by news reports or by the evidence of the real countryside, available to those who lived or travelled in it. There was also an alternative tradition—stronger in literature than in art—which emphasized the hardships of the labourer's life and mocked some of the poetic illusions surrounding it. W. J. Keith has dubbed this tradition a "counter-myth": "Myths regularly provoke counter-myths. The pastoral tradition, in substituting Arcadia or Eden for the realities of country life, is not likely to pass unchallenged for long, but the concentration upon squalor and misery need be no more accurate than an emphasis on charm and ease."[59] In the late eighteenth century the most important literary manifestation of this counter-myth was the poetry of George Crabbe. In *The Village* (1783) he denied that rural life had any charms except for the farmer or the landowner; the labourers, "the poor laborious natives" of the countryside, were joyless and sullen, neglected or callously exploited by their superiors, worn down by hard labour and disease, and given to drunkenness and riotous behaviour.[60] Thomson had described the sight of a cornfield as "a calm of plenty," a "heart-expanding view," but Crabbe was more cynical:

> Where Plenty smiles—alas! She smiles for few—
> And those who taste not, yet behold her store,
> Are as the slaves that dig the golden ore—
> The wealth around them makes them doubly poor.[61]

In 1783 Crabbe's reaction against the pastoral myth has a tone of indignation, which many have seen as anticipating the mood of the French Revolution. By 1807, however, when he came to write "The Parish Register," his tone is different: he makes a sharp distinction between those labourers who are virtuous and those who are improvident and vicious. The good labourers are industrious, read the Bible and have prints of Louis XVI, Marie Antoinette and Charles I on their walls; their "indulgent" lord has allotted them garden ground on which they grow fruits, vegetables and herbs. The improvident labourers are dirty, drunken wife-beaters whose garden ground is full of weeds and whose sons and daughters sleep together, close to their parents: "Toil, care and patience bless th'abstemious few, / Fear, shame and want the thoughtless herd pursue."[62] In this poem Crabbe presents as his ideal labourer one Isaac Ashford, "A wise good man contented to be poor."[63] In the end, then, Crabbe comes close to the purveyors of rural myths in his emphasis on the virtues needed to maintain social stability.

From the 1840s onwards, the counter-myth of rural misery becomes more insistent in literature and, eventually, in painting, too. Disraeli's novel *Sybil* (1845) follows Crabbe in underlining the contrast between the visual attractiveness of the country-side and the suffering of its poor inhabitants. The rural town of Marney, Disraeli wrote, was a "beautiful illusion! For behind that laughing landscape penury and disease fed upon the vitals of a miserable population."[64] Charles Kingsley, in *Yeast* (1848), used remarkably similar language when he remarked that "picturesque villages are generally the perennial hotbeds of fever and ague, of squalid penury, sottish profligacy, dull discontent too stale for words."[65] Articles by Richard Jefferies, published in the 1870s, stressed the monotony, hard labour, and immorality of life in the countryside, to such an extent that one compiler of his writings claimed that, as a result of Jefferies and his contemporaries, "the 1870s saw the dispersal of the pastoral-idyllic myth as far as descriptions of the farm labourer's life were concerned."[66] Exhibition reviewers, however, from around 1850, were increasingly critical of the pastoral-idyllic myth.

16. WALTER HOWELL DEVERELL
The Irish Vagrants, 1853–54. Oil on canvas, 24¹⁵⁄₁₆ × 30⅜ (63.4 × 77.2 cm.). Johannesburg Art Gallery.

Perhaps the truth is that throughout this period the two myths coexisted: the "rural misery" myth was more plausible, but substantial sections of the population had good reasons for wishing to believe the idyllic myth.

The emphasis on rural misery was always more suited to literary than artistic expression. Writers could exploit the contrasts between pastoral poetry and contemporary reality, but artists had a vested interest in making their images attractive. Victorian picture-buyers and critics particularly liked "pleasing" images that provided refreshment in the bustle and ugliness of city life. As John Eagles put it in 1848: "Is the man of business, in this weary turmoil of the daily world, to return to his house, after his labour is over, and see upon his walls nothing but scenes of distress, of poverty, of misery, of hard-heartedness—when he should indulge his sight and his mind with every thing that would tend to refresh his worn spirits, avert painful fears, either for himself or others, and should tune himself, by visible objects of rational hilarity, into the full and free harmonies of a vigorous courage, and health of social nature?"[67] It seems highly likely that the "painful fears" Eagles refers to included the fear of revolutionary unrest (the article was published in February 1848, the month when revolution broke out in France). In the same article Eagles made a scathing attack on realism in landscape painting and described even Gainsborough as a painter of the "low natural."

There are, however, some paintings of agricultural landscape and labourers that could be classed as counter-pastoral rather than idyllic. In the late eighteenth and early nineteenth centuries a number of artists, including James Ward, Thomas Barker of Bath and George Morland, produced closely observed studies of rural figures which emphasize the hard labour and poverty of rural life (cat. 1, 2, 54). Something of their viewpoint survives in the figures that people the landscapes of J. M. W. Turner and John Linnell in the first decades of the nineteenth century (cat. 8, 12). In the 1850s the more explicit social protest of the Pre-Raphaelites produced some memorable images of rural poverty. Deverell's *Irish Vagrants* (fig. 16) even looks like a deliberate comment on Collins's *Rustic Civility* (see fig. 8), replacing an image of deference and paternalism with one showing callous indifference on the part of the gentry and sullen defiance on the part of the poor. This tendency towards "social realism" gathered strength in the 1860s and 1870s, culminating in the work of George Clausen in the early 1880s.

Such paintings, however, were always in the minority. Many more are related to the pastoral-idyllic myth, which was undoubtedly the dominant myth of the period (especially before 1850) and had a deep influence on the representation of agricultural life and labour in the visual arts. This myth was an updated combination of the ancient myths of the greater happiness and virtue of rural as opposed to urban life: its main claim was that the rural working class was contented, industrious, pious, deferential and full of family affection, and thus provided a secure foundation for a stable social system. It appealed particularly to those who supported the social and moral prestige of a paternalistic aristocracy and gentry, but it was also a comforting idea for all members of the middle class who were fearful of revolution. In addition, it could appeal to radicals and socialists attacking the evils of capitalism and industrialisation, and to all Victorian town dwellers, rich or poor, who felt that their roots were in the countryside.

Chapter Three
Paintings of the
Agricultural Landscape

The main stylistic developments in the representation of agricultural landscape from 1780 to 1890 fall into three periods, divided by the political watersheds of the ending of the Napoleonic Wars in 1815 and the revolutionary year 1848. In the first period, there was a move away from artificial, arcadian pastorals to studies of actual labourers, paralleled by an increasing interest in topographical landscapes and plein-air naturalism. From 1816 to 1848, naturalistic agricultural landscapes are found mainly in the work of the watercolourists, especially Peter DeWint and David Cox; in the same period, sentimental rural genre paintings, the escapist idylls of Palmer, or rural scenes set in the eighteenth century all seem to reflect disenchantment with contemporary rural society and the need for reassurance in a time of threats of revolution. After 1848, a new mood of optimism meant that idyllic harvest scenes became very popular; but at the same time, growing publicity about rural conditions produced a trend towards "social realism," beginning with the Pre-Raphaelites. This realist strain was encouraged by the influence of contemporary French painting from the mid-1850s and culminated in the work of George Clausen in the early 1880s.

The paintings, watercolours and drawings in the exhibition range from sketchbook studies to highly finished exhibition pictures. Most of the latter were first exhibited in London, at the Royal Academy (founded 1768) or the Society of Painters in Water-Colours (founded 1804 and known popularly after 1832 as the Old Water-Colour Society). During the course of the nineteenth century, many other exhibiting societies grew up (such as the British Institution and the Society of British Artists), but the Royal Academy maintained its primacy for most of the century. At the Academy, paintings tended to be more carefully composed and more laden with meaning than at the other exhibiting societies—thanks partly to the efforts of its first president, Sir Joshua Reynolds, who encouraged its students to aspire to history painting and to be conscious of their role as founders of a new British school of painting. The Society of Painters in Water-Colours, by contrast, always had a bias towards less ambitious landscapes, and particularly topographical landscapes. Hence the most unaffected treatments of agricultural landscape are often to be found in watercolour rather than oil—especially in the early part of the period. From 1813 to 1820 the Society of Painters in Water-Colours became the Society of Painters in Oil and Water-Colours and accepted oils as well, thus providing a useful forum for naturalistic landscape painting in oils: both John Linnell and G. R. Lewis showed paintings there.

Exhibitions were extremely important for landscape painters, because very few works were done on commission. Agricultural landscapes were only commissioned if they were of particular places (such as the patron's house or his estate); most were painted as a speculation and then exhibited in the hope of finding a buyer; later on in the nineteenth century, they might be sold to a dealer. The interests of the buyers, or patrons, were thus exerted only indirectly: artists were not told what to paint, but they had a vested interest in finding subjects that were appealing and in treating them in ways that would please their patrons.

The buyers of agricultural landscapes were, in the first period, usually from the aristocracy and gentry, but from the 1820s they were more likely to be from the newly enriched middle classes—merchants, manufacturers and industrialists.[1] This does not necessarily mean that the artistic view of rural life becomes more "urban" or less accurate after 1820, or that agricultural scenes lost their meaning. Andrew Hemingway, in his study of landscape painting and criticism in the early nineteenth century, found that there was no clear demarcation between aristocratic and bourgeois taste. The gentry should not be seen as representing an exclusively rural perspective. They may have had country estates, but they spent much of their time in town houses in London, and they may well have hung their agricultural landscapes in their town houses to remind themselves of the countryside.[2] As we have seen, the myths associated with rural life appealed to the new as well as the old sections of the ruling classes. A further complication is a renewed interest in plein-air study and in agriculture in the 1850s and 1860s, which meant that artists and critics of this period, despite being based in the city, had a surprisingly detailed knowledge of agricultural practices. Changing patterns of patronage did, however, mean that social realism had more chance of success after 1820 (and especially after 1850, when fears of revolution abated), whereas earlier it would have had little appeal for landowners, whose wealth was derived from the labours of the rural poor.

Agricultural landscape is relatively rare in the history of European landscape painting before the nineteenth century, and as such it may have seemed, in the early years of the Royal Academy, to offer distinctive subject matter for a new national school. The available artistic precedents reinforced the religious and patriotic associations of agricultural landscape. It appears in paintings of the seasons, which developed from illustrations in prayer books, or in the backgrounds to religious paintings, or else in paintings illustrating good government or good estate management.[3] Flemish painters—Joachim Patinir, Pieter Breugel, Peter Paul Rubens, Jan Siberechts—seem to have been especially attracted to it. Rubens and Siberechts spent time working in Britain, and indeed many of the landscape painters in England in the late seventeenth and early eighteenth centuries were Flemish immigrants. On the other hand, agricultural landscape is rather rare in Dutch painting, although it does appear in the work of Jacob van Ruisdael, an artist who was much admired by Gainsborough and Constable.

However, in academic theory at least, the Dutch and Flemish schools were regarded as inferior to the classical landscape tradition, epitomised by the paintings of Claude Lorraine, of which there were many in British collections by the early nineteenth century. This tradition generally excludes agriculture, as does the work of its followers, such as the entire oeuvre of Richard Wilson in the eighteenth century and much of the output of J. M. W. Turner in the nineteenth century. In the hierarchy of the arts, landscape occupied a subordinate position; classical subject matter could "elevate" it, but agricultural landscape was a particularly "low" form. Influential theorists, including William Gilpin and John Ruskin, advised artists to paint "sublime" subjects, such as mountains, instead. For Gilpin, writing in the late eighteenth century, "haymaking—harvesting—and other employments of husbandry" were "low vulgarisms," suited only for "inferior modes of landscape."[4] The taste for the "picturesque," which became fashionable in the late eighteenth century—partly as a result of Gilpin's writings and partly, as Ann Bermingham has argued, as a "compensatory response" to enclosure—encouraged the aesthetic appreciation of uncultivated nature, of woodlands rather than fields and of idle rather than working figures.[5] In the first volume of *Modern Painters* (1843), Ruskin similarly exhorted artists to paint "nature in her liberty, not as servant of all work in the hands of the agriculturist." He thought that Constable's work, with its emphasis on cultivated landscape, showed "a morbid preference for subjects of a low order," reserving his highest praise for painters of grand mountain scenery, particularly Turner.[6]

Nevertheless, popular taste did rate agricultural landscape highly. In addition to the social and political reasons for this (discussed in chapter 2), popular literature also provides evidence of the appreciation of the variety of colours and textures to be found in cultivated landscape, backed up by a surprisingly detailed understanding of agricultural practices. William Hone's *Every-day Book* (1826), for example, contains precise observations on the appearance of the landscape in late July:

> The cornfields are all redundant with waving corn—gold of all hues—from the light yellow of the oats (those which still remain uncut) to the deep sunburnt glow of the red wheat. But the wide rich sweeps of these fields are now broken in upon, here and there, by patches of the parched and withered looking bean crop; by occasional bits of newly ploughed land, where the rye lately stood; by the now darkening turnips—dark, except where they are being fed off by sheep flocks; and lastly by the still bright-green meadows, now studded everywhere with grazing cattle, the second crops of grass being already gathered in.[7]

For the artist, then, the agricultural landscape had considerable appeal: it was widely appreciated, both on purely aesthetic grounds and for its political, moral and religious connotations. But it also had the stigma of being low subject matter, and a persistent study of it could involve a certain degree of resistance to prevailing aesthetic theories and academic hierarchies. Some artists found that painting naturalistic agricultural landscapes did little for their careers; others attempted to elevate agricultural subject matter by stressing its classical or biblical associations.

The earliest works of the first period are near in date to those of the French painter François Boucher (1703–1770), whose paintings represent the pastoral tradition in its most artificial form. Boucher's shepherds and shepherdesses wear silk and satin and are symbols of aristocratic fantasies of the simple life (see fig. 7), a product of a society that wore pastoral dress for court balls and in which Marie Antoinette used to play at being a milkmaid in the Petit Trianon. In England, this rococo form of pastoral was never taken to such extremes. It did, however, exert an influence on opera and the theatre, and on Francis Hayman's decorations for Vauxhall Gardens in London in the 1740s.[8] Some of Gainsborough's early works are stylistically similar to Boucher's pastorals, and there was a fashion for the rich to have themselves portrayed in the character of gleaners or cottagers.[9] Gainsborough's *Peasant Girl Gathering Faggots* (fig. 17), for example, is a portrait of a girl of the Abdy family, who owned a country house. In the 1780s and 1790s several paintings and drawings depict labourers with a degree of grace, elegance and refinement that suggests an affinity either with aristocrats amusing themselves or with the peasants of opera choruses. Most of Thomas Rowlandson's harvesters, for example, could almost be part of the crowd at the Assembly Rooms in Bath; and the figures depicted by Julius Caesar Ibbetson and Thomas Hearne, similarly, are elegantly dressed and graceful in their movements (cat. 40, 41, 43). Gainsborough's late landscapes and fancy pictures have been persuasively linked by Marcia Pointon with the fashion for "retirement" in the late eighteenth century and thus with aristocratic yearnings for the simple life. In 1814 William Hazlitt criticised Gainsborough for having "led the way to that masquerade style, which piques itself on giving the air of an Adonis to the driver of a hay-cart, and models the features of a milkmaid on the principles of the antique."[10]

17. Thomas Gainsborough
Peasant Girl Gathering Faggots, 1782. Oil on canvas, 66½ ×
48½ in. (169 × 123 cm.). Manchester City Art Galleries.

Gainsborough's late rural pictures, however, are extremely complex images. In the
Peasant Girl, as in other pictures of the 1770s and 1780s, there is a strong hint of the
charity theme: this poor girl could be waiting for a benevolent observer to press a coin
into her hand, and, as eighteenth-century observers looked at the painting, they might
experience all the pleasurable emotions associated with sensibility, without any of its
practical drawbacks. The figures in his late paintings are not always so refined: right at
the end of his career Gainsborough was making careful studies of actual labourers, like
his celebrated *Woodman*. Such pictures, therefore, represent much more than aristocratic fantasies or masquerades, and it is not surprising that they have been seen as a
parallel to Wordsworth's poetry, as well as to the poetry of retirement. George Stubbs's
agricultural scenes are equally difficult to categorise. His *Reapers* are very fashionably
dressed and excessively neat and clean, yet they seem to have the features, not of actors
or aristocrats, but of real labourers. Stubbs was primarily a sporting painter who
painted his subjects from nature. He painted portraits of his patrons' stable lads and

hunt servants, so it is possible that the first versions of his *Reapers* and *Haymakers* were the result of a similar commission. Nevertheless, his reworking of the subjects and his very fastidious style give the paintings an artificial air that is curiously combined with their more documentary elements.[11]

In the 1790s, as Marilyn Butler has pointed out, the sentimental yearning for the simple life came to seem old-fashioned and potentially dangerous or subversive.[12] There is a corresponding change in depictions of rural life, which begin to concentrate less on the fantasies of the rich and more on the character and morality of the labourers themselves. This was the decade immediately following the French revolution—a decade of repression, and of attempts to persuade the English poor to be "contented" so that the social order could be maintained. Paintings by Francis Wheatley and Richard Westall represent the virtues of the peasantry, but with contrasting emphasis. Westall treated his *Storm in Harvest* (cat. 5) like a history painting, giving the labourers an "elevated" air, especially the old man who, despite his rustic features, has the stoicism of a Roman. Westall's picture was very successful, and he painted several versions as well as reproducing it in the form of a print. Interestingly, two of the would-be purchasers were prominent Whig M.P.s of Radical tendencies, Samuel Whitbread and Richard Payne Knight, who may have appreciated the way Westall attributes "noble" emotions to the labourers.[13] Writing about the picture, Payne Knight described it as "affecting" and a stimulus to "tender" and "pathetic" feelings, indicating that it also appealed to the sentiments of charity and benevolence.[14] Wheatley's series *The Four Times of Day* (cat. 6, 7) stresses, rather, the "desirable" virtues of the poor—those that would prevent revolution, such as piety, family affection, industriousness and self-sufficiency—and thus anticipates much of the didactic painting of the early to mid-nineteenth century. In the same period George Morland produced some images that emphasized didacticism, some that illustrated charity, and others that, as John Barrell has shown, indicated the real class conflict underlying the acceptable image of the rural poor.[15] Curiously, though, Morland seems to have painted no real agricultural landscapes. Indeed, agricultural landscape (rather than genre) was somewhat out of fashion in the 1780s and 1790s, partly as a result of the influence of theories of the picturesque.

Even the labourers of Westall and Wheatley, however, are not based on studies of real labourers. Mrs Wheatley apparently posed for the pretty young women in the *Times of Day*, and Westall probably used professional models. In all these paintings the standard of accuracy in the representation of agricultural detail is not very high. Robert Bloomfield, the poet, wrote that he had never seen a Suffolk codger like the young man in the *Storm in Harvest*, and he could not work out whether the crop was barley or wheat.[16] There are, however, some indications, towards the end of the century, of a search for greater authenticity in images of rural life. Gainsborough's *Woodman* was followed by Thomas Barker's picture of the same title, which was painted from an actual woodman (cat. 1): in the 1790s, Barker did many portrait-like studies of beggars and peasants, usually of old men and women.[17] In the first decade of the nineteenth century such "documentary" images of rustic figures became very widespread. They are found not only in painting but also in book illustrations and drawing manuals. This movement is linked to documentary pictures of agriculture, which became common in the late eighteenth and early nineteenth centuries, years of intensive agricultural progress. Landowners, from the King downwards, took an active interest in "improvement," and many commissioned artists to record their livestock, implements and agricultural events. These decades were also years of war with France, when agriculture was an integral part of the war effort, and thus inherently patriotic.

The best-known results of this flowering of documentary art are the livestock portraits—paintings of incredibly fat sheep and cattle—but several artists who did livestock portraits also did similarly careful studies of rural labourers. Livestock portraits were highly regarded and even shown regularly at the Royal Academy; Stubbs did them, as did James Ward.[18] Ward was a close associate of W. H. Pyne, whose *Microcosm* (cat. 98) includes illustrations of many different agricultural processes, as well as studies of rustic figures in a variety of occupations. Ward and Pyne, with Robert Hills, founded the Sketching Society in 1800, a group of artists who met weekly at each other's houses and made sketching expeditions into the countryside.[19] Pyne and Hills were amongst the founding members of the Society of Painters in Water-Colours in 1804, whose early exhibitions included many studies of rustic figures and agricultural landscapes by Joshua Cristall, Thomas Uwins, David Cox, Peter DeWint, William Turner of Oxford, and John and Cornelius Varley. In comparison to later paintings, the figure studies of the Pyne circle seem to be approached in a detached, objective way. Even here, however, idealisation, didacticism and reassurance are not entirely absent. Pyne's *Microcosm* had an avowedly patriotic motive; the inscription on Ward's *Wiltshire Peasant* (cat. 54) stresses the virtue of industriousness, and Cristall's figures often have classical features. As a critic wrote of Cristall's work in 1812, they were "such as we wish to meet in every village," raising "in the mind of the spectator none but images of pleasure," with no hint, evidently, of distress, discontent or injustice: "The gleanings are from a golden harvest, and are not scattered with a sparing hand."[20]

This intensive study of the rustic figure was the background to the agricultural landscapes of the "decade of naturalism": works by Constable, Turner, DeWint, Cox, Lewis and Linnell. The term was coined by John Gage and applied to the decade from 1810 to 1820.[21] As far as agricultural landscape is concerned, however, 1807–1816 is a more accurate range—from Turner's studies on the Thames to the harvest scenes exhibited by Lewis and Constable in 1816. In this decade plein-air studies became common amongst the more adventurous British landscape painters. Just as the figure painters had left their studios to find authentic models in the countryside, so the landscapists, too, were painting entire pictures from nature or making open-air sketches, in oil or watercolour, on which exhibition pictures were closely based. Accurate detail became a matter for pride, and several pictures (including Lewis's harvest

PLATE 1. THOMAS BARKER
Old Man with a Staff, c. 1790. Oil on canvas. (cat. 2)

PLATE 2. GEORGE STUBBS
Reapers, 1795. Enamel on Wedgwood biscuit earthenware. (cat. 4)

PLATE 3. RICHARD WESTALL
A Storm in Harvest, 1796. Oil on card, loosely mounted on canvas. (cat. 5)

PLATE 4. FRANCIS WHEATLEY
Noon, 1799. Oil on canvas. (cat. 6)

PLATE 5. JOSEPH MALLORD WILLIAM TURNER
Ploughing Up Turnips, near Slough, 1809. Oil on canvas. (cat. 8)

Plate 6. Thomas Barker
Sheep Shearing, c. 1812. Oil on canvas. (cat. 9)

PLATE 7. JOHN CONSTABLE
Golding Constable's Kitchen Garden, 1815. Oil on canvas. (cat. 11)

PLATE 8. PETER DeWINT
The Cornfield, c. 1815. Oil on canvas. (cat. 13)

PLATE 9. GEORGE ROBERT LEWIS
Hereford, Dynedor and the Malvern Hills from the Haywood Lodge, Harvest Scene, Afternoon. Painted on the Spot,
1815–16. Oil on canvas. (cat. 14)

PLATE 10. JOHN CONSTABLE
Landscape: Ploughing Scene in Suffolk, c. 1825. Oil on canvas. (cat. 16)

PLATE 11. GEORGE VINCENT
Trowse Meadows, near Norwich, 1828. Oil on canvas. (cat. 17)

PLATE 12. JOHN LINNELL
Shepherd Boy Playing a Flute, 1831. Oil on panel. (cat. 19)

PLATE 13. SAMUEL PALMER
The Harvest Moon, 1833. Oil on paper, laid on panel. (cat. 20)

PLATE 14. JOHN LINNELL
The Harvest, 1850–53. Oil on canvas. (cat. 24)

PLATE 15. FORD MADOX BROWN
Carrying Corn, 1854–55. Oil on panel. (cat. 26)

PLATE 16. FORD MADOX BROWN
The Hayfield, 1855–56. Oil on panel. (cat. 27)

PLATE 17. JOHN FREDERICK HERRING, SR.
Harvest, 1857. Oil on canvas. (cat. 29)

PLATE 18. JOHN BRETT
The Hedger, 1859–60. Oil on canvas. (cat. 33)

PLATE 19. GEORGE VICAT COLE
Harvest Time, 1860. Oil on canvas. (cat. 34)

PLATE 20. HEYWOOD HARDY
Corn Stooks by Bray Church, 1872. Oil on paper laid on board. (cat. 37)

PLATE 21. SIR GEORGE CLAUSEN
Winter Work, 1883–84. Oil on canvas. (cat. 38)

PLATE 22. SIR GEORGE CLAUSEN
The Mowers, 1891. Oil on canvas. (cat. 39)

PLATE 23. THOMAS HEARNE
Autumn (Palemon and Lavinia), c. 1783. Pen, grey ink and watercolour. (cat. 40)

PLATE 24. ROBERT HILLS
Studies of Haymakers, c. 1804–10. Pencil and
watercolour. (cat. 49)

PLATE 25. JOSHUA CRISTALL
Hop-picking, 1807. Watercolour. (cat. 51)

PLATE 26. DAVID COX
Haymaking, c. 1810. Watercolour over pencil. (cat. 53)

PLATE 27. THOMAS UWINS
Haymakers at Dinner, 1812. Watercolour. (cat. 59)

PLATE 28. ROBERT HILLS
A Village Snow Scene, 1819. Watercolour with touches of body colour and scraping out over pencil. (cat. 62)

PLATE 29. SAMUEL PALMER
Harvesting, c. 1851. Watercolour and body colour. (cat. 72)

PLATE 30. WILLIAM TURNER OF OXFORD
Haymaking, Study from Nature, in Osney Meadow, near Oxford, Looking towards Iffley, 1853–54. Watercolour and body colour. (cat. 73)

PLATE 31. DANIEL ALEXANDER WILLIAMSON
Ploughing, 1865. Watercolour. (cat. 77)

PLATE 32. GEORGE JOHN PINWELL (attributed)
Hop-picking, c. 1870. Watercolour with body colour. (cat. 79)

PLATE 33. GEORGE WALKER
Lowkers, from *The Costume of Yorkshire*, 1814. Hand-coloured aquatint. (cat. 101)

Plate 34. John William North
Gleaners, Coast of Somerset, 1890. Watercolour with body colour. (cat. 83)

scenes) had the words "painted on the spot" incorporated in the titles printed in exhibition catalogues. Agricultural subject matter provided a useful source of foreground incident for these works.

Constable might seem to be the quintessential painter of the cultivated English countryside—especially since the rediscovery of his *Wheatfield* (see fig. 4). But in adopting harvest subject matter he was following fashion, not initiating it. Exhibition catalogues show agricultural landscapes starting to be popular in 1807. Several of Turner's sketches from a boat on the Thames feature agriculture, which also figures in some of the large-scale oils exhibited in Turner's gallery in his own house in 1809 (cat. 8). Turner's studies of agriculture seem to have been stimulated by the war with France. His poetry shows that he was aware of the connection between home agricultural production and Napoleon's blockade, and the years from 1807 to 1809, when the blockade was at its most effective, were also the years in which Turner's paintings and sketches show the strongest interest in agriculture. Agriculture, like the planting of woodlands, which was also seen as having patriotic significance during these years, was a part of the war effort: timber was needed to build the warships, corn to feed the troops and reduce Britain's dependence on imports.[22] Turner's agricultural studies are not confined to harvest but illustrate a whole range of activities, including winter work, and, as John Barrell has pointed out, he generally manages to avoid the stereotypes in his depiction of the labourers.[23] Constable's most intensive studies of agriculture date from somewhat later, the summers of 1813, 1814 and 1815—years when he was spending long periods at home in East Bergholt and devoting much time to plein-air study. His interest in agriculture follows a sequence—from the ploughing and manuring of the ground to the eventual harvest—which is obviously connected with his own thorough understanding of agriculture and its place in the local economy. Many of the fields that he painted, as well as such buildings as water mills, belonged to his family. Constable was so scrupulously accurate in his depiction of agriculture that it is possible to date his sketches and paintings exactly by reference to the crops growing and the activities taking place in the fields. Indeed, the standard of accuracy in all the agricultural studies of the decade of naturalism is high, reflecting the fact that so many of them were made in the open air.

In the summers of 1814 and 1815—after Napoleon's exile to Elba and after his final defeat at Waterloo—several artists painted harvest scenes in oils. Michael Rosenthal has argued that these works, by DeWint (cat. 13), Lewis (cat. 14), and Constable, reflect relief and patriotic pride in the victories, and this does seem highly likely, especially as the cornfield was a symbol of peace.[24] The classic composition for the harvest scene evolved during these years, and it was popularised by printed illustrations such as those in Cox's treatise on landscape painting in watercolour (cat. 100). The formula made the most of the variety to be found in harvest landscapes. Workers engaged in different activities represent a balance between rest and labour; standing corn, sheaves and waggons to be loaded are all shown simultaneously; harvesters and gleaners are often shown in the same field; and all this is depicted against a backdrop of trees, hedges and distant views, whose colours contrast with what might otherwise be the monotonous gold of the harvest field. A comparison with the harvest scenes painted in the 1850s and 1860s, by George Vicat Cole or Richard Redgrave (cat. 34, 35), shows how influential this formula continued to be. In this earlier period, however, patrons did not give much encouragement to naturalistic agricultural landscapes, except in watercolour. Most of Constable's agricultural scenes of this period remained unsold, as far as we know, as did Turner's; DeWint's *Cornfield* of 1815 similarly failed to find a purchaser. Linnell's works sold for low prices, often to fellow artists or long after they were painted,[25] and there is no evidence of whether G. R. Lewis's harvest scenes were sold. After the war ended, depression set in, causing problems for artists as well as in the countryside, and a number of artists turned away from this type of subject matter after 1816.

Between 1816 and 1848 naturalistic agricultural landscapes continued to be painted, but they were rarely exhibited at the Royal Academy. Instead, they survive in the work of some painters of the Norwich school, such as Stark and Vincent (cat. 15, 17); and also in that of the watercolourists Cox, DeWint and William Turner of Oxford. Constable turned away from agricultural subjects to concentrate on canal scenes after 1816. (*The Cornfield* of 1826 [National Gallery, London] is an important exception, but even in this painting the actual agricultural activity is not a dominant theme.) J. M. W. Turner abandoned oil sketching from nature and painted no more large agricultural scenes after 1813, but he continued to depict agricultural landscape in watercolours, in the illustrations for his engraved series, *Picturesque Views in England and Wales* (cat. 64, 91). In the work of Cox, DeWint and the two Turners a certain nostalgia for the open fields (now disappearing fast as a result of enclosure) can be detected. In their watercolours the figures are small, the fields are large and there is often a feeling of boundless space that reflects the open-field system; occasionally, the topographical details prove that they were actually painting land which was still farmed on the open field system.[26] All four first became interested in agriculture in the 1801–1810 decade. Cox and DeWint helped ensure that agricultural landscape was a staple theme in the Old Water-Colour Society's exhibitions throughout the first half of the nineteenth century.

There are interesting contrasts between the agricultural landscapes of Cox and DeWint. DeWint specialised in cornfields, whereas Cox, at least later in life, preferred to paint hay fields or pictures of workers going to and from their work, often walking across windswept commons. DeWint's workers are industrious, modestly dressed, often placed in a landscape that has a church or cathedral in the background (cat. 63). His patrons were often from the landed gentry and aristocracy.[27] Cox, on the other hand, was a Radical in politics, an admirer of William Cobbett, and his patrons more often seem to have come from the urban middle class.[28] The rural workers he depicts appear to have more freedom and individuality than DeWint's do. There are hints of social protest in some of DeWint's early works, but in general his figures are much closer to "model labourers" than those of Cox, reflecting differences both in their personal views and in the market they were painting for.

Another artist who specialised in agricultural landscape during these years was Samuel Palmer. His personal views, however, produced a very individual interpretation of agricultural landscape, which met with incomprehension and indifference (except amongst his friends) in the 1820s and 1830s but has been highly regarded in this century. Palmer's starting point was naturalistic landscape—he admired Cox and was a close friend of John Linnell—but Linnell also introduced him to the poet and visionary artist William Blake and to the study of fifteenth-century engravings. Under these influences he decided that Cox was not "profound" and withdrew from the London art world. His aim was to use landscape painting to reveal the spiritual world that lay behind the material world and was accessible in moments of "vision." The landscape of agriculture was particularly suited to this purpose: the religious significance of harvest was widely recognised, and a harvest scene could be viewed as a perfect illustration of God's benevolence. The landscapes that Palmer painted in his Shoreham period (c. 1825–1835) are overflowing with plenty and abundance (see fig. 14). It is easy to exaggerate their archaic aspects: in the sepias of 1825 the implements and practices are medieval or imaginary; but once Palmer settled permanently in Shoreham, much of his work does reflect contemporary agricultural practice in the area, although it is made otherworldly through his exploitation of magical light effects: glowing twilights and velvety moonlights (cat. 20, 67–69). In contrast to the broad, open landscapes of the watercolourists, Palmer emphasizes the boundaries of hills and trees, creating the effect of a protected, enclosed world, "A little village, safe, and still, / Where pain and vice, full seldom come, / Nor horrid noise of warlike drum," as he wrote in his sketchbook in 1824.[29]

Yet pain, vice and the equivalent of warlike drums did come to Shoreham during Palmer's residence there: Kent was badly affected by the incendiarism of the Swing riots of 1830. Palmer's departure from Shoreham, and his change to a more conventional style, have been attributed to the riots, but they certainly did not drive him out immediately, and he was still painting visionary cornfields in 1833 and 1834. The lack of patronage and a growing consciousness of rural distress were, perhaps, more decisive factors. Politically, Palmer was a Tory who deplored the reforms of the 1830s in church and state and feared the annihilation of "Old England." As the century progressed, his approach to rural life became more nostalgic and his general outlook more pessimistic, ending the ecstatic enthusiasm that had made possible his intensely poetic paintings of the 1820s and early 1830s. While at Shoreham, his enthusiasm influenced the more prosaic Linnell and was shared by his younger contemporary, Edward Calvert, whose images of agriculture are much more remote from the contemporary world than Palmer's (cat. 92, 93).

The decades following 1830 were depressing years in the countryside. Indeed, the period from 1815 to the 1850s has been described as "the most dreadful time of the English agricultural labourer's existence."[30] Rick burning continued, the new Poor Law gave rise to much resentment and opposition to the Corn Laws was gathering strength. Bad harvests and recession in the years 1837 to 1842 produced distress in

18. WILLIAM FREDERICK WITHERINGTON
Stacking Hay, 1840. Oil on canvas, 40 × 50 in. (101.6 × 127 cm.). Formerly Nettlefold Collection. Present
location unknown.

town and country, earning the following decade the appellation of the "Hungry For-
ties." To many, a celebration of agriculture would have seemed out of place—a reminder of divisions within the ruling classes rather than a symbol of social harmony. At
Academy exhibitions in these years agricultural landscapes are rare, and those that
were exhibited are often set in other European countries or in the eighteenth century,
accompanied by quotations from James Thomson or Oliver Goldsmith. One reviewer
thought this interest in eighteenth-century agricultural life might imply that there
were "no more cakes and ale—no more 'English harvests' in our day."[31] The efforts
made by the clergy to institute the Harvest Festival in this decade could be seen as an
attempt to restore a more joyous and socially unifying approach to the harvest, which
was to bear fruit in the paintings of the 1850s and 1860s.

Rural genre painting, on the other hand, was very popular in these years. The genre
scenes of William Collins (cat. 18) and W. F. Witherington (fig. 18) occasionally
include agricultural landscape backgrounds, although happy groups of children, or
families, dominate the foreground. Comments in reviews suggest that this emphasis
on the "domestic affections" of the agricultural labourer was readily believed by

members of the upper and middle classes, and welcomed in a time of threats to the social order intensified by Chartism at home and revolutions on the Continent. Publicity about conditions in factories, which accompanied the legislation of the 1830s and 1840s, made rural children seem fortunate by comparison, and even a source of national pride. One reviewer described the children in Collins's paintings as "those merry-tongued, stout limbed, honest-hearted urchins, which make us so proud of leading foreigners through our hamlets and homesteads."[32] Collins and other artists of this period also stressed the piety of the English agricultural labourer. Wilkie Collins's biography of his father makes it clear that Collins did study rural labourers closely, but also that his work was appreciated because he tactfully avoided both incongruous refinements and the "fierce miseries" of rural life: "His villagers . . . are not fine ladies and gentlemen, masquerading in humble attire; but genuine poor people . . . stamped with the thorough nationality of their class."[33] Thus, his work could seem authentic in comparison with the masquerades of the 1780s, but it also did much to give visual form to the myth of the virtuous peasant—contented, pious, devoted to family life and hence impervious to the temptations of revolution.

Towards the end of the 1840s a series of events altered the mood of the country. The Corn Laws were repealed in 1846; in 1848, the "year of revolutions" on the Continent, Britain escaped serious unrest; in 1851 the Great Exhibition was held. A new mood of optimism marked the beginning of the 1850s, based on pride in Britain's social harmony and industrial achievements. Palmerston claimed, in a famous speech in 1850, that Britain had "shown the example of a nation in which every class of society accepts with cheerfulness the lot which Providence has assigned to it."[34] Fears of revolution, which had been so strong between 1790 and 1848, declined. Harvest scenes could once more be viewed as an expression of patriotic pride. In his *Year-Book of the Country* (1850) William Howitt wrote that, as a result of the repeal of the Corn Laws, people could "again hail the month of harvests with unmingled joy. . . . Never was there a generation that had more cause to put forth their reaping and rejoicing hands, and sing as heartily, as ours. . . . Let us go out and rejoice amid the sunshine, and the wheat stooping to the sickle . . . and to the certain assurance that the loaf never was cheaper than it shall be, never the heart of labour more strengthened with abundance."[35]

At the same time, however, the late 1840s and 1850s brought a new awareness of rural distress. A series of articles in the *Morning Chronicle* in 1850, for example, revealed appalling living conditions in cottages, stimulating demands for the provision of new cottages and allotments.[36] Elsewhere in his *Year-Book* Howitt declared that rural labourers were living on "boiled horse-beans and turnip-tops . . . instead of the roast beef and plum pudding of old England" owing to years of neglect.[37] In the early 1850s, then, optimism about the future was combined with a new consciousness of rural poverty, which was perhaps easier to accept—and get indignant about—than it would have been in the more threatening times of the first half of the century.

Both elements find expression in the paintings of the Pre-Raphaelites, the new group founded in 1848. Holman Hunt reacted against the rural idylls of the 1830s and

1840s in his *Hireling Shepherd* (see fig. 3): reviewers were shocked, but at the same time alerted to over-idealisation in other depictions of rural labourers. At about this time, they start to be cynical, not only about representations of dainty labourers and pretty cottages, but also about displays of peasant virtues and paternalism.[38] Henry Wallis's *Stonebreaker* (see fig. 1) and Walter Deverell's *Irish Vagrants* (see fig. 16), similarly, were conscious rejections of the earlier approach to rural happiness and virtue. The patrons of the Pre-Raphaelites were mainly middle-class merchants, industrialists and professionals, who perhaps shared the anti-aristocratic sentiments, similar to those of the Benthamites and the Anti-Corn Law League, that occasionally surface in the reviews of the period.[39]

As well as taking a critical approach to social problems in the countryside, the Pre-Raphaelites pursued a style of open-air naturalism that produced some very fresh agricultural landscapes, which resembled those of the decade of naturalism but emphasized fine detail rather than breadth. Hunt's *Hireling Shepherd* includes a meticulously observed cornfield on the right, but also, in the background, a field of stooked beans—an unusual subject, and one that was taken up as a major motif by Ford Madox Brown in *Walton-on-the-Naze* (see fig. 6). The latter painting, despite its small size, encompasses the history and economy of a whole area, in a way that is reminiscent of Constable's Stour Valley landscapes; its inclusion of a warship, Martello tower and flag also refer to the patriotic connotations of agriculture at a time when Napoleon III's exploits in Italy raised fears of a new war against France. In two other small landscapes, *Carrying Corn* and *The Hayfield* (cat. 26, 27), Brown produced closely observed depictions of agriculture, with a choice of unusual effects reminiscent of Palmer's work.

Other painters associated with the Pre-Raphaelites who painted notable agricultural landscapes were Richard Burchett, William Davis, John Brett and G. P. Boyce. Burchett's *View across Sandown Bay, the Isle of Wight* (fig. 19), like Brown's *Walton-on-the-Naze*, includes middle-class figures strolling in the landscape rather than farm labourers, reflecting a rather urban idea of the countryside as a source for leisure (but also a way of avoiding the depiction of stereotypical "model labourers"). Boyce's farmyard scenes concentrate on the beauty of old barns threatened by mechanisation and a newly prosperous "high" (progressive) farming (cat. 75). Brett and Davis anticipated future artistic developments in pictures that stressed the dreary hardships of winter work on the land, in a further reaction against the idylls of previous painters (cat. 33). Davis's *Harrowing* (fig. 20) was especially appreciated by Tennyson, who said he could not look at it without tears.[40] Davis was original in his choice of subject matter: in contrast to the many paintings of cheerful country children, he emphasizes the hard and lonely labour of a rural childhood, a theme taken up by Frederick Shields in his provocatively titled watercolour, *One of Our Breadwatchers* (fig. 21). Child labour and winter work were to become important themes in the paintings of the 1860s and 1870s.

The Pre-Raphaelite emphasis on minutely detailed open-air naturalism also affected other painters of the 1850s and 1860s, such as George Vicat Cole, J. F. Herring,

19. RICHARD BURCHETT
View across Sandown Bay, The Isle of Wight. Oil on canvas, 13½ × 22½ in. (34.3 × 57.2 cm.). Victoria and
Albert Museum, London.

20. WILLIAM DAVIS
Harrowing, c. 1859. Oil on canvas, 17¼ × 26 in. (43.8 × 66 cm.). Present location unknown.

21. FREDERICK JAMES SHIELDS
One of Our Breadwatchers, 1866. Watercolour, 15½ × 22¾ in. (39.4 × 57.8 cm.). Manchester City Art Galleries.

William Maw Egley and Richard Redgrave. These artists, with John Linnell (who continued to paint in a broader style despite his dealers' complaints) produced many cheerful harvest landscapes. Indeed, this period can be seen as the heyday of the sunny harvest scene. The pursuit of "high" farming initiated the so-called golden age of British farming—a name applied to the period in retrospect but anticipated in the titles of many paintings, such as Vicat Cole's *Summer's Golden Crown* (1866). In the optimistic mood of the 1850s the cornfield was a symbol of national unity; its patriotic associations were underlined by wars and threats of war, in 1854–1856 (the Crimean War) and 1859–1860. These harvest scenes are similar in composition to those of the decade of naturalism, but the figures are larger and reflect the genre painting of the 1830s and 1840s, with the emphasis on happy family groups.

   Another important contrast with the naturalism of the early nineteenth century is that these paintings sold very well. Artists were able to specialise in harvest scenes, and Linnell and Vicat Cole particularly made a comfortable living from them. Some landscape painters of this period could even adopt the life-style of the gentry: Linnell bought arable fields around his house at Redhill in Surrey,[41] and J. F. Herring depicted

22. FRED WALKER
The Violet Field, 1867. Watercolour, 9¾ × 15¼ in. (24.8 × 40 cm.). Present location unknown.

his own elegant house and parkland in the background of his *Harvest* of 1857 (cat. 29)—perhaps even including himself in the painting as a country squire riding across the fields. Many of these harvest scenes were based on open-air study: Vicat Cole apparently painted entire agricultural landscapes on the spot, working from a hut. His biographer (who was also his brother-in-law) claimed that farmers "would leave in the fields patches of corn uncut, stooks uncarted, and waggons ready-loaded, until the artist had finished what he wanted of them."[42] Egley's *Hullo! Largesse* is contemporary with these works, all of which, more or less explicitly, celebrate the virtue and contentment of the rural labourer as well as the bounty of Providence.

This type of picture continued to be painted after the 1860s. It coexisted increasingly, however, with agricultural landscapes of a very different kind: depictions of downtrodden labourers, often solitary, in dreary landscapes, which are melancholy rather than cheerful in mood. As we have seen, this type of painting was initiated by the Pre-Raphaelites, but it was accelerated by the influence of contemporary French paintings of rural life, which were exhibited regularly in London from 1854 onwards. At first, the classicising paintings of Jules Breton exerted an influence on a group of four painters who were well known in their lifetimes but are largely forgotten today: George Heming Mason, Fred Walker, G. J. Pinwell and J. M. North. These artists produced some socially conscious pictures in the 1860s and early 1870s (fig. 22; cat.

23. FRED WALKER
The Plough, 1870. Oil on canvas, 56½ × 83¾ in. (143.5 × 212.7 cm.). Tate Gallery, London.

24. GEORGE HEMING MASON
The Harvest Moon, 1872. Oil on canvas, 33⅜ × 91 in. (84.6 × 231.1 cm.). Tate Gallery, London.

80), which aroused the admiration of Vincent Van Gogh during his stay in England between 1873 and 1876.[43] However, their two most important paintings of agricultural landscape, Walker's *The Plough* (1870; fig. 23) and Mason's *Harvest Moon* (1872; fig. 24), are timeless and idyllic, reflecting the influence of the aesthetic movement and of a sophisticated preference for musical, poetic art rather than for "vulgar naturalism."[44] In these paintings the labourers have the graceful movements of those of Breton, although the subject matter is firmly grounded in the English tradition. Mason's work echoes the poetic intensity of Palmer's at Shoreham, and indeed Palmer himself was exhibiting etchings at this time which recaptured, to some extent, the Shoreham mood (cat. 95). There is a further link in the work of William Linnell and William Blake Richmond, sons of Palmer's friends at Shoreham, who were exhibiting paintings of a similar style to Mason's in the 1860s. Mason, Pinwell and Walker all died within a few years of each other in the early 1870s; in retrospect, their work was seen as thoroughly English although we can now detect the influence of Breton, and also of Millet.[45]

In the 1870s a number of paintings attacked rural social issues in a more direct way: the pictures of R. W. Macbeth and J. R. Reid are a parallel to those of the better-known urban social realists, Frank Holl, Hubert Herkomer and Luke Fildes. Macbeth's *Lincolnshire Gang* (1876; now known only from an engraving) focussed on the agricultural gangs operating in the eastern counties, in which children as young as four were employed. One reviewer commented: "So humiliating a representation shows what an immense field yet awaits the sickle of the social philanthropist."[46] In fact, Macbeth's protest was rather out of date: the Gangs Act of 1867 had legislated against the worst abuses of the system, prohibiting gangs of mixed sex and the employment of children under eight years of age.[47] This was a period, however, when legislation concerned with limiting child labour on the land, and providing a nationwide system of primary education, was being discussed and implemented, so in that sense the issue was still a topical one. J. R. Reid's *Toil and Pleasure* (1879; fig. 25) also appears to show an agricultural gang of old men, women and children watching in delight as huntsmen trample the crops (although the gangmaster, evidently, is not amused).[48] The emphasis in this painting on the discomforts of winter work on the land, with the women's faces, in particular, blue and blotchy with cold, is in striking contrast to the sunny harvest scenes of Linnell, Vicat Cole and other artists.

The movement towards social realism in the depiction of rural life reached a peak in the work of George Clausen in the early 1880s. Inspired by the paintings of Jules Bastien-Lepage (fig. 26) and by the work of Walker and Reid, Clausen settled at Childwick in Hertfordshire and produced, between 1882 and 1884, a series of paintings that were regarded by his contemporaries as being in a style of "thorough-going realism."[49] He used photographs of labourers and chose subjects that emphasized hard, unglamorous labour, such as turnip cultivation and weeding.[50] This style was harshly criticised; some artists and critics associated it with socialism.[51] *Winter Work* (cat. 38) remained unsold after it was first exhibited; Clausen then added the girl with a hoop, perhaps in an attempt to make the painting less of a stark comment on rural

25. JOHN ROBERTSON REID
Toil and Pleasure, 1879. Oil on canvas, 38½ × 71½ in. (97.8 × 181.6 cm.). Tate Gallery, London.

26. JULES BASTIEN-LEPAGE
Les Foins (Hay Harvest), 1878. Oil on canvas, 70⅞ × 76¾ in. (180 × 195 cm.).
Musée du Louvre, Paris. Photo R.M.N.

27. JEAN-FRANÇOIS MILLET
Le Semeur (The Sower). Oil on canvas, 40 × 32½ in. (101.6
× 82.6 cm.). Gift of Quincy Adams Shaw through Quincy
A. Shaw, Jr., and Mrs. Marian Shaw Haughton. Courtesy
Museum of Fine Arts, Boston.

hardship and to suggest a family group, like the very successful sunny harvest scenes of some of his contemporaries. In 1893 George Moore wrote of another of Clausen's paintings from this period, "Mr Clausen has seen nothing but the sordid and mean," and declared that "the mission of art is not truth, but beauty. . . . The common workaday world . . . can be only depicted by a series of ellipses through a mystery of light and shade."[52] After the mid-1880s Clausen seems to have come to a similar conclusion, and his later work draws on the influence of Millet and the French Impressionists (fig. 27), concentrating on light effects and the "noble" aspects of rural labour, rather than on those elements that Moore found "sordid and mean."

The history of Clausen's work in the early 1880s illustrates the fundamental dilemma that faced all painters of agricultural life and labour. The public appreciated "truth to nature," yet there were certain unpalatable truths about rural life that they did not want to be told, preferring the comforting myth of the labourer's contentment and virtue within a stable social hierarchy. Agricultural landscape, if depicted too literally, risked being stigmatised as low, vulgar or mean. In addition, the stark reality was not, perhaps, suitable material for art. Clausen's contemporary Richard Jefferies declared in 1874 that "in the life of the English agricultural labourer there is absolutely no poetry, no colour."[53] In the period between 1780 and 1890 English painters of agricultural landscape swung between various degrees of realism and idealisation, reacting against the artificiality of earlier artists or modifying their work to suit the public's taste, using classical, literary and religious references to extract the maximum amount of poetry from their subject matter. The result is a body of work that is immensely varied, sometimes strikingly truthful, sometimes poetic, sometimes mythical, but nearly always rich in meaning.

Notes

Introduction

1. In nineteenth-century England *corn* was a generic term that was applied to cereals such as wheat, barley and oats. It should not be confused with the modern American usage of *corn* to mean maize or sweet corn.

2. R. Williams, *The Country and the City* (London, 1973), pp. 9–12.

3. J. Barrell, *The Dark Side of the Landscape: The Rural Poor in English Painting, 1730–1840* (Cambridge, 1980); D. Solkin, *Richard Wilson: The Landscape of Reaction* (exh. cat.; Tate Gallery, London, 1982); M. Rosenthal, *British Landscape Painting* (London, 1982) and *Constable: The Painter and His Landscape* (New Haven and London, 1983); A. Bermingham, *Landscape and Ideology: The English Rustic Tradition, 1740–1860* (Berkeley, Los Angeles and London, 1986). Barrell's book was the most deliberately polemical, but all have upset traditionalists, not least because they share a more or less avowedly Marxist standpoint. In my view, this leads Barrell to overemphasize the effects of capitalism and the belief in industriousness as the chief working-class virtue while underestimating the importance of aesthetic factors, such as Picturesque theory. Solkin, similarly, stresses the political significance of Wilson's use of figures in his landscapes at the expense of other issues. Rosenthal and Bermingham, however, adopt a more subtle and balanced approach.

4. See, for example, G. E. Mingay, *Rural Life in Victorian England* (London, 1977); K. D. M. Snell, *Annals of the Labouring Poor: Social Change and Agrarian England, 1660–1900* (London, 1985); and A. Howkins, *Reshaping Rural England: A Social History, 1850–1925* (London, 1991). James Caird's famous survey of 1850–51 was also concerned with English, rather than British, agriculture.

5. Modern historians feel less confident than their nineteenth-century predecessors about their abil-

ity to separate myth from history, interpretation from "facts." Since history depends on contemporary observers, who have their own idea (perhaps mistaken or biased) of what was happening, it is itself a form of myth. Even "facts" that look like the result of detached, scientific investigation, such as statistics, result from selection, firstly by contemporaries, secondly by historians. Thus, although I have tried to deal separately with actual conditions and people's perceptions of those conditions, I do recognize that the distinction is an artificial one. Critics could argue, quite reasonably, that my "history" in chapter 1 is influenced by what I identify as the countermyth of rural poverty and distress in chapter 2, and that this has also affected many twentieth-century historians. My defence would be that the countermyth has a closer relationship to reality than the idyllic myth, which dominates the visual arts.

Chapter One: The English Countryside

1. J. Caird, *English Agriculture in 1850–1* (London, 1852), frontispiece and p. 510. Caird declared that "it is in the strictly corn districts of the south and east that the labourer's condition is most depressed" (p. 487).

2. W. Howitt, *The Year-Book of the Country; or the Field, the Forest and the Fireside* (London, 1850), p. 377.

3. Mingay, *Rural Life in Victorian England*, p. 31.

4. Williams, *Country and the City*, p. 186.

5. Howkins, *Reshaping Rural England*, pp. 7–8.

6. J. H. Clapham, *An Economic History of Modern Britain: Free Trade and Steel, 1850–1886* (London, 1967), p. 3.

7. This is the opinion of Mingay, *Rural Life in Victorian England*, p. 63.

8. Caird, *English Agriculture*, p. 510.

9. J. Glyde, *Suffolk in the Nineteenth Century* (London, 1856), p. 356, gives an example of a family budget from Cosford in Suffolk: the man earned 9/- per week, his wife 9d., his sons, ages 12, 11 and 8, 2/-, 1/- and 1/-, respectively. There were two smaller children, ages 6 and 4. The

family spent 9/- on bread, 1/- on potatoes, 1/2d. on rent, 9d. on coal and wood and minimal amounts on other foodstuffs (3d. on cheese, 3½d. on sugar) out of the total expenditure of 13/9d.

10. P. Horn, *The Victorian Country Child* (Kineton, 1974), pp. 16–17.

11. W. Cobbett, *Rural Rides* (Everyman ed., 1912; repr. 1973), vol. 2, p. 266; J. D. Chambers and G. E. Mingay, *The Agricultural Revolution 1750–1880* (London, 1966), p. 192.

12. E. Chadwick, *Report on the Sanitary Condition of the Labouring Population of Great Britain* (London, 1842), quoted in P. Horn, *Labouring Life in the Victorian Countryside* (London, 1976), p. 182.

13. D. Morgan, "The Place of Harvesters in Nineteenth Century Village Life," in R. Samuel, ed., *Village Life and Labour* (Oxford, 1975), pp. 36–37.

14. R. Jefferies, "Field Faring Women" (first published in *Fraser's Magazine*, 1874), in *Toilers of the Field* (London, 1892), p. 147; and "Women in the Field," *Graphic*, 11 September 1875, p. 263.

15. E. J. Hobsbawm and G. Rudé, *Captain Swing* (London, 1969), p. 198.

16. Ibid., pp. 262–63.

17. R. B. Beckett, ed., *John Constable's Correspondence* (Ipswich, 1962–68), vol. 6, p. 88.

18. Glyde, *Suffolk*, p. 126.

19. This is suggested by Howkins, *Reshaping Rural England*, pp. 61–65.

20. P. Horn, *Joseph Arch* (Kineton, 1971), pp. 69–70, 109.

21. Cobbett, *Rural Rides*, vol. 1, pp. 267–68.

22. Peel thought that prosperity was the best means of calming discontent. He wanted "to promote so much of happiness and contentment among the people that the voice of disaffection should no longer be heard, and that thoughts of the dissolution of our institutions should be forgotten in the midst of physical enjoyment" (N. Gash, *Reaction and Reconstruction in British Politics, 1832–52* [Oxford, 1965]). Brian Harrison has pointed out that rises in charitable activity coincided with periods of unrest, and that supporters

of charity openly acknowledged their hope that it would improve class relations and prevent agitation (Harrison, "Philanthropy and the Victorians," *Victorian Studies*, vol. 9 [1966], pp. 353–74).

23. J. L. Hammond and B. Hammond, *The Village Labourer, 1760–1832: A Study in the Government of England before the Reform Bill* (London, 1913), p. 191.

24. An example of the first type of painting is a pair exhibited by Edward Prentis in 1837: "*Fruits of Idleness*—a wounded poacher with his terrified family—and *Fruits of Industry*, a cottage dinner" (review in *Athenaeum*, 25 March 1837, p. 219).

25. *Athenaeum*, 1 May 1858, p. 567.

26. *Athenaeum*, 29 May 1841, p. 427, described the subject as "the application of a widow to the guardians of the public purse for bread," and portrayed the guardians as "the country gentlemen, who lounge about or listen, as they are selfish or benevolent—the deaf farmer on one side the table, the thin, sallow, but humane-looking clergyman on the other, and behind him, the young gentleman, who finds the whole transaction 'such a bore' that he takes that opportunity to pare his nails, screened by the standing figure, who avails himself of the cheery blaze of the board-room fire, in the distinctive attitude of John Bull."

27. M. E. Rose, *The English Poor Law, 1780–1930* (Newton Abbot, 1971), pp. 40–41.

28. Chambers and Mingay, *Agricultural Revolution*, p. 77.

29. Hammond and Hammond, *Village Labourer*, argued that it was catastrophic. J. H. Clapham, in *An Economic History of Modern Britain: The Early Railway Age, 1820–1850* (Cambridge, 1939), considered regional variations and concluded that "it is doubtful whether, averaged over Britain, the loss in well-being due to enclosure of commons would have amounted to very much" (p. 126). His analysis was challenged by E. P. Thompson in *The Making of the English Working Class* (London, 1963), pp. 213–33. Chambers and Mingay, *Agricultural Revolution*, argue that it was not enclosure but the population increase that was the basic cause of worsening rural poverty in the late eighteenth century. Snell, *Annals of the Labouring Poor*,

supports the Hammonds' view and gives a particularly good account of the social effects of enclosure (pp. 144–80). A useful summary of the debates over enclosure is in M. Turner, *Enclosures in History, 1750–1830* (London, 1984), which also cites recent research tending to support the Hammonds' case.

30. Snell, *Annals of the Labouring Poor*, pp. 149–54.

31. Hammond and Hammond, *Village Labourer*, pp. 128–29, 130–31; G. Bourne, *Change in the Village* (London, 1912), pp. 133–34.

32. R. Southey, *Essays, Moral and Political* (London, 1832), vol. 1, pp. 179, 180–83.

33. A. Young, *Inquiry into the Propriety of Applying Wastes to the Better Maintenance or Support of the Poor* (London, 1801), quoted in E. W. Martin, *The Secret People: English Village Life after 1750* (London, 1954), p. 156.

34. Norman McCord, *The Anti-Corn Law League, 1838–46*, 2d ed. (London, 1968), p. 21.

35. Ibid., pp. 23, 204.

36. Gash, *Reaction and Reconstruction*, p. 139; C. R. Fay, *The Corn Laws and Social England* (Cambridge, 1932), p. 196. Only one-third of the Conservative party voted with Peel on the Corn Laws.

37. Fay, *Corn Laws*, p. 202.

38. Kay Dian Kriz, "An English Arcadia Revisited and Reassessed: Holman Hunt's *The Hireling Shepherd* and the Rural Tradition," *Art History*, vol. 10, no. 4 (December 1987), pp. 475–91.

39. Rev. J. J. Blunt, *The Duties of the Parish Priest* (London, 1856), pp. 177, 181.

40. G. Kitson Clark, *Churchmen and the Condition of England: 1832–1885* (London, 1973), pp. 178–80.

41. L. C. B. Seaman, *Victorian England: Aspects of English and Imperial History, 1837–1901* (London, 1973), p. 282.

42. For reaping tools, see E. J. T. Collins, *Sickle to Combine: A Review of Harvest Techniques from 1800 to the Present Day* (University of Reading, 1969), pp. 12–15. On the use of the sickle and scythe, see E. Hostettler, "Gourlay Steele and the Sexual Division of Labour," *History Workshop Journal*,

1977, pp. 95–100; and M. Roberts, "Sickles and Scythes: Women's Work and Men's Work at Harvest Time," *History Workshop Journal*, 1979, pp. 3–28.

43. T. Hardy, *Tess of the d'Urbervilles* (1891), chap. 14 (London: Wordsworth Classics, 1992), p. 107; Morgan, "Place of Harvesters," p. 31.

44. In an article first published in 1874, Richard Jefferies says: "In harvest time, the superintendence of work continues until late, and in the autumn labour is not unfrequently prolonged into the moonlight, in order to carry the corn" (R. Jefferies, *The Toilers of the Field* [London, 1892], p. 25). T. Hennell, in *Change in the Farm* (London, 1934), declares: "There are labourers still working in Somerset and Gloucestershire who have many times been up all night reaping by moonlight" (quoted in Denys Thompson, *Change and Tradition in Rural England* [Cambridge, 1980], p. 130). T. Hardy, *The Mayor of Casterbridge*, chap. 27 (London: Macmillan, 1924), p. 233.

45. J. Gage, ed., *Collected Correspondence of J. M. W. Turner* (Oxford, 1980), p. 129; Leigh Hunt, *The Months, Descriptive of the Successive Beauties of the Year* (London, 1821), p. 72.

46. Leviticus 23:22; Ruth 1–4; P. King, "Customary Rights and Women's Earnings: The Importance of Gleaning to the Rural Labouring Poor, 1750–1850," *Economic History Review*, vol. 44, no. 3 (1991), pp. 461–76.

47. T. Ruggles, "Picturesque Farming," *Annals of Agriculture*, vol. 9 (1788), p. 13.

48. W. H. Pyne, *Microcosm . . . to Which Are Added, Explanations of the Plates . . . by C. Gray* (2d ed., 1806), p. 3. The italicized words refer to the prescription in Leviticus 23:22 exhorting farmers to leave gleanings for the poor.

49. "Harvest," *Cornhill Magazine*, vol. 12 (1865), p. 360. On gleaning, see also Christiana Payne, "Boundless Harvests: Representations of Open Fields and Gleaning in Early Nineteenth Century England," *Turner Studies*, vol. 11, no. 1 (Summer 1991), pp. 7–15. Jules Breton and Jean-François Millet produced celebrated paintings of gleaners in France in the 1850s: on these, see especially G. Weisberg, ed., *The Realist Tradition: French Painting and Drawing, 1830–1900* (Cleveland Museum of Art, 1981).

50. Cobbett, *Rural Rides*, vol. 1, pp. 265–66. On this issue, see also Howkins, *Reshaping Rural England*, pp. 42–44.

51. See R. Bloomfield, *The Farmer's Boy* (1800), "Summer," ll. 323–72; and J. Clare, *The Shepherd's Calendar* (1827), ed. E. Robinson and G. Summerfield (Oxford, 1964), pp. 68–69. (This edition includes the lines cut by the editor from the published edition because he thought them too politically controversial.)

52. V. Surtees, ed., *The Diary of Ford Madox Brown* (London, 1981), p. 84 (entry for 22 August 1854).

53. Sarah Uwins, *A Memoir of Thomas Uwins, R.A.* (1858, repr. West Yorkshire, 1978), p. 35 (letter from Uwins to his brother, Zechariah, from Farnham, 5 September 1811).

54. For example, a reviewer wrote in 1859 or 1860 of hop picking as "that lively, rollicking, sunshiny scene of English country life—where, however, light and laughter thinly veil so much vagrant vice and houseless misery" (*The Fine Arts*, vol. 5 [1859–60]; press cuttings, item Z0 in library of Courtauld Institute of Art, London).

55. In 1845 an essay on the farming of Kent records threshing machines only in Sheppey: G. Buckland, "On the Farming of Kent," *Journal of the Royal Agricultural Society of England*, vol. 6 (1845), pp. 251–302.

56. Pyne, *Microcosm*, pp. 30–31.

57. Mingay estimates that in 1866–67 less than 2 percent of the arable acreage was steam-tilled: G. E. Mingay, ed., *The Agricultural Revolution: Changes in Agriculture, 1650–1880* (London, 1977), pp. 42–43.

58. Ibid., p. 46.

59. Morgan, "Place of Harvesters," p. 62.

60. P. Horn, *The Rural World: Social Change in the British Countryside, 1750–1850* (London, 1980), p. 238.

61. Mingay, *Rural Life in Victorian England*, p. 68.

62. "The weald is the only part of the country where oxen are generally used for draught . . .

frequently ten oxen, without any horse, are seen drawing a plough" (John Boys, *General View of the Agriculture of the County of Kent* [1796], p. 157); in 1845 G. Buckland ("On the Farming of Kent") stated that oxen were still employed as workers in many places in the wealds of Kent and Sussex.

63. "Harvest," *Cornhill Magazine*, vol. 12 (1865), p. 361.

64. R. Jefferies, *The Life of the Fields* (1884; repr. London, 1947), pp. 163–64.

65. Hardy, *Tess of the d'Urbervilles*, chap. 47, pp. 365–66.

Chapter Two: Rural Myths and Values

1. J. Thomson, *The Seasons* (rev. ed., 1746), "Summer," ll. 353–57; "Autumn," ll. 153–54. On the Georgic tradition in poetry, see J. Chalker, *The English Georgic* (London, 1969).

2. W. Cowper, *The Task* (1785), bk. 1, l. 749.

3. Williams, *Country and the City*, pp. 9–12; Bermingham, *Landscape and Ideology*, pp. 81–82. An example that Bermingham cites here is the popularity of pictures of industrious cottagers in the late eighteenth century, which ostensibly celebrate the old rural order yet emphasize the virtues of hard work, thrift and sobriety, which are needed by the new order of industrial capitalism.

4. Cowper, *The Task*, bk. 3, ll. 740–63; W. Wordsworth, *The Excursion* (1814), bk. 8, ll. 232–51.

5. O. Goldsmith, *The Deserted Village* (1770), ll. 1–2, 63–64, 74.

6. See, for example, R. Bloomfield, *The Farmer's Boy* (1800), bk. 2, ll. 333–400; and J. Clare, "Enclosure," in J. W. Tibble, ed., *The Poems of John Clare* (London, 1935), pp. 419–20.

7. Fred Walker prepared himself for painting *The Plough* (1870; Tate Gallery, London) by reading Thomson's *Seasons* and Bloomfield's *Farmer's Boy* (J. G. Marks, *Life and Letters of Frederick Walker, A.R.A.* [London, 1896], p. 192).

8. W. Wordsworth, *Lyrical Ballads* (1800), preface, p. xi.

9. G. Eliot, "The Natural History of German Life," *Westminster Review*, 1856: T. Pinney, ed., *Essays of George Eliot* (London, 1963), p. 269.

10. M. Howitt, ed., *Pictorial Calendar of the Seasons* (1854), pp. 391–93.

11. W. Howitt, *The Book of the Seasons, or, The Calendar of Nature* (2d ed., 1833), pp. 212, 214. For the life of William Howitt, see Amice Lee, *Laurels and Rosemary: The Life of William and Mary Howitt* (London, 1955).

12. "Harvest," *Cornhill Magazine*, vol. 12 (1865), pp. 358–60.

13. W. E. Houghton, *The Victorian Frame of Mind* (London, 1957), p. 55.

14. W. Howitt, *Book of the Seasons*, p. 177. For William Howitt's eyewitness account of the burning of Nottingham Castle, see Lee, *Laurels and Rosemary*, pp. 86–87.

15. Hobsbawm and Rudé, *Captain Swing*, pp. 219ff.

16. *Athenaeum*, 12 May 1832, p. 309.

17. On 26 November 1831 Collins wrote to the Reverend R. A. Thorpe: "I have, since the spring, as usual, projected many *great* works. What is to become of them; whether we shall have another exhibition at all, or whether, if we do, 'The House of Delegates' will demand the produce of it. . . . I know not" (Wilkie Collins, *Memoirs of the Life of William Collins, Esq., R.A.* [1848; repr. London, 1978], vol. 2, pp. 3–4). *Rustic Civility* was sold to the Duke of Devonshire for 250 gs. in 1832 (Ibid., appendix).

18. Review of Royal Academy exhibition, *Art Journal*, 1 July 1871, p. 173.

19. Barrell, *Dark Side of the Landscape*, p. 77.

20. Reviewed in the *Athenaeum*, 25 March 1837, p. 219. The pictorial contrast between industry and idleness, and between their effects, had precedents in the work of Hogarth and Morland.

21. See Jennie Kitteringham, "Country Work Girls in Nineteenth Century England," in R. Samuel, ed., *Village Life and Labour* (Oxford, 1975), esp. pp. 97, 111.

22. For example, an article on agricultural gangs, *Quarterly Review*, vol. 123, no. 243 (July 1867), p. 187.

23. Kay Dian Kriz, "An English Arcadia Revisited and Reassessed: Holman Hunt's *The Hireling Shepherd* and the Rural Tradition," *Art History*, vol. 10, no. 4 (December 1987), pp. 475–91.

24. Quoted in O. Chadwick, *The Victorian Church* (1971), part 1, p. 353 (from *Politics for the People* [1848], the journal of the Christian Socialists).

25. Arthur Young, in 1798, begged Parliament to build more churches, saying that "the true Christian will never be a leveller, will never listen to French politics, or to French philosophy" (Quoted in K. S. Inglis, *Churches and the Working Class in Victorian England* [London, 1963], p. 6).

26. W. Howitt, *Book of the Seasons*, p. 187. Hazlitt said that the rural labourers were superstitious and bigoted but had no real idea of religion (in an article first published in the *Examiner* (1819), "Character of the Country People," in P. P. Howe, ed., *Complete Works of William Hazlitt* vol. 17 [London, 1933], pp. 69–70). Cobbett declared that "the labouring people have, in a great measure, ceased to go to church," partly because their clothes were too shabby (Cobbett, *Rural Rides*, vol. 1, pp. 226–30).

27. *Athenaeum*, 23 May 1846, p. 527; 16 May 1846, p. 503.

28. Ibid., 16 May 1846, p. 503.

29. Thomas Bernard, *Reports of the Society for Bettering the Condition and Increasing the Comforts of the Poor* (1798–1814), vol. 1 p. 262, quoted in Nigel Everett, "Country Justice: The Literature of Landscape Improvement and English Conservatism, with Particular Reference to the 1790s" (Ph.D. diss., Cambridge University, 1977), p. 229.

30. Everett, "Country Justice"; S. Daniels, "Humphrey Repton and the Morality of Landscape," in J. R. Gold and J. Burgess, eds., *Valued Environments* (London, 1982), pp. 124–44.

31. Bermingham, *Landscape and Ideology*, pp. 207–8, n. 92, gives examples of depictions of rustic charity and notes that they proliferated during the period of enclosure. A good example of a text that describes the pleasures of sensibility is a novel by Henry Mackenzie, *The Man of Feeling* (1771).

32. "Charitable Institutions," *Westminster Review*, vol. 2 (1824), p. 107; reprinted in A. W. Coats, ed., *Poverty in the Victorian Age*, vol. 3, *Charity, 1815–70* (London, 1973).

33. David Owen, *English Philanthropy, 1660–1960* (Oxford, 1965), p. 112.

34. John Aikin, *Calendar of Nature* (1785), p. 55.

35. *The Harvest Home* (Cheap Repository for Moral and Religious Tracts, 1795), p. 7 and p. 15.

36. Howitt, *Year-Book of the Country*, p. 225. An example of a hymn based on Psalm 65 is no. 484 in *Hymns Ancient and Modern* (1861; rev. ed. London, 1972), which includes the lines: "Bright robes of gold the fields adorn, / The hills with joy are ringing, / The valleys stand so thick with corn / That even they are singing."

37. *Somerset House Gazette*, vol. 2 (1824), p. 143, quoted in Hammond Smith, *Peter DeWint* (London, 1982), p. 65.

38. R. Lister, ed., *The Letters of Samuel Palmer* (Oxford, 1974), vol. 1, p. 25; A. T. Story, *The Life of John Linnell* (London, 1892), vol. 1, p. 308.

39. Howitt, *Book of the Seasons*, p. 213.

40. P. G. Hamerton, *Landscape* (London, 1885), p. 341.

41. *Christian Observer*, October 1842, p. 640. The Harvest Festival also began in the 1840s, although there is disagreement as to which clergyman was the first to celebrate it. See Chadwick, *Victorian Church*, part 1, p. 517.

42. Salmacida Spolia, 1640, f. B4v., quoted in J. Turner, *The Politics of Landscape* (Oxford, 1979), p. 11.

43. Thomson, *The Seasons*, "Summer," ll. 1454–55.

44. See I. C. Stuebe, *The Life and Works of William Hodges* (New York, 1979), pp. 72–77, 351–54. To Hodges's dismay, the Duke of York thought the pictures politically subversive (since England was at war with Revolutionary France) and had the exhibition closed.

45. Creswick's *England* is described in "British Artists: Their Style and Character," no. 14, "Thomas Creswick, R.A.," *Art Journal*, 1 May 1856, p. 144; Dearle's *English Landscape* was ex-

hibited at the British Institution and reviewed in *Art Journal*, 1 March 1856, p. 82.

46. Ibid., 1 March 1859, p. 81.

47. Ibid., 1 June 1865, p. 161.

48. M. Wiener, *English Culture and the Decline of the Industrial Spirit, 1850–1980* (Cambridge, 1981), p. 56.

49. Ibid., pp. 8, 127.

50. A. Howkins, "The Discovery of Rural England," pp. 62–88, in R. Colls and P. Dodds, eds., *Englishness: Politics and Culture, 1880–1920* (London, 1986).

51. Wiener, *English Culture*, p. 27.

52. J. Morley, *Life of Richard Cobden* (London, 1881), vol. 2, pp. 481–82; quoted in Wiener, *English Culture*, p. 14.

53. E. H. Hunt, *British Labour History, 1815–1914* (London, 1981), pp. 58–59, 68–9, 206–10.

54. Cobbett, *Rural Rides*, vol. 1, p. 136; R. Southey, *Essays, Moral and Political* (London, 1832), vol. 1, pp. 296–304.

55. Everett, "Country Justice," p. 310.

56. *Athenaeum*, 2 February 1846, p. 202.

57. W. E. Houghton says that the romantic love of nature in the mid-Victorian city passed into a new phase: "It became the nostalgia for a lost world of peace and companionship . . . of country peace and unifying belief" (Houghton, *Victorian Frame of Mind*, pp. 79, 71). Froude's remarks, quoted by Houghton, p. 344, are from *The Nemesis of Faith* (1849), p. 116.

58. A. Hemingway, "Discourses of Art and Social Interest: The Representation of Landscape in Britain, c. 1800–1830," (Ph.D. diss., University of London, 1989), pp. 286–87.

59. W. J. Keith, "The Land in Victorian Literature," in G. E. Mingay, ed., *The Victorian Countryside* (London, 1981), vol. 1, p. 147.

60. G. Crabbe, *The Village* (1783), in *Poetical Works of George Crabbe* (Oxford, 1908), pp. 34–36, 39.

61. Crabbe, *The Village*, p. 35; Thomson, *The Seasons*, "Autumn," ll. 34, 40.

62. Crabbe, *Poetical Works*, pp. 51, 53.

63. Ibid., p. 75.

64. B. Disraeli, *Sybil, or, The Two Nations* (1845; London: Macmillan, 1895), p. 59.

65. C. Kingsley, *Yeast: A Problem* (London, 1866) p. 40 (first published in *Fraser's Town and Country Magazine*, 1848).

66. R. Jefferies, *Landscapes and Labour*, with an introduction by John Pearson (Bradford-on-Avon, 1979), p. 12.

67. John Eagles, "Subjects for Pictures: A Letter to Eusebius," *Blackwood's Edinburgh Magazine*, no. 63 (February 1848); reprinted in J. C. Olmsted, ed., *Victorian Painting: Essays and Reviews*, vol. 1, *1832–48* (London, 1980), p. 641.

Chapter Three: Paintings of the Agricultural Landscape

1. On this development, see Peter Ferriday, "The Victorian Art Market: The New Connoisseurs," *Country Life*, vol. 139, 6 June 1966, pp. 1456–58; also Brian Allen, "Patronage of British Painting, c. 1800–1850" (M.A. report, Courtauld Institute of Art, London, 1975).

2. Hemingway, "Discourses of Art and Social Interest," esp. pp. 39–67. An example of an agricultural landscape that was commissioned by a member of the gentry yet probably hung in a town house is Constable's *View of Dedham* (Museum of Fine Arts, Boston), which was described by the artist as "a present for Miss G. to contemplate in London," although "Miss G." (Philadelphia Godfrey, the daughter of a neighbour) was marrying Thomas Fitzhugh, who had an estate in Denbighshire (Beckett, ed., *John Constable's Correspondence*, vol. 2, pp. 134–35).

3. For example, Ambrogio Lorenzetti's fourteenth-century fresco cycle *The Effects of Good Government in the City and the Country* (Sala della Pace, Palazzo Pubblico, Siena), includes cultivated fields, with peasants at work. In seventeenth- and eighteenth-century England, estate views that include agricultural landscape carried a similar meaning, illustrating the beneficial effects of the country house on its surrounding estate.

4. W. Gilpin, "Instructions for Examining Landscapes" (Unpublished manuscript, Fitzwilliam Museum, Cambridge); quoted in C. P. Barbier, *William Gilpin* (London, 1963), p. 112.

5. Bermingham, *Landscape and Ideology*, p. 66. On the picturesque, see C. Hussey, *The Picturesque* (1927; repr. London, 1947) and Malcolm Andrews, *The Search for the Picturesque: Landscape Aesthetics and Tourism in Britain, 1760–1800* (Aldershot: Scolar Press, 1989).

6. J. Ruskin, *Modern Painters*, in E. T. Cook and A. Wedderburn, eds., *The Works of John Ruskin* (London: 1903–1912), vol. 1, pp. 627n and 191.

7. W. Hone, *The Every-Day Book* (1826), vol. 2, p. 1046; quoted from *The Mirror of the Months* (1826), p. 179.

8. For example, Francis Hayman, *The Milkmaid's Garland, or, Humours of May-Day* (Victoria and Albert Museum, London).

9. Perhaps the most Boucher-like of Gainsborough's works are the two landscapes at Woburn Abbey, *Peasant with Two Horses* and *Landscape with a Woodcutter Courting a Milkmaid*. Gainsborough painted his daughters as gleaners (a portrait of one of them is now in the Ashmolean Museum, Oxford); Reynolds depicted Thomas Macklin's wife and daughter, with a Miss Potts, as *The Cottagers* in 1788 (Detroit Institute of Arts).

10. M. Pointon, "Gainsborough and the Landscape of Retirement," *Art History*, vol. 2, no. 4 (December 1979), pp. 441–54; W. Hazlitt, "On Gainsborough's Pictures," *Champion*, 31 July 1814, in Howe, ed., *Complete Works of William Hazlitt*, vol. 2, p. 36.

11. For a comparison of Gainsborough with Wordsworth, see E. Waterhouse, "Gainsborough's Fancy Pictures," *Burlington Magazine*, June 1946, pp. 134–40. It has been shown that Stubbs's labourers are wearing contemporary working clothes, in N. McKendrick, *The Birth of a Consumer Society* (London, 1982), pp. 60–62.

12. M. Butler, *Romantics, Rebels and Reactionaries: English Literature and Its Background, 1760–1830* (Oxford, 1981), p. 36.

13. K. Garlick and A. Macintyre, eds., *The Diary of Joseph Farington, R.A.*, vol. 2, p. 552 (19 May 1796) and p. 588 (24 June 1796).

14. R. Payne Knight, *An Analytical Enquiry into the Principles of Taste* (1805; 4th ed., 1808, repr. in facsimile, 1972), p. 311.

15. Barrell, *Dark Side of the Landscape*, p. 128.

16. *The Remains of Robert Bloomfield* (1824), vol. 2, p. 112–13.

17. Edward Harington, *A Schizzo on the Genius of Man; in which, among various subjects, the merit of Mr Thomas Barker, the celebrated young painter of Bath, is particularly considered* (Bath, 1793), p. 141 (on *The Woodman*) and p. 184–85 (on Barker's painting of a match woman).

18. For example, Stubbs's *Lincolnshire Ox* (1790; Walker Art Gallery, Liverpool); James Ward exhibited paintings of *A Staffordshire Cow* and *A Staffordshire Bull* at the Royal Academy in 1797 (nos. 172 and 183).

19. M. Hardie, *Watercolour Painting in Britain*, vol. 2 (London, 1967), p. 140.

20. R. Ackermann, *Repository of the Arts*, May 1812, p. 304, quoted by Basil Taylor in *Joshua Cristall, 1768–1847*, catalogue of an exhibition held at the Victoria and Albert Museum (London, 1975), p. 33.

21. J. Gage, *A Decade of English Naturalism*, catalogue of an exhibition at Norwich Castle Museum (London, 1969).

22. An example of Turner's awareness of the connection between home agricultural production and Napoleon's blockade come in these lines from the draft letterpress to the *Southern Coast* series: "Why should the Volga or the Russians / Be coveted for hemp? . . . / Have we not soil sufficient rich? . . . / Plant but the ground with seed instead of gold. / Urge all our barren tracts with agricultural skill, / And Britain, Britain, British canvas fill; / Alone and unsupported prove her strength / By means her own to beat the direful length / Of continental hatred called blockade" (W. Thornbury, *The Life of J. M. W. Turner, R.A.* [3d ed., London, 1897], p. 215). Turner's example here is hemp, but the lesson could well be applied to corn, home production of which had to be increased to beat the blockade. For the patriotic significance of timber, see S. Daniels, "The Political Iconography of Woodland in Later Georgian

England," in D. Cosgrove and S. Daniels, eds., *The Iconography of Landscape* (Cambridge, 1988), p. 47.

23. Barrell, *Dark Side of the Landscape*, p. 154.

24. Rosenthal, *British Landscape Painting*, pp. 110–12.

25. See Christiana Payne, "The Agricultural Landscape in English Painting c. 1785–1885" (Ph.D. diss., University of London, 1985), pp. 132–34.

26. See Payne, "Boundless Harvests."

27. The buyers of DeWint's works between 1827 and 1849 are recorded in a list held in the Usher Gallery, Lincoln (item L1). They include Lady Clive, Lord Lonsdale, Earl Brownlow, Lady Belhaven and Mr Heathcote of Connington Castle, amongst others.

28. For Cox's political opinions, see F. Gordon Roe, *Cox the Master: The Life and Art of David Cox* (London, 1946), pp. 39–40, and A. J. Finberg, *The Drawings of David Cox* (London, 1939), p. 13. For Cox's patrons, see N. N. Solly, *Memoir of the Life of David Cox* (London, 1873), esp. pp. 24, 327–332.

29. M. Butlin, ed., *Samuel Palmer's 1824 Sketchbook* (London, 1962), p. 127.

30. A. J. Peacock, "Village Radicalism in East Anglia, 1800–1850," in J. P. Dunbabin, ed., *Rural Discontent in Nineteenth Century Britain* (London, 1974), p. 59.

31. *Athenaeum*, 13 May 1837, p. 219. The critic was discussing J. P. Knight's paintings, shown at the Royal Academy: *The English Harvest: A Dream of the Olden Times: Ploughing* (no. 335), *Reaping* (no. 460) and *Harvest Home* (no. 541).

32. *Athenaeum*, 14 May 1836, p. 348.

33. Wilkie Collins, *Memoirs of the Life of William Collins, Esq., R.A.* (1848, repr. London, 1978), vol. 2, pp. 311, 314.

34. From a speech in the House of Commons, June 1850, in J. Ridley, *Lord Palmerston* (London, 1970), p. 387.

35. Howitt, *Year-Book of the Country*, pp. 226–27.

36. See, for example, *Morning Chronicle*, 28 October 1850.

37. Howitt, *Year-Book of the Country*, p. 171.

38. For example, on 29 May 29 1852 (*Athenaeum*, p. 607) a reviewer wrote of E. T. Parris's *Faith, a Companion to Hope and Charity* (a picture of a farm labourer's family reading the Bible in a cottage): "No pastoral poem was ever more unreal—nor can we guess the country in which this pious poetical prize peasant family was raised." On 19 May 1860 (*Athenaeum*, pp. 689–90) a discussion of T. F. Marshall's *The Prop of the Family* includes this passage: "An old farmer . . . as he well may, smiles benignantly upon the youth [a boy of fourteen who supports his mother and younger brothers and sisters by reaping], whose exertions to lessen the Poor's-rates are so praiseworthy, and may, by the time he is eighty years of age, entitle him to a new pair of shoes and a sovereign in this world, if he will but condescend to make a show of himself before a row of boozy farmers and a benevolent peer." This writer said that Wallis's *Stonebreaker* had shown "the obverse side of this medal."

39. E.g. the reviewer quoted in note 38.

40. H. C. Marillier, *The Liverpool School of Painters* (London, 1904), p. 102.

41. Linnell bought 31 acres in about 1854, including three arable fields, which he let to farmers; by 1862 he owned about 80 acres (Story, *Life of John Linnell*, vol. 2, pp. 33–34).

42. R. Chignell, *The Life and Paintings of George Vicat Cole* (London, 1898), vol. 1, pp. 68, 10.

43. R. Pickvance, *English Influences on Vincent Van Gogh* (Arts Council, 1974–1975), p. 19.

44. For example, in 1871 Mason was grouped with William Blake Richmond, Thomas Armstrong and Albert Moore as painters whose work was "a timely protest against the vulgar naturalism, the common realism, which is applauded by the uneducated multitudes who throng our London exhibitions" (*Art Journal*, 1871, p. 177).

45. In 1897 Mason, Walker and Pinwell were described as a "budding school . . . which had that special quality, the value of which cannot well be overestimated, that it remained in its innovations national in feeling and character" (Claude Phillips, *Frederick Walker and his Works* [London, 1897], pp. 5–6.)

46. *Art Journal*, July 1876, p. 214.

47. In the catalogue to the Royal Academy exhibition of 1876, Macbeth published an explanation of his picture which seems to derive from an article on agricultural gangs in the *Quarterly Review* of July 1867.

48. The *Athenaeum* said that it showed "country folks, girls, bumpkins and boys in a mangold wurzel field, witnessing with delight the galloping of the fox-hunters, who destroy the hedges and trample the crops" (31 May 1879, p. 703).

49. In 1890 R. A. M. Stevenson wrote that Clausen's *Field Hand* (1883; sold at Sotheby's, London, 19 May 1982) was "admired by some and hated by others as a piece of thorough-going realism, unusual in England at that time, when peasants were represented as unnaturally clean, coquettish, and simperingly pretty" ("George Clausen," *Art Journal*, October 1890, p. 292).

50. For example, *A Field Gang Hoeing Turnips* (1883; sold at Christie's, London, 13 June 1980).

51. For example, see P. H. Calderon, "Realism in Art," *Art Journal*, February 1884, p. 58.

52. George Moore, *Modern Painting* (London, 1893), pp. 118, 121.

53. R. Jefferies, "The Labourer's Daily Life" (1874), reprinted in *The Toilers of the Field* (London, 1892), p. 95.

Catalogue

The catalogue is divided into five sections, covering oil paintings, watercolours and drawings, prints, illustrated books and photographs. Within these sections the items are listed in chronological order.

In the catalogue entries dimensions are given in inches, followed by centimetres in brackets; height precedes width. The bibliographical references are selective; in many cases a recent monograph or catalogue is cited in which further references may be found.

The following abbreviations are used in the catalogue:

A.O.W.S.	Associate of the Old Water-Colour Society (Society of Painters in Water-Colours, founded in 1804)
A.R.A.	Associate of the Royal Academy
A.R.S.A.	Associate of the Royal Scottish Academy
F.S.A.	Fellow of the Society of Antiquaries
N.W.S.	New Water-Colour Society (New Society of Painters in Water-Colours, founded in 1831)
O.M.	Order of Merit
O.W.S.	Old Water-Colour Society
P.O.W.S.	President of the Old Water-Colour Society
P.R.A.	President of the Royal Academy
R.A.	Royal Academy
R.W.S.	Royal Watercolour Society (name taken by the Old Water-Colour Society from 1881)

Oil Paintings

1

Thomas Barker 1769–1847

1

The Woodman, c. 1790
Oil on canvas
89 x 49 (226 x 124.5)
Provenance: By descent to present owner
References: E. Harington, *A Schizzo on the Genius of Man* (Bath, 1793), esp. pp. 140–45 and 184–85

The Lord Barnard, Raby Castle

Thomas Barker, usually known as Barker of Bath, established a reputation in the 1790s for his portrait-like studies of old labourers and beggars painted from life. A child prodigy, he was taken up by Charles Spackman, a rich coach-builder of Bath, who made him copy Old Masters and sent him to Italy to study.

His most famous painting, *The Woodman*, exists in several versions.[1] Its immediate inspiration was Thomas Gainsborough's *Woodman*, which was painted in 1787 and exhibited in London in 1789, after Gainsborough's death. This represented something of a new departure in Gainsborough's art, and it was a picture of which Gainsborough himself was particularly proud. Barker's *Woodman* also matches the description of the woodman in William Cowper's poem *The Task* (bk. 5, ll. 11.41–57).

Edward Harington's account of meeting the model for *The Woodman*, George Kelson, stresses the fidelity of Barker's depiction: he claims to have recognised him while out on a walk, as a result of seeing the painting, in which "the visage of this woodman is wonderfully expressive of his laborious occupation, rough and weather-beaten" (p. 141). It is clear, however, from Harington's account that the painting was read as a comforting or didactic display of virtuous poverty. Kelson was "sober, honest, industrious, sensible,

and inoffensive," and Harington told him that he was "a proper subject for a picture" because "virtue in poverty is far more distinguished, and will be more eminently rewarded, than even the virtue of the rich!" (p. 145). Harington was writing in 1793, soon after the French Revolution, at a time when it seemed particularly important to encourage virtue in the poor.

Nottingham only

---

1. The earliest would seem to be the version at the Tate Gallery (no. 792), which is very close to the Gainsborough. There is also a version belonging to the Torfaen Museum Trust, which may be the painting sold to Thomas Macklin on which the Bartolozzi engraving of 1792 was based (*The Barkers of Bath* [Victoria Art Gallery, 1986], no. 10).

Thomas Barker 1769–1847

2

Old Man with a Staff, c. 1790
Oil on canvas
30 x 24⅞ (76.2 x 63.2)
Provenance: Thomas Agnew and Sons, 1965

Yale Center for British Art, Paul Mellon Collection

Like *The Woodman* (cat. 1), this painting combines realism and didacticism. The old man's patched clothes, dishevelled hair and wrinkled face are painstakingly delineated, but they are clean. His oak staff is symbolic of his character, stressed by his proud stance and unflinching gaze. Like an oak, he is typically English, able to withstand the storms of life and yet remain erect. He can be seen, therefore, as an emblem of peasant virtue, the bedrock of the national character.[1]

Although Barker's paintings of beggars and labourers are, in many respects, typical

(see pl. 1)

of their period, their portrait-like accuracy looks forward to the rustic figures of W. H. Pyne and his circle in the early nineteenth century.

Yale only

---

1. Stephen Daniels has discussed the symbolism of oaks in the art and discourse of this period. See S. Daniels, "The Political Iconography of Woodland in Later Georgian England," in D. Cosgrove and S. Daniels, eds., *The Iconography of Landscape* (Cambridge, 1988), pp. 48–57.

FRANCIS WHEATLEY (R.A.) *1747–1801*

3
The Hay Cart, 1790
Signed and dated 1790
Oil on canvas
40 x 49 (101.6 x 124.4)
Provenance: Maskelyne Collection;
Christie's, 6 February 1953 (no. 139)

References: M. Webster, *Francis Wheatley* (New Haven and London, 1970), p. 140, no. 71

Government Art Collection of the United Kingdom

Wheatley's rural scenes were strongly influenced by contemporary French painters, prints of whose work were readily available in late eighteenth-century London. From artists such as François Boucher and Jean-Baptiste Greuze he adopted the pastoral notion of the countryside as a place of relaxation and flirtation. In this painting, the rather contrived composition balances a carefully delineated waggon and horses against a group of attractive, youthful haymakers who are evidently in the process of pairing up into three couples. The actual work is far away, in the background. Artists and poets often presented haymaking as an opportunity for lovemaking: the work was lighter than at corn harvest, there was less danger of the crop being spoilt by such distractions and it was in any case less valuable. Couples often appear in depictions of haymaking, whereas at harvest time the presence of children as gleaners seems to have encouraged artists to concentrate on family groups instead.

Yale only

GEORGE STUBBS (A.R.A.) *1724–1806*
4
Reapers, 1795
Signed and dated 1795, lower right
Enamel on Wedgwood biscuit earthenware
30¼ x 40½ (77 x 102), oval
Provenance: . . . Major A. E. W. Malcolm;
Mrs Malcolm, Sotheby's, 18 November 1959 (no. 43), P. and D. Colnaghi, 1959
First exhibited: British Institution, 1806 (no. 56)

3

4 (see pl. 2)

References: Bruce Tattersall, *Stubbs and Wedgwood: Unique Alliance between Artist and Potter*, exh. cat. (Tate Gallery, London, 1974), p. 106; J. Egerton, *The Paul Mellon Collection: British Sporting and Animal Paintings, 1655–1867* (London, 1978), no. 95; J. Egerton, *George Stubbs, 1724–1806*, exh. cat. (Tate Gallery, London, 1984), no. 126

Yale Center for British Art, Paul Mellon Collection

Stubbs was primarily a sporting painter. His agricultural scenes were painted at a time in his life when he was trying to widen the scope of his art and experimenting with the smooth finish and lasting colours that could be achieved through enamel painting. Three versions of *The Reapers* are extant: two oils (1782, Upton House, and 1785, Tate Gallery), both of these paired with oils of *The Haymakers*; and this ceramic plaque, produced in association with the potter Josiah Wedgwood. The 1785 versions became the basis for mezzotints that do not, however, appear to have been successful commercially (see cat. 86). The Yale *Reapers* is the largest of the ceramic plaques produced by Stubbs and Wedgwood to survive. There are also two ceramic plaques at the Lady Lever Art Gallery, Port Sunlight: *Haymakers*, 1794, and *Haycarting*, 1795 (Tattersall, *Stubbs and Wedgwood*, pp. 105 and 109).

As he worked on successive versions, Stubbs gradually refined his compositions to produce the harmonious, rhythmical effects evident in the Yale *Reapers*. The cleanliness and fashionable clothing of his field workers have often been remarked upon, but they may have as much to do with Stubbs's meticulous style as with his attitudes toward rural life.

The Reapers shows successive stages in the harvesting of wheat. The labourer on the right grasps the stalks of wheat, ready to cut them, the labourer to the left of him is bending down to make the cut, the woman makes a straw rope to bind the sheaves and the man to the right of her sets them up. The scene is, however, rather contrived: the stubble is much too short for a crop that is being cut by sickle, there are no swathes of unbound corn lying on the ground, and no one binds the sheaves. Stubbs's careful, accurate depiction of agricultural detail was tempered, therefore, by the exclusion of any details that might suggest disorder or untidiness.

The labourers are undoubtedly very well dressed: the men wear buckled shoes and their breeches have not been unbuttoned to allow them to bend more easily (cf. cat. 5); the woman's hat is fashionable. On the other hand, she wears buff-coloured sleeves to protect her arms from scratchy stubble, unlike the women in harvest scenes by Wheatley and Thomas Rowlandson, and the men, at least, have the features of individuals rather than types. Drawings for *The Reapers* and *The Haymakers* were in Stubbs's studio sale of 1807 but have since disappeared. Their existence suggests that the pictures were based on careful study from nature and should thus be seen as anticipating the "rustic figures" of 1800–1810 instead of belonging to the more artificial rococo pastorals of Stubbs's contemporaries such as Thomas Hearne and Wheatley.

The church spire, small and distant though it is, occupies an important place in the composition. It is almost in the centre and is lined up with the central figure and the tie on the straw rope in the foreground, reminding the observer of the religious associations of harvest. It also stands between the mounted farmer or overseer on the right and the labourers at either side of the stooks on the left, as if emphasizing the parallels between the master-servant relationship and the relationship between God and man.

It has been thought that this plaque was identical with a work included in Stubbs's sale of 27 May 1807 (no. 93), but as the latter was catalogued as *Landscape with Hay Field and Hay Makers*, this seems unlikely. The Yale *Reapers* had been exhibited a year earlier as *Harvest*, and in the early nineteenth century cataloguers were much more aware of the difference between haymaking and wheat harvesting than we are today.

Yale only

RICHARD WESTALL (R.A.) *1765–1836*

5

A Storm in Harvest, 1796
Signed on barrel, lower left, "RW/1796"
Oil on card, loosely mounted on canvas
23¾ x 31 (58.8 x 78)
Provenance: Richard Payne Knight; by descent to present owner
References: M. Clarke and N. Penny, eds., *The Arrogant Connoisseur: Richard Payne Knight, 1751–1824* (Manchester, 1982), no. 200

Private collection

Richard Westall was primarily a painter of literary and historical subjects. From the mid-1790s onwards, however, he produced rustic scenes that proved to be very popular.

A Storm in Harvest was one of his most successful compositions. The first version, in watercolour (untraced), was painted for W. Chamberlayne and exhibited at the Royal Academy in May 1796 (no. 652). The second (exhibited here) is an oil version which Westall had completed by June of the same year. Samuel Whitbread tried, unsuccessfully, to buy first the watercolour and then the oil, but the latter was sold to Payne Knight instead. There was such widespread interest in the picture that a spurious print

was made of it, according to Farington, based on a drawing by an artist who "went 22 times to the Academy to make copies of parts by stealth." In 1802 Farington reported that 1600 impressions had been taken of the official print by R. M. Meadows, and in the Royal Academy exhibition of that year Westall showed a picture entitled "A woman and a child in a storm, part of the principal group of the 'Storm in Harvest.'"[1]

Evidently, then, the composition had wide appeal. The subject would have been familiar to readers of James Thomson's *Seasons*, which describes a storm in harvest.[2] Westall, however, has invested the group of labourers with the dignity and profound emotions normally reserved for heroes in history paintings, and this may have appealed to viewers with democratic sympathies. It is significant that both Payne Knight and Whitbread were Whig members of Parliament with Radical tendencies: Whitbread had even proposed a bill to fix minimum wages for farm labourers (9 December 1795).

Payne Knight had a high opinion of the painting. In his treatise on taste he grouped it with Benjamin West's *General Wolfe* and Joseph Wright's *Soldier's Tent* as "some of the most interesting and affecting pictures, that the art has ever produced," in which, he argued, the pathos was much improved "by the characters and dresses being taken from common familiar life." Elsewhere in the treatise he declared that "it is the dignified elevation of the sentiments of the actors or sufferers, that separates the interesting, or the pathetic, from the disgusting, or the ridiculous."[3] In other words, the painting appealed to the emotions involved in "sensibility": it invited sympathy with the labourers (who, if they were not mere employees, stood to lose the products of a year's labour in the storm) but "elevated"

5 (see pl. 3)

them sufficiently to avoid "disgusting" the viewer. The features of most of the figures are certainly refined, suggesting that Westall studied them from professional models, not from real rural labourers. His understanding of agricultural practice also seems rather superficial. The poet Robert Bloomfield was critical of the watercolour version of *A Storm in Harvest* on both these counts: he could not tell whether the sheaves were meant to be barley or wheat but thought they were "a bad crop"; he described the young man in the centre as "an Abelard—never saw a Suffolk codger like him," although he preferred the old man and woman and thought "the old man's hand to his chin *right good.*"[4]

1. K. Garlick and A. Macintyre, eds., *The Diary of Joseph Farington* (New Haven and London, 1978–

1984), vol. 2, p. 588 (24 June 1796); p. 598 (9 July 1796); vol. 3, p. 675 (10 October 1796); and vol. 5, p. 1764 (6 April 1802).

2. J. Thomson, *The Seasons* (rev. ed., 1746), "Autumn," ll. 311–52.

3. R. Payne Knight, *An Analytical Enquiry into the Principles of Taste* (4th ed., London, 1808), pp. 311–12, 361.

4. *The Remains of Robert Bloomfield* (London, 1824), vol. 2, pp. 112–13.

FRANCIS WHEATLEY (R.A.) *1747–1801*

6

Noon, 1799
Oil on canvas
17½ x 21½ (44.5 x 54.5)
Provenance: Arthur Tooth and Sons, 1961
First exhibited: Royal Academy, 1801 (no. 70)

6 (see pl. 4)

References: Mary Webster, *Francis Wheatley* (New Haven and London, 1970), no. 120; John Barrell, "Francis Wheatley's Rustic Hours," *Antique Dealer and Collector's Guide*, December 1982, pp. 39–42

Yale Center for British Art, Paul Mellon Collection

With its companion, *Evening* (cat. 7), this is one in a series of four "rustic hours," showing rural activities appropriate to different times of day, all of which are now in the Yale Center for British Art.

John Barrell has stressed the function of this series in showing the deserving poor— industrious, neat, clean and domesticated. The series also hints at rural piety: in *Evening* the father's spade points to the church, and in *Noon* the older woman (the grand-mother?) folds her hands, apparently saying grace before the meal.

Noon is one of the earliest representations of workers lunching in the harvest field, which was later to become a common foreground motif (cf. cat. 12 and 13). But in contrast to later paintings the emphasis is very much on family life rather than work. The loaded waggon in the background contains much more wheat than this man could have harvested on his own, yet there are no other workers to be seen. His wife and children look as if they have come out only to bring lunch, not to bind or glean: they do not, for example, wear arm protectors to prevent their arms from being scratched by stubble, as the woman in Stubbs's *Reapers* does. Three generations of the family are shown, but the man is anonymous, as he is in other paintings in the series. We see his face only once, and it is the attractive female members of the family who look directly at us.

The details suggest that the man's labour is richly rewarded. His wife apparently brings cold roast beef to the field (instead of the more likely bread and cheese), and spotlessly clean linen cascades out of the basket in the foreground. The overall effect, in fact, is of a delightful picnic, not a break from labour.

Yale only

FRANCIS WHEATLEY (R.A.) *1747–1801*
7
Evening, 1799
Oil on canvas
17½ x 21½ (44.5 x 54.5)
Provenance: Christie's, 8 February 1946;
Arthur Tooth and Sons, 1961
First exhibited: Royal Academy, 1801 (no. 87)

References: Mary Webster, *Francis Wheatley* (New Haven and London, 1970), no. 119; John Barrell, "Francis Wheatley's Rustic Hours," *Antique Dealer and Collector's Guide,* December 1982, pp. 39–42

Yale Center for British Art, Paul Mellon Collection

See cat. 6.

Yale only

JOSEPH MALLORD WILLIAM TURNER (R.A.) *1775–1851*
8
Ploughing Up Turnips, near Slough, 1809
Oil on canvas
40 x 51¼ (102 x 130)
Provenance: Bequeathed by the artist, 1856
First exhibited: Turner's Gallery, 1809 (no. 9)

7

8 (see pl. 5)

References: M. Butlin and E. Joll, *The Paintings of J. M. W. Turner* (New Haven and London, 1984), no. 89

Tate Gallery, London

From around 1806 to 1813 Turner produced a number of oil paintings of agricultural scenes ranging from small sketches to full-scale exhibition pieces like this one. The impetus for his study of agriculture in this period seems to have come from two sources: a realisation of the patriotic significance of agriculture in wartime and an intensive phase of plein-air painting. The war also meant that Turner was unable to travel to Europe and thus, like many of his contemporaries, concentrated on English landscape. As Michael Rosenthal has pointed out, *Ploughing Up Turnips* is especially patriotic since (despite Turner's idiosyncratic title) the building in the background is Windsor Castle, residence of the King, who was noted for his encouragement of agriculture.[1] The mes-

sage is clear: the King is at the apex of the nation and farm labourers are at its base, but both are united in their common effort against the French.

Ploughing Up Turnips illustrates the stages in the four-course rotation introduced in Norfolk in the eighteenth century, which made an important contribution to the agricultural revolution by increasing the fertility of the soil and the resulting crop yields. Turnips were grown in between cereal crops, restoring soil fertility without the need for a bare fallow; once harvested, they were fed to cattle, whose manure in turn contributed to the richness of the soil. Turner's painting shows the turnips being harvested and the land being prepared for the sowing of the next crop, probably barley. Two women on the right are putting turnips into sacks; the men in the centre are preparing to plough the field; it will then be rolled, using the roller on which the woman sits in the left foreground. As soon as the soil is prepared, the sower, who stands in a central position in the painting, will broadcast seed from the seedlip he carries on his hip and, finally, the field will be harrowed to cover up the seed. A harrow is just visible to the left of the lighter-coloured cow, being held upright by the man standing behind the women who are gathering turnips. J. F. Herring's *Seed Time* (cat. 28) shows a similar series of operations being performed successively in the same field.

In a sense, then, this painting is a celebration of agricultural improvement. But the four-course rotation was hardly new in 1809, and the implements and number of horses used would have seemed old-fashioned to a modern progressive farmer.[2] Turner's figures, too, are not the efficient automata of some agricultural scenes. They rest, converse, watch the observer, feel the cold and, in the case of the old man holding the plough, display the arthritic effects of hard labour in the open air. Turner thus seems to have taken a stronger interest in the human aspects of the agricultural landscape than in its technological progress.

1. M. Rosenthal, *Constable and the Valley of the Stour* (Ph.D. diss., London University, 1978), p. 310.
2. This has been pointed out by A. Hemingway, *Landscape Imagery and Urban Culture in Early Nineteenth Century Britain* (Cambridge, 1992), pp. 230–31.

THOMAS BARKER *1769–1847*

9

Sheep Shearing, c. 1812
Oil on canvas
17½ x 23 (44.5 x 58.5)
Provenance: Sir T. W. Holburne, by 1867
First exhibited: ?British Institution, 1812 (no. 58)
References: *The Barkers of Bath* (Victoria Art Gallery, Bath, 1986), no. 59

9 (see pl. 6)

Holburne Museum and Crafts Study
Centre, Bath

In 1812 Barker exhibited two pairs of paintings of sheep washing and sheep shearing at
the British Institution: this may be no. 58,
the dimensions of which (including the
frame) were given as 2.0 x 2.5 feet. His interest in rustic figures links him with the circle of W. H. Pyne. Barker made pen and
wash copies of scenes from Pyne's *Microcosm*;
and Pyne, in his turn, recommended
Barker's set of 40 lithographic impressions,
selected from his studies of *Rustic Figures after Nature* (1813) as works from which the
student might copy.[1]

   Sheep Shearing, however, is far removed
from the documentary style of Pyne's illustrations of rustic occupations. Barker uses
chiaroscuro and swirling brushstrokes to
dramatise the subject, setting it out of doors,
apparently in open countryside, rather than
in the more likely surroundings of a barn or
farmyard. Although the labourers wear contemporary clothes—gaiters, shirts, waistcoats and breeches—the picture shows the
influence of the Old Masters, such as
seventeenth-century Dutch and Flemish
painters and the Spanish painter Bartolomé
Murillo, whose work Barker is known to
have copied. Yet the result is a painting that
conveys more of the effort of rural labour
than many British paintings, and its dark
palette, chiaroscuro and approach to labour
anticipate the work of Millet in the mid-
nineteenth century.

1. See, for example, *Barker of Bath: An Exhibition
of Paintings and Drawings by Thomas Barker, 1769–
1847* (Victoria Art Gallery, Bath, 1962), no. 67;
W. H. Pyne, *Rustic Figures for the Embellishment of
Landscape* (London, 1815), p. 8.

JOHN CONSTABLE (R.A.) *1776–1837*
10
Studies of Two Ploughs, 1814
Inscribed "2d. Novr. 1814"
Oil on paper with a brown ground
6¾ x 10¼ (17.2 x 26)

10

Provenance: Given to the Victoria and Albert Museum by Isabel Constable, the artist's daughter, in 1888

References: G. Reynolds, *Catalogue of the Constable Collection at the Victoria and Albert Museum* (London, 1960), no. 136; M. Rosenthal, *Constable: The Painter and His Landscape* (New Haven and London, 1983), p. 12

The Board of Trustees of the Victoria and Albert Museum, London

This study was made in 1814, the year that Constable exhibited the first version of his *Landscape: Ploughing Scene in Suffolk* (cat. 16) at the Royal Academy. The main sketch shows a high gallows wheel plough, of the same type as the plough shown in the painting. Michael Rosenthal has pointed out that the second plough, a Suffolk swing plough, was a type used in the heavier lands around East Bergholt but not in the village itself, and that when Constable came to paint *The Cornfield* in 1826 (National Gallery, Lon-

don) he combined the features of both ploughs, creating an unlikely composite type in a painting that, in contrast to his work of the 1810s, showed relative indifference to accuracy of agricultural detail.

The careful documentary record of the implements is typical of this period, not only in Constable's work but in British art in general: it can be compared with Pyne's careful recording of agricultural processes in the *Microcosm* (cat. 98).

JOHN CONSTABLE (R.A.) *1776–1837*

11

Golding Constable's Kitchen Garden, 1815
Oil on canvas
13 x 20 (33 x 50.8)
Provenance: By descent to Charles Golding Constable; Christie's, 11 July 1887, bought by Agnew for Sir Cuthbert Quilter; Christie's, 26 June 1936, bought by Gooden and Fox; . . . Ernest Cook, by whom bequeathed to Ipswich through the National Art Collections Fund, 1955

11 (see pl. 7)

References: M. Rosenthal, "Golding Constable's Gardens," *Connoisseur*, vol. 187, October 1974, pp. 88–91; L. Parris and I. Fleming-Williams, *Constable* (Tate Gallery, London, 1991), no. 26

Ipswich Borough Council Museums and Galleries

This is one of a pair of paintings that Michael Rosenthal has shown were painted in the summer of 1815, the year in which Constable's *Wheatfield* (see fig. 4) was first exhibited at the Royal Academy. Constable is known to have been in East Bergholt from 7 to 31 July and again from 6 August. In the *Kitchen Garden* the wheat in the field adjoining the garden is not quite ripe, but in the companion picture, *Golding Constable's Flower Garden*, it is being reaped. It seems likely, then, that the *Kitchen Garden* was painted in July and its companion in August.

Both pictures were painted from nature with meticulous attention to detail, from upstairs windows in Constable's father's house. They were neither exhibited nor sold in Constable's lifetime and appear to have been painted as an exercise in finishing from nature. Many commentators have stressed the strong personal associations of their subject matter: not only his father's gardens but also the elder Constable's arable fields and windmill are included in the view, and the house just to the right of the centre, in the middle distance, is the Rectory, the home of Dr Rhudde, who opposed Constable's marriage to his granddaughter, Maria.

This painting is a good example of the contrasting colours and textures to be found in cultivated landscape. In the far distance and middle distance on the left, fields of wheat can be seen in at least two different stages of ripeness. The farthest is being harvested, and a loaded waggon and the white shirts of the labourers can just be made out.

In front of this field there are three fields, each of a different colour: meadows, perhaps, or green wheat just starting to whiten in the sun. The nearest field, in front of the wooden fence, contains a wheat crop that is very nearly ripe. The individual stalks of wheat are suggested by narrow strokes of impasto, giving a ridged effect, a technique Constable also used in *The Wheatfield;* and Constable applied horizontal strokes in some areas to indicate that the crop has been partly "laid," that is, beaten down by rain.

The painting as a whole is a celebration of a well-ordered, richly productive landscape in which the village on the right is balanced by the harvest fields on the left, and the good husbandry of the vegetable garden is echoed throughout the landscape.

Nottingham only

JOHN LINNELL *1792–1882*
12
The Haymakers' Repast: A Scene in Wales, 1815
Oil on panel
15½ x 28½ (39.3 x 72.5)
Provenance: Mr Peacock; Mr Lopez; Mr Thomson; Mr Rought, 1850s; . . . Spink and Co., 1973, from whom bought by present owner
First exhibited: Society of Painters in Oil and Water-Colours, 1815 (no. 152)
References: K. Crouan, *John Linnell: A Centennial Exhibition*, exh. cat. (Cambridge, 1982), no. 28

Private collection

Between 1813 and 1820 the Society of Painters in Water-Colours became the Society of Painters in Oil and Water-Colours, accepting oils as well as watercolours for its annual exhibitions. It seems to have become

12

quite a centre for plein-air naturalism: Linnell became a member of it in this period, and his friend G. R. Lewis also exhibited oils there.

This painting was based on a watercolour study done on Linnell's trip to Wales in the company of Lewis in 1813.[1] The watercolour only included the haymakers in the background, and for the oil Linnell added a rather self-conscious foreground, combining naturalistically observed details, such as the man stretched out on the ground and two men with hats pulled down over their faces, with more conventional features, such as the framing tree and the girl with a pot on her head, both of which give it a rather Italianate air. The serious mood of the foreground figures, however, suggests some awareness of rural hardships and is very different from the jollity of his later harvest scenes, with their happy family groups.

Linnell's landscape sketchbook records that this painting was retouched for a Mr Wrought in 1850.[2] The sky particularly is in Linnell's later, broader style. It is also recorded that the painting went to a Mr Peacock; it may then be the "View in Wales"

that Linnell records having given to Mr Peacock "in exchange for an old picture early Italian" in 1825.[3] If so, then it remained unsold for ten years.

Nottingham only

1. Crouan, *John Linnell*, no. 27.
2. Linnell's landscape sketchbook, p. 20 (British Museum).
3. Linnell's journal (Private collection), 13 September 1825.

PETER DeWINT (o.w.s.) *1784–1849*
13
The Cornfield, c. 1815
Oil on canvas
41¼ x 64½ (104.8 x 163.8)
First exhibited: Royal Academy, 1815
(no. 290)
Provenance: Given to the Victoria and Albert Museum by Mrs P. Tatlock, the artist's daughter, in 1872
References: H. Smith, *Peter DeWint* (London, 1982), pp. 65–69; R. Parkinson, *Catalogue of British Oil Paintings, 1820–1860*

13 (see pl. 8)

This painting was probably the one exhibited at the Royal Academy in 1815 (no. 290), but it found no purchaser and was still in DeWint's collection at his death.

In a panoramic landscape in Lincolnshire, workers are engaged in a variety of occupations: having a lunch break in the foreground, pitching sheaves onto a waggon in the background and raking loose corn into heaps in the centre while the women to the left and right are gleaning. It was becoming standard practice to include all these occupations in the same picture, although it is unlikely that they would all have happened simultaneously. Gleaners were generally not allowed to glean until the fields were cleared; it is likely that all the workers would have had lunch at the same time, at the hottest time of day; sheaves were left in the field to dry for days or even weeks and

would not have been loaded onto a waggon while wheat in the same field remained uncut.

The heaps in the centre of the painting are an unusual feature. At first it looks as if haymaking or barley harvest is going on in another part of the field. C. Gray, however, in his commentary to Pyne's *Microcosm*, mentions the practice of raking the fields after the sheaves have been carried, to collect up any loose stalks missed by the reapers, and attributes this to the "repulsive selfishness" of the farmers (because raking meant that little was left behind for the gleaners).[1] In DeWint's painting, the gleaners on the right hold very meagre gleanings, and one looks pointedly across at the raked heaps of corn, as if contrasting the few stalks she holds in her hand with the bounty that ought to have been left to the gleaners. Like Gray, then, DeWint may have been making a comment on the conflict between ancient rights on the one hand and modern commercial practice on the other. Further support is given to this interpretation by Constable's choice of a couplet to accompany his *Wheatfield* (see fig. 4),exhibited a year later, which declares that the fields are *not* raked in Suffolk: "No rake takes here what Heaven to all bestows— / Children of want, for you the bounty flows!"[2]

---

1. See Introduction, p. 00.
2. R. Bloomfield, *The Farmer's Boy*, 1800, "Summer," ll. 137-38.

GEORGE ROBERT LEWIS *1782–1871*

14

Hereford, Dynedor and the Malvern Hills from the Haywood Lodge, Harvest Scene, Afternoon. Painted on the Spot, 1815–16
Oil on canvas
16¼ x 23½ (41 x 59)
Provenance: . . . Rev. Stopford Brooke, by whom given to the Tate Gallery, 1904
First exhibited: Society of Painters in Oil and Water-Colours, 1816 (no. 139)
References: *Landscape in Britain, 1750–1850*

(Tate Gallery, London, 1973), no. 247; J. Barrell, *The Dark Side of the Landscape* (Cambridge, 1980), pp. 115–17

Tate Gallery, London

In 1816 G. R. Lewis exhibited two medium-sized and twelve small landscape paintings (the latter shown in four frames, three paintings to a frame) at the exhibition of the Society of Painters in Oil and Water-Colours. Four of these are now in the Tate Gallery. All were painted in Herefordshire and have specific topographical titles; each title notes the time of day and includes the words "painted on the spot." The Haywood Lodge is a substantial farmhouse, situated on a ridge a few miles out of Hereford, which was let to a tenant farmer, a widow, Mrs Theresa Price, in 1815.[1] The fields depicted in this harvest scene are part of the lands belonging to the farmhouse, and nearly all of the other subjects mentioned in the titles of this series of paintings could be seen from the Haywood Lodge. It seems likely, then,

14 (see pl. 9)

that Lewis stayed at the Haywood Lodge in the summer of 1815 and made plein-air studies of the cornfields and employees of a friend or patron.

Lewis has transcribed the landscape with great accuracy and regard for agricultural detail. The field in the foreground has been reaped and stooked, and only then are the sheaves loaded onto a waggon. Other artists, such as DeWint (cat. 13), liked to maximise the variety and appeal of the harvest scene by showing different operations going on in the same field, and women and children working alongside the men. Lewis, however, shows reaping going on only in a separate field in the background and depicts women gleaning, but in a separate study (now in the Tate Gallery).

Despite the claim in Lewis's title that the picture was "painted on the spot," it seems likely that at least some of the foreground figures were added at a later date. They have undergone changes, which are obvious now that the pentimento of a man in a jacket, left of centre, has begun to show through the top layer of paint. In its original form the foreground group may have consisted of only three men: the man holding a barrel, the man with a pitchfork, and the man in a jacket, who was subsequently painted out by Lewis. These three figures all appear to have individualised features and could be portraits of employees of Mrs Price; the other figures are noticeably more anonymous, fit rather awkwardly with the rest of the figures, and are clearly painted over the completed landscape. The man in a jacket, who has no hat, is presumably supervising rather than working and appears to be a bailiff or overseer.

The changes in the figures may have been motivated by the faulty perspective of the "bailiff," but they also have the effect of transforming the workers into a convivial group and toning down the element of confrontation that must have been evident in the original version of the painting. In 1816, when the painting was exhibited, the optimism of the summer of 1815, following the final defeat of Napoleon, had given way to fears of popular revolt in the wake of economic depression, and Lewis may have worried that his original composition would have looked too threatening.

His harvest scene can be compared with other plein-air studies from the summers of 1814 and 1815, by Constable, Peter DeWint and John Linnell, the last of whom had accompanied Lewis on a sketching tour of Wales in 1813.

---

1. Belmont Papers, including deeds of Haywood Lodge, ref. C.38/14, Herefordshire County Record Office.

JAMES STARK 1794–1859

15

Sheep Washing at Postwick Grove, Norwich, c. 1822
Oil on panel
17 x 21 (43 x 53.5)
Provenance: Henry Hirsch; Christie's, 23 March 1934; Thomas Agnew and Sons, 1964
First exhibited: ?Norwich Society, 1822 (no. 8)

Yale Center for British Art, Paul Mellon Collection

Stark was one of the Norwich school of artists, who had their own flourishing exhibiting society and local patrons in East Anglia, although many of them also exhibited, or lived for varying periods, in London. Stark himself had been in London from 1814 to 1820 and had studied at the Royal Academy schools.

The main stylistic influence on their work came from seventeenth-century Dutch artists, hence their concentration on woodland

15

and river scenes. They painted surprisingly
few agricultural landscapes, despite the fact
that agriculture was both prosperous and
progressive in Norfolk and had made an important contribution to the agricultural revolution of the eighteenth century.

In *Sheep Washing* the sheep are being
washed in the river before shearing so that
the fleeces will be clean. Hurdles have been
placed to direct them through the river and
out onto the bank.

Stark produced at least five paintings of
this subject throughout his career. Paintings
with this title were exhibited twice at the
Norwich Society (1822 and 1849) and three
times at the British Institution in London
(1824, 1848 and 1858).

Yale only

John Constable (r.a.) *1776–1837*
16
Landscape: Ploughing Scene in Suffolk, c. 1825
Oil on canvas
16¾ x 30 (42.5 x 76)
Provenance: John Allnutt; Christie's, 20 June
1863, bought by Cox; Christie's, 14 July
1944; L. Neville Long until 1961; Leggatt
Bros., 1962
References: R. B. Beckett, "'A Summerland'
by John Constable," *Art Quarterly*, vol. 27
(Summer 1964), pp. 176–82; J. Barrell, *The
Dark Side of the Landscape* (Cambridge,
1980), pp. 149–53; M. Rosenthal, *Constable:
The Painter and His Landscape* (New Haven
and London, 1983), pp. 69–78; G. Reynolds,
*The Later Paintings and Drawings of John
Constable* (New Haven and London, 1984),
no. 24.81

16 (pl. 10)

Yale Center for British Art, Paul Mellon Collection

This painting is a replica of a picture bought by John Allnutt in 1815. Allnutt had the sky altered by John Linnell,[1] but some years later he asked Constable to restore it and reduce its size to match another painting in his collection. Constable instead painted a slightly smaller replica, free of charge, as a mark of gratitude to Allnutt for "buying the first picture he ever sold to a stranger." The original version was taken back and used by Constable as the basis for David Lucas's mezzotint *A Summerland*. The title of the mezzotint implies that this field has been left fallow over the summer and is being ploughed in the autumn to make ready for sowing the next crop.

When Constable exhibited the first version of the painting at the Royal Academy in 1815, he accompanied it with lines from Robert Bloomfield's *The Farmer's Boy*: "But, unassisted through each toilsome day / With smiling brow the ploughman cleaves his way." The ploughman is ploughing with only two horses and no plough-boy—an efficient, modern mode of ploughing, of which progressive agriculturists could approve. Bloomfield's verses make it clear, however, that this modern practice involves hardship for the labourer: his day is "toilsome" and he is "unassisted." In this context, "smiling" surely means lined or furrowed rather than implying that the labourer works cheerfully.

Michael Rosenthal discovered a review in the *East Anglian* magazine that indicates how an agriculturist might view the painting: "Its exhibition in the metropolis, as showing that mode of performing the operation in that county, contrasted with the inferior practice in many others, of ploughing with three or even four horses at *length*, instead of two *abreast*, may be serviceable to the interests of agriculture."[2] To such a reviewer, Turner's *Ploughing up Turnips* (cat. 8) might seem to represent the "inferior practice," although it could perhaps be justified on heavier soils.

Yale only

1. In an entry in his cash book for 5 July 1815, Linnell recorded that he "recd. of Mr Robson— for painting a new Sky to a Picture by Mr Constable belonging to Mr Olnet [*sic*] of Clapham

3–3–0" (Linnell Trust Manuscripts, private collection).

2. *East Anglian*, 1814, no. 4, p. 210; quoted in Rosenthal, *Constable: The Painter and His Landscape*, p. 19.

GEORGE VINCENT *1796–1832*

17

Trowse Meadows, near Norwich, 1828
Oil on canvas
28¾ x 43⅛ (73 x 109.5)
Provenance: William Davey; bought from him by J. J. Colman, 1891; J. J. Colman Bequest, 1899
First exhibited: ?Norwich Society, 1828 (no. 107 or 142)
References: A. Moore, *The Norwich School of Artists* (Norfolk Museums Service, 1985), p. 46

Norfolk Museums Service (Norwich Castle Museum)

George Vincent, like Stark, belonged to the Norwich school. This painting is a rare example of an agricultural landscape by one of this group, although even here the river and woodland take prominence over the hay field and hay cart in the middle distance. A very fully loaded hay wain, with a man lying on top to steady the load, prepares to cross the river. Another wain can be seen behind, being loaded, while haymakers are visible amongst the haycocks in the middle distance on the right. The general composition is reminiscent of Constable's *Hay Wain* (National Gallery, London), which Vincent could have seen when it was shown at the Royal Academy in 1821. Two other smaller versions of this composition are known: one in Norwich Castle Museum (27.939) and another in a private collection in Australia.

WILLIAM COLLINS (R.A.) *1788–1847*

18

Sketch in a Kentish Hop-Garden, 1829
Signed on cradle rocker
Oil on panel
15⅜ x 19½ (39.1 x 49.5)
Provenance: Bought from the artist by the 12th Duke of Norfolk for 150 guineas

17 (see pl. 11)

18

First exhibited: Royal Academy, 1829 (no. 103)

References: Wilkie Collins, *Memoirs of the Life of William Collins, Esq., R.A.* (1848; repr. London, 1978), vol. 1, pp. 316–17

His Grace the Duke of Norfolk

William Collins was very successful in the 1820s, 1830s and 1840s with his rural genre scenes, which usually focussed on children and family life. Stylistically, they look back to the painting of the late eighteenth century, but such subjects acquired additional significance in this period, when factory reform made rural children seem fortunate by comparison and fears of revolution created a demand for portrayals of peasant virtue.

The title of this work implies that it has been painted on the spot, or at least based closely on open-air sketches. Collins stayed with a patron, Mr Wells of Redleaf, in Kent, and could have observed hop picking near his home.[1] He was influenced by the fashion for open-air painting in the 1810s, as well as by the interest of other artists, such as Joshua Cristall, in the subject (cf. cat. 51). As in other paintings of hop picking, the emphasis is on the women and children who normally did the work. Collins, however, focusses on the foreground incident, giving the painting the character of a latter-day holy family or nativity, with the actual work well in the background. The mother and baby are reminiscent of a holy family by Rembrandt, such as *The Holy Family with the Angels* (1645; The Hermitage, St. Petersburg). The young girl kneels like an attendant angel, and the baby seems to radiate light, which is reflected in the face of his Correggio-like mother, who wears the blue of the Madonna.[2] It seems likely, then, that Collins was deliberately trying to make the painting appealing to a collector who owned Old Masters.

In his biography of his father, Wilkie Collins described this painting as a "charming English country scene" and pointed out the inclusion of "the curious Kentish 'hop-cradle,' formed of clumsy sticks covered with a red cloak, and used by the women to hold their children while they are at work."[3] Collins was a Tory, and his sympathies for the rural poor were paternalistic: he admired the charitable activities of his patrons but disliked the degree of "equality, or attempts at it, in the common people" in Norwich. His son's biography provides some amusing but rather patronising anecdotes of Collins's contacts with the models for his rural scenes.[4]

1. Collins, *Memoirs*, vol. 1, p. 237.
2. Compare, for example, Correggio's *Adoration of the Shepherds* (1522; Gemäldegalerie, Dresden).
3. Collins, *Memoirs*, vol. 1, pp. 316–17.
4. Ibid., vol. 1, pp. 237, 78, 220–23.

JOHN LINNELL *1792–1882*
19
Shepherd Boy Playing a Flute, 1831
Signed and dated 1831, bottom left
Oil on panel
9 x 6½ (23 x 16.5)
Provenance: Mrs Florence Donald; L. J. Drew, Esq.; P. and D. Colnaghi, 1962
References: K. Crouan, *John Linnell: A Centennial Exhibition*, exh. cat. (Cambridge, 1982), no. 68

Yale Center for British Art, Paul Mellon Collection

This is probably a smaller replica of *The Farmer's Boy*, exhibited at the Royal Academy in 1830. Linnell, in his journal, mentions work on an oil painting, *The Shepherd Boy*, but he seems to have changed the title to *The Farmer's Boy* before it was exhibited, perhaps hoping to capitalise on the fame of Robert Bloomfield's poem of that name. Confusingly, the composition appears in his

19 (see pl. 12)

landscape sketchbook under the original title of *The Shepherd Boy*. In his journal for December 1830 he mentions "a small pic of Farmer's Boy for the engraving to be made from": presumably this is a reference to cat. 19.[1]

The painting is based on a study, apparently from life, made at Shoreham, perhaps on a visit with George Richmond in 1829.[2] The influence of Palmer and his friends is very evident: the piping shepherd boy is in an idyllic landscape reminiscent of Palmer's Shoreham landscapes, and the composition carries overtones of the Christian symbolism of the good shepherd, as well as echoing the frontispiece for Blake's *Songs of Innocence*. The boy's smock, neckerchief, hat and sunburnt face, however, are authentic details that reflect Linnell's careful study of his model.

The original version of *The Farmer's Boy*, which measured 24 x 18 in., belonged to Richard Redgrave in 1883: for further links between Redgrave and the Palmer circle, see cat. 35 and 67.[3]

Yale only

---

1. Linnell's journal for 1830, Linnell Trust Manuscripts, private collection; Linnell's landscape sketchbook, British Museum, p. 46.
2. K. Crouan, *Linnell*, no. 66.
3. *Winter Exhibition of Works by Old Masters and Deceased Masters of the English School, including . . . John Linnell* (Royal Academy, London, 1883), no. 76.

SAMUEL PALMER (R.W.S.) *1805–1881*

20

The Harvest Moon, 1833
Signed, lower left
Oil on paper, laid on panel
8¾ x 10⅞ (22.2 x 27.6)
Provenance: Samuel Palmer; A. H. Palmer; Christie's, 20 March 1909, no. 84, bought by

Eyre; . . . Christie's, 23 June 1972, no. 65, bought by John Baskett Ltd.
References: R. Lister, *Catalogue Raisonné of the Works of Samuel Palmer* (Cambridge, 1988), no. 168

Yale Center for British Art, Paul Mellon Collection

Palmer's son, A. H. Palmer, wrote of this panel: "There is nothing out of place in the laden waggon with its team of oxen, or in the harvest labourers, for their dress proclaims them labourers of long ago."[1] Neither the oxen nor the smocks worn by the labourers, however, were as anachronistic as A. H. Palmer makes out. Oxen continued to be used in some parts of Britain throughout the nineteenth century, and smocks were standard dress in this period, although they tended to be worn by poorer labourers to cover up shabby clothing.

This painting is typical of Palmer's "Shoreham period" in its visionary intensity, expressed through otherworldly lighting, rich colours, an enclosed composition and insistent detail. The moonlight adds a magical effect to the scene but also emphasizes the hard labour of harvesting, with the workers still busy late at night. Palmer's arrangement of the figures in the foreground, however, suggests aesthetic rather than documentary concerns. They are embedded jewel-like in the golden corn, men and women together, with no open space to set up the sheaves that they are apparently cutting and binding. This crowded effect must be deliberate, since it contributes to the impression of the overflowing plenty of harvest, which was regarded by Palmer as a reflection of God's benevolence towards man.

Yale only

---

1. A. H. Palmer, *Life and Letters of Samuel Palmer* (London, 1892), p. 47.

20 (see pl. 13)

John Wilson Carmichael *1799–1868*

21

Corby Viaduct, the Newcastle and Carlisle Railway, 1836
Signed and dated 1836, bottom left
Oil on canvas
8 x 12 (20 x 30.5)
Provenance: Browse and Darby; Charles Glazebrook
Engraved by J. W. Archer for J. Blackmore, *Views on the Newcastle and Carlisle Railway* (London, 1839), pl. 21
References: *Carmichael Centenary Exhibition,* (Laing Art Gallery, Newcastle, 1968)

Yale Center for British Art, Paul Mellon Fund

J. W. Carmichael was a Newcastle-based painter who specialised in marine views. In 1837 he completed a set of drawings for *Views on the Newcastle and Carlisle Railway,* one of the first and most important of the illustrated railway books that began to appear from this time onwards; nine pencil sketches for this project are in the Carlisle Museum, and *Corby Viaduct* was painted for one of the illustrations to the book.

The cornfield in the painting is unusually well supervised: there are two men on horseback as well as a third man who inspects the stooks, perhaps to ensure that the wheat is dry enough to be cut or to assess its quality. Women are shown doing most of the work, reaping as well as binding: this is unusual, although not unheard-of, and more common in areas where industrialisation provided a competing source of employment for the men.

The composition emphasizes the contrast between old and new, juxtaposing the railway and the carriage and riders on the road. There may also be an implied contrast between the old and new sources of wealth—

21

land and industry—whose representatives were engaged in political conflicts over parliamentary reform, the Factory Acts and the Corn Laws in this decade.

The engraving follows the painting closely except that the man inspecting the stooks is omitted in the engraving, his place being taken by a picturesque arrangement of a keg, hat, sickle and piece of clothing. The accompanying letterpress states that the viaduct crosses "a valley on the estate of Henry Howard, Esquire, of Corby Castle, whose carriage road to it and the village of Corby passes under the centre arch." In the engraving, it can be seen that there are two women in the carriage, with a servant behind: presumably these are members of the Howard family.

Yale only

WILLIAM HOLMAN HUNT (A.R.S.A., R.W.S., O.M.) *1827–1910*

22

Cornfield at Ewell, 1849
Inscribed on label on verso by Gladys Holman-Hunt: "*Ewell,* at his uncle's farm, by W. Holman Hunt 1846"
Oil on millboard
7¹⁵⁄₁₆ x 12½ (20.2 x 31.8)
Provenance: D. G. Rossetti in 1854; . . . Gladys Holman-Hunt in 1951; private collection, London, 1979–1988; presented anonymously to the Tate Gallery, 1988
References: J. Bronkhurst, "New Light on Holman Hunt," *Burlington Magazine,* vol. 129, no. 1016 (November 1987), p. 739; and *William Holman Hunt: A Catalogue Raisonné* (New Haven and London, forthcoming), no. 59

Tate Gallery, London

22

The inscription, as Judith Bronkhurst has shown, must be erroneous: the Pre-Raphaelite Brotherhood journal mentions a study in colour of a cornfield, made by Hunt at Ewell in August 1849.[1] At that time Hunt was about to start on the landscape of *A Converted British Family Sheltering a Christian Missionary from the Persecution of the Druids* (Ashmolean Museum, Oxford). Although *Cornfield at Ewell* is not a direct study for the painting, Hunt may have wanted to study a cornfield as preparation for the standing corn on the extreme right of the picture.

The sketch must have been painted on the spot, and it would appear that the field was empty when Hunt painted it, perhaps because a shower had interrupted work. The solitary reaper was a later addition, which explains why he has no companions and why there is no one to bind the wheat into sheaves.

G. P. Boyce saw *Cornfield at Ewell* in Rossetti's rooms in March 1854 and described it as "a lovely hasty rub in of a cornfield against a deep blue sky."[2]

---

1. W. E. Fredeman, ed., *The P. R. B. Journal, William Michael Rossetti's Diary of the Pre-Raphaelite Brotherhood, 1849–1853* (Oxford, 1975), p. 12.
2. V. Surtees, *The Diaries of George Price Boyce* (Norwich, 1980), p. 12.

DAVID COX (O.W.S.) *1783–1859*

23

Sheep Shearing, 1849
Signed and dated, lower right
Oil on canvas
10½ x 15 (26.7 x 38.1)
Provenance: Bequeathed by Joseph H. Nettlefold, 1882
References: S. Wildman, R. Lockett, and J. Murdoch, *David Cox 1783–1859* (Birmingham Museums and Art Gallery, 1983), no. 88

Birmingham Museums and Art Gallery

23

Between 1844 and 1856 Cox made annual
visits to Bettws-y-Coed in Wales from his
native Birmingham, to which he had returned after periods of living in London and
Hereford. It is clear from the tall hats of his
sheep shearers that this scene is set in
Wales, and it is likely that it was painted
near Bettws-y-Coed.

It is unusual to see women shearing
sheep, and also unusual to see the shearers
sitting down as they work. Sheep shearing
was a strenuous job that was usually done by
men, often by gangs who travelled round
the country at shearing time. Cox's depiction of the subject may be compared with
Barker's (cat. 9), in which there is much
more emphasis on the effort needed to re-
strain the struggling sheep.

Cox taught himself to paint in oils in the
1840s and was delighted by the results. He
made especially effective use of creamy impasto here to depict the fleeces of the sheep.

He was evidently pleased with this composition, since he repeated it in watercolour in
the following year (British Museum, no.
1915–3–13–15).

JOHN LINNELL *1792–1882*
24
The Harvest, 1850–53
Signed and dated "1850x53," lower right
Oil on canvas
28 x 35½ (71 x 90.2)
Provenance: Joseph Gillott; Hooper and
Wass by 1854; Charles Butler by 1883; . . .
Fine Art Society, from whom bought by
present owner
References: K. Crouan, *John Linnell: Truth to
Nature (A Centennial Exhibition)* (Martyn
Gregory Gallery, London, 1982), no. 104

Private collection

After concentrating on portraiture in the 1820s, 1830s and early 1840s, Linnell returned to landscape painting in the late 1840s and early 1850s. In 1851 he moved to Redhill, Surrey, where he had a house built at Redstone Wood. In 1854 he bought land around the house, which he rented out to farmers.[1] From this time until his death in 1882 he produced a steady stream of landscapes, often harvest scenes, which he sold to dealers who in turn sold them to northern merchants and industrialists. *The Harvest* is the first harvest scene recorded in his landscape sketchbook from this later period in his life.[2]

Linnell's later harvest scenes are very different from those he produced in the 1810s: in the early examples the workers are shown hard at work or else exhausted by their labours (cat. 12). In the harvest scenes of the 1850s and later, however, the countryside is a much jollier place, with plump, attractive women and children, such as the gleaners leading the way out of the field in this painting, very much in evidence. Linnell remained a Radical all his life, and probably knew more about the harsh realities of rural life in his later years, but he was skilled at gauging the taste of his patrons, and his idyllic harvest scenes were much more successful commercially than the more naturalistic landscapes of the 1810s.

The Harvest was commissioned by the pen manufacturer Joseph Gillott, who may have had some influence over Linnell's decision to turn to harvest subject matter around 1850: his collection, sold at his death in 1872, included agricultural scenes by A. W. Callcott, William Collins and David Cox.[3] Gillott also acted as a dealer, and he sold *The Harvest* four years later.

In this painting, the richly textured load

24 (see pl. 14)

on the waggon and the boys in smocks are reminiscent of Palmer, whose harvest scenes were an important influence on Linnell.

1. A. Story, *The Life of John Linnell* (London, 1892), vol. 2, pp. 33–34. By 1862 Linnell owned about 80 acres of land.
2. Linnell's landscape sketchbook, British Museum, p. 83. For Joseph Gillott, see B. Denvir, "Pens and Patronage," *Connoisseur Year-book*, 1958, pp. 71–77. Linnell's northern patrons are discussed in a fascinating article by E. Firestone, "John Linnell and the Picture Merchants," *Connoisseur*, vol. 182, February 1973, pp. 124–31.
3. Joseph Gillott sale, Christie's, 19 April–4 May 1872, lots 271, 275 and 401.

DAVID COX (O.W.S.) *1783–1859*

25

Going to the Hayfield, 1853
Signed and dated 1853, lower left
Oil on millboard
10 x 13¼ (25.5 x 33.6)

Provenance: Thomas Agnew and Sons, 1965
References: M. Cormack, *Oil on Water: Oil Sketches by British Watercolorists* (Yale Center for British Art, New Haven, 1986), p. 22, fig. 12

Yale Center for British Art, Paul Mellon Collection

The theme of workers going to the hay field was one of Cox's favourite subjects in the 1840s and 1850s.[1] Cox adopted a standard composition in which the actual haymaking is in the background, while in the foreground workers walk along a track or ride and lead horses (presumably so that the horses can be harnessed to a waggon loaded with hay for transport from the field to the farmyard). The weather is usually breezy, and the figures' clothing is blown by the wind. The figures are seen from behind, but nevertheless they seem to have more individuality than the industrious harvesters of, for example, DeWint's cornfields: Cox's hay

25

fields are less didactic images, which tempt the viewer to empathise with the labourers in their struggle against the wind rather than admire their virtues.

The choice of weather was deliberate. Talking of one of these paintings, Cox said to a friend, "I want to show a proper hay-making day, bright and sunny, of course, but with a brisk, drying wind sweeping across the fields, and making the fleecy clouds speed along the sky at a greater pace than they seem to be going now."[2] The wind would help dry the hay as the haymakers turned and tedded it, making it ready for stacking all the sooner.

Yale only

1. Pictures with this title were exhibited by Cox at the Royal Academy in 1844 and at the Old Water-Colour Society in 1839, 1848, 1851 and 1860. He also painted pictures entitled *Going to the Cornfield* or *Going to Plough*.
2. W. Hall, *A Biography of David Cox* (London: 1881), p. 141.

FORD MADOX BROWN *1821–1893*
26
Carrying Corn, 1854–55
Inscribed: "F. Madox Brown Finchley/54"
Oil on panel
7¾ x 10⅞ (19.7 x 27.6)
Provenance: Sold to White, 27 June 1855; B. G. Windus; Christie's, 1862, bought by Tebbs; H. Virtue Tebbs; Christie's, 10 March 1900, bought by Radley; Christie's, 20 April 1934, bought by Martin; bought by Tate Gallery, 1934
First exhibited: Russell Place, 1857 (no. 11)
References: *The Pre-Raphaelites* (Tate Gallery, London, 1984), no. 61

Tate Gallery, London

Carrying Corn and *The Hayfield* date from a period in Brown's life when he was doing small landscapes in an attempt to produce paintings that could be finished quickly and sold easily. But the laborious Pre-Raphaelite technique that he adopted as a result of his contacts with Hunt, Millais and Rossetti

26 (see pl. 15)

meant that he spent much more time on them than he intended, and the prices were often disappointing. In his diary he records 21 visits to the field to paint *Carrying Corn* and about 70 hours of painting, yet the dealer, White, paid only £12 for it.

The diary also records Brown's ecstatic response to the beauties of the agricultural landscape, suggesting that he may have found some solace in these landscapes at a time of financial insecurity and depression. On a bus ride to St Albans in August 1854, he and his wife were entranced by the colour of turnip leaves: "One field of turnips against the afternoon sky did surprise us into exclamation with its wonderful emerald tints."[1] It is the unusual contrast between the green of the turnips and the golden yellow of the corn that provides the central theme of *Carrying Corn*, a painting that looks remarkably modern for its date, partly because of the way the figures merge into the landscape and partly because it eschews the usual space-creating devices of traditional landscape composition, such as framing trees in the foreground or lines of stooks seen in perspective.

The history of Brown's work on the painting vividly illustrates some of the problems faced by artists who wanted to paint agricultural landscape "from nature." On 5 September Brown began work on a landscape "of surpassing loveliness," with "corn shocks in long perspective" and a farm, hay ricks and steeple seen between them. But "by the time I had drawn in the outline they had carted half my wheat," and when he went back the next day it was all gone. A few days later he began a little landscape, presumably *Carrying Corn*, "in a hurry & fluster attempting to paint corn sheaves and cart while they were going."[2] This hurry may explain the odd appearance of the sheaves in the painting, some of which are rounded in shape like haycocks. It may also explain why

so much of the painting is devoted to turnips, which were still growing and were not liable to be carted off. But by the time Brown had nearly finished, in October, men were at work pulling up turnips, and Brown found the gate nailed up and brambled.[3]

Such long periods of study in the fields tended to shatter any illusions Brown might have had about the charms of rural life. On his last day in the field, "a labourer came and looked and stuttering fearfully expressed admiration which ended in his supposing he *could not beg half a pint of beer*, one whom I used to look on as a respectable man. I gave the degraded wretch twopence and scorn."[4] Brown's agricultural landscapes, therefore, focus on the aesthetic charms of the landscape itself, not on the supposed virtues of the labourer which were such an important theme for many of his contemporaries.

1. V. Surtees, ed., *The Diary of Ford Madox Brown* (New Haven and London, 1981), p. 84.
2. Ibid., p. 90.
3. Ibid., p. 102.
4. Ibid.

Ford Madox Brown *1821–1893*

27

The Hayfield, 1855–56
Inscribed "F. MADOX BROWN, HENDON 1855"
Oil on panel
9 7/16 x 13 1/16 (24 x 33.2)
First exhibited: *Art Treasures,* Manchester, 1857 (Modern Pictures, no. 319)
Provenance: Bought by William Morris, 24 August 1856, for £40; Major Gillum by 1865; by descent to John Gillum, Esq.; bought by Tate Gallery, 1974
References: *The Pre-Raphaelites* (Tate Gallery, London, 1984), no. 68

Tate Gallery, London

Like *Carrying Corn* (cat. 26), this painting was inspired by Brown's observation of the

27 (see pl. 16)

countryside. He wrote in his diary on 21 July 1855: "What wonderful effects I have seen this even[in]g in the hayfields, the warmth of the uncut grass, the greeny grey-ness of the unmade hay in furrows or tufts, with lovely violet shadows . . . & one moment more & cloud passes and all the magic is gone." A few days later he "saw in twilight what appeared a lovely bit of scenery with the full moon behind it just risen."[1] He referred to the painting as the "Moon Piece." Brown pursued his usual laborious methods, making many visits to the field, but most of the specifically agricultural details could not have been painted on the spot. The hay must have been carted soon after he started work on the painting, and he put in the cart and figures in December, including the figure of the artist in the left foreground, complete with palette, umbrella and paint box.

The landscape is full of incident and variety: behind the artist, a mounted farmer talks to his workers, the cart in the foreground is being made ready to carry away the haycocks and, in the distance on the right, another cart is almost full. The haycocks and the remaining hay on the ground contrast with the rich green of the cut grass, which has obviously put forward new growth since it was originally cut. Brown explained this colour contrast in the catalogue to his one-man exhibition in 1865: "The stacking of the second crop of hay had been much delayed by rain, which heightened the green of the grass, together with the brown of the hay. The consequence was an effect of unusual beauty of colour, making the hay by contrast with the green grass, positively red or pink, under the glow of the twilight here represented."[2]

Thus, a sequence of events that would not have pleased an agriculturist (for the hay must have been spoiled by being left out in the rain), has produced an unusual and poetic effect. The figure of the artist in the foreground conveys Brown's enthusiasm for the magical effects in agricultural landscape, in a composition that is strongly reminiscent of Samuel Palmer. Brown was acutely conscious of the English landscape tradition, although he does not actually mention Palmer in the diary.

All three of Brown's agricultural landscapes exploit intense colour contrasts—reminiscent of stained glass—which, together with his interest in rarely painted crops and effects, makes them very original. His dealer, White, refused to buy *The Hayfield*—he said "the hay was pink and he had never seen such"—but Rossetti brought William Morris to Brown's studio and Morris bought the painting, drawn to it, perhaps, by its almost medieval effects.

---

1. V. Surtees, ed., *The Diary of Ford Madox Brown* (New Haven and London, 1981), p. 145.
2. *The Exhibition of Work, and Other Paintings, by Ford Madox Brown* (191 Piccadilly, 1865). Catalogue by the artist.

JOHN FREDERICK HERRING, SR. *1795–1865*
28
Seed Time, 1854–56
Signed and dated, lower right
Oil on canvas
42 x 72 (106.7 x 183.1)
Provenance: John Tyson; Christie's, 1872; Tom Nickalls; Christie's, 4 June 1909; presented to the Victoria and Albert Museum by Miss Mercy Mayhew, 1915
References: R. Parkinson, *Catalogue of British Oil Paintings, 1820–1860* (Victoria and Albert Museum, 1990), p. 126

The Board of Trustees of the Victoria and Albert Museum, London

J. F. Herring was primarily a sporting painter, who moved out of London in 1853 to live at Meopham Park in Kent, a nine-bedroom Georgian mansion with a 30-acre

28

park, orchard, kitchen garden and farmyard. While at Meopham he produced several paintings of agricultural scenes, some of which were engraved in pairs or as a series showing different farming occupations. *Seed Time* is the same size as *Harvest* (cat. 29), so they may have originally been conceived as a pair.

Seed Time illustrates the processes involved in preparing the land and sowing the seed. In the foreground the earth can clearly be seen changing from turf to the furrows left by the plough, then to the levelled ground ready for the sower. Men and teams of horses plough, roll, sow and harrow in quick succession—the same sequence of operations as in Turner's *Ploughing Up Turnips* of 1809 (cat. 8).

It is tempting to connect this painting with the new scientific agriculture of the 1850s—the so-called high farming that increased crop yields through the use of new implements and machinery, land drainage and fertilizers. The horses look well cared for, the men are well dressed and their implements apparently carefully maintained. To a progressive farmer of the period, however, this scene would have looked old-fashioned. Broadcast sowing was still practised in many areas, but seed drills had long been available; cast-iron ploughs were superseding the heavy wooden types; and the number of horses pulling each implement seems excessive (cf. cat. 16). Like the harvest scenes of this period, then, the painting shows the traditional farming that was threatened by the new developments.
Not exhibited

JOHN FREDERICK HERRING, SR. *1795–1865*

29
Harvest, 1857
Signed and dated 1857, bottom centre
Oil on canvas
41 13/16 x 73 3/16 (106.2 x 183.3)

Provenance: Sold by the artist to Edward Shayer, 14 July 1859; . . . Hutchinson; Speelman, 1973
References: J. Egerton, *The Paul Mellon Collection: Sporting and Animal Paintings, 1655–1867* (London, 1978), no. 333; O. Beckett, *J. F. Herring and Sons: The Life and Works of J. F. Herring, Sr. and His Family* (London, 1981), p. 126

Yale Center for British Art, Paul Mellon Collection

This painting shows Herring's house and park in the background on the right, and thus bears an uncanny resemblance to eighteenth-century country house views with agricultural scenes in the foreground, such as Paul Sandby's *Hackwood Park* (fig. 28). In this case, however, the "squire" (shown riding across the cleared field, with two hunting hounds) is not one of the traditional gentry but a nouveau-riche artist from the city.

The painting shows successive stages in the harvesting of wheat: reapers in standing corn on the left, stooks standing in the field, a waggon being loaded, and, in the foreground, horses straining as they pull another waggon up the hill. It is unlikely that all these operations would have been carried out simultaneously in the same field, but artists often did combine them for the sake of variety.

The group of figures in the foreground is puzzling. The three on the left look sufficiently individual to be portraits and sufficiently refined to be middle-class observers: indeed, Herring often included portraits of members of his family in farmyard scenes. The woman on the right, however, wears a red cloak, feeds her baby and has a sheaf beside her, which is tied up with material rather than a straw rope. She must, therefore, be a poor gleaner, and Herring has

Fig. 28. PAUL SANDBY

Hackwood Park, Hampshire, 1764. Oil on canvas, 40³/₁₆ × 50¼ in. (102.1 × 127.6 cm.). Yale Center for British Art, Paul Mellon Fund.

29 (see pl. 17)

clearly taken pains to show her as separate from the other three, who are rather awkwardly placed in the landscape.

It has often been remarked that the bright colours and minute detail of this painting show Pre-Raphaelite influence. Yet *Harvest* is also comparable to some of Constable's paintings in its display of a panoramic landscape, including the various elements in the rural economy: mansion and village, park and woodland, arable fields and enclosed meadows, all harmoniously combined, just as the rich and poor seem to mingle happily in the foreground.

Herring found it financially advantageous to settle in the country. He wrote to a family friend in America in 1855: "In consequence of the light and facilities in landscape, Rural figures etc. which we can command by a call or a whistle . . . the pictures are enhanced at least 50 per cent in the Market, since we have been here. . . . I have only to send a Letter or two to London and say I have

something to show, and down come the dealers, and clear the deck" (Beckett, *Herring and Sons*, pp. 82–83). In the same period other artists, such as John Linnell or George Vicat Cole, were finding that landscapes painted on the spot found a ready market in London. Herring's reference to "Rural figures" suggests that he rather enjoyed playing the role of the squire and lording it over the local rustics, and the pictorial conventions on which he has drawn in *Harvest* suggest the same conclusion.

Yale only

JOHN LINNELL *1792–1882*
30
A Finished Study for "Reaping," 1855–1858
Signed and dated 1858, lower right
Oil on panel
8¼ x 13 (21 x 33)
Provenance: Gooden and Fox, 1964

30

Yale Center for British Art, Paul Mellon
Collection

This panel is probably Linnell's "first
sketch" for a large oil, *Reaping*, 1855 (34 x
26 in.). In his landscape sketchbook (British
Museum, p. 116) he records finishing this
sketch in 1858 for the dealer William
Wethered, who had commissioned *Reaping*.
In the 1850s and 1860s Linnell was painting
many harvest scenes for dealers such as
Gambart, Hooper and Wass, Louis Huth,
and Thomas Agnew. He often painted rep-
licas or finished sketches, so that many of
his compositions exist in several versions.
Like his contemporaries George Vicat Cole
and J. F. Herring, he evidently found that
cheerful, sunny harvest scenes were easily
saleable in this period.

Yale only

NEVIL OLIVER LUPTON *1828–after 1877*
31
The Harvest Field, 1858
Signed and dated 1857–58, bottom left, and
initialled NOL/58 on the cask
Oil on canvas
16 x 24 (41 x 61)
Provenance: Purchased in 1943
First exhibited: Royal Academy, 1858 (no.
194)

The Visitors of the Ashmolean Museum,
Oxford

This is a typical example of a harvest scene
from the 1850s, which may be compared
with works by better-known artists such as
Vicat Cole and Linnell. It contains the classic elements of harvest scenes of this period:
sunshine, careful detail based on study from
nature, children, a church spire in the dis-

31

tance and an overall impression of a peaceful, productive landscape.

The harvest field serves as the background for a charming group of children, one of whom has been picking wildflowers in the corn. They look chubby, healthy and well dressed, with boots in particularly good repair, and there is no indication that they have been gleaning. Lupton gives little hint, therefore, of the poverty of such rural children. The oldest girl (presumably the older sister) looks after the two little ones, and they are also observed by one of the women binding sheaves on the left of the painting, the implication being that she is their mother. One of the two men scything the wheat could be the father. Harvest labour thus appears to provide an opportunity for whole families to be together in pleasant surroundings and fresh air.

The painting was described by a reviewer as "an unqualified transcript from a simple passage of English scenery, the principal section of the plan being an extensive harvest-field, with the corn in sheaf."[1]

---

1. *Art Journal*, 1 June 1858, p. 164.

WILLIAM DAVIS *1812–1873*

32
A Field of Green Corn, c. 1860
Signed
Oil on panel
12 x 15½ (30.5 x 38.2)
Provenance: James Leathart; Colonel Gillum; by descent to present owner
First exhibited: ?Liverpool Academy, 1860 (no. 55)
References: *The Pre-Raphaelites* (Tate Gallery, London, 1984), no. 115

32

Private collection

William Davis was a Liverpool painter who became friendly with the Pre-Raphaelites, and particularly with Madox Brown, in the mid-1850s. He was acknowledged by his contemporaries to have a faulty grasp of linear perspective.[1] This may have hampered his career, but it produced spatial effects in his landscapes which now seem to us preciously modern. Like Ford Madox Brown's landscapes, Davis's have high horizons and often lack the usual perspectival devices, resulting in a flattened, primitive effect. Like Brown, too, he depicted crops in great detail and had an eye for unusual effects, such as this field of unripe corn.

This painting is also unusual in showing an agricultural landscape without any human presence. Because the corn is unripe and the field uninhabited, the rabbits in the foreground can feed undisturbed: once the field is reaped, they will be under threat from sportsmen. The painting represents a rather urban view of the beauties of agricultural landscape. To a city dweller, the rabbits are a charming foreground motif, but to an agriculturist of the time, they were pests nibbling the green shoots of corn and reducing crop yields.

Nottingham only

1. F. G. Stephens, "William Davis, Landscape Painter, of Liverpool," *Art Journal*, 1884, p. 328.

JOHN BRETT (A.R.A.) *1831–1902*

33
The Hedger, 1859–60
Signed and dated 1860
Oil on canvas
35 7/16 x 27 9/16 (90 x 70)
Provenance: Bought by B. G. Windus; . . . Sotheby's, Belgravia, 23 March 1981, no. 22
First exhibited: Royal Academy 1860 (no. 360)

References: *The Pre-Raphaelites* (Tate Gallery, London, 1984), no. 107

Private collection

John Brett seems to have regarded *The Hedger* as a sequel to *The Stonebreaker* (fig. 29). His first sketch for *The Hedger* is dated "18 May 58."[1] Work on *The Hedger*, however, was interrupted by Brett's trip to Switzerland and his painting of *The Val d'Aosta* (1858; Private collection), and he began the actual painting of *The Hedger* in April 1859.

Whereas the earlier painting showed a boy at work on a heap of stones in an idyllic summer landscape, *The Hedger* shows an older man, in an occupation that was relatively well paid[2] but nevertheless took place in cold, wintry conditions. The idea of showing two stages in a rural labourer's life may have been inspired by the old man and boy in Gustave Courbet's famous *Stonebreakers* (1851), of whom Courbet wrote: "Alas, in labour such as this, one's life begins that way, it ends the same way."[3]

The early sketches place the hedger in the centre of the composition, under an arched top, suggesting that Brett saw the labourer as a kind of hero or secular saint. The intended meaning of the painting was thus similar to that of Henry Wallis's *Stonebreaker* (see fig. 1). The existence of the latter painting precluded Brett from painting an older stonebreaker as a sequel, but it may also have directly inspired *The Hedger*: when he drew the first sketch, he had just attended a meeting of the Hogarth Club at which Wallis was present, and he would have seen Wallis's painting at the Academy exhibition in May 1858.

From Brett's title it would appear that the man is laying a hedge, that is, slashing through saplings with his billhook, bending them at right angles, and weaving them into the hedge, where they will continue to grow. This was the traditional way of making a

33 (see pl. 18)

Fig. 29. JOHN BRETT
The Stonebreaker, 1857–58. Oil on panel, 20 × 27 in. (51.3 × 68.5 cm.). Trustees of the National Museums and Galleries on Merseyside. Walker Art Gallery, Liverpool.

very strong and thick hedge. Reviewers, however, misunderstood the subject and thought that he was repairing a wattled fence.[4] John Ruskin, who was trying to persuade Brett to concentrate on landscape at this stage in his career, also misunderstood, or lacked interest in the subject. In 1875 he praised Brett's "conscientious painting of the Stonebreaker and Woodcutter," and in a letter to Brett in 1860 he referred to "your wood cutter (hedgemaker, or whatever he is)."[5]

The first sketch for the painting shows a young man neatly dressed in a short jacket and waistcoat. In the final painting, however, the man is older and he wears a smock and patched trousers; the young girl holding a baby and bringing lunch to her father are added to the composition. These changes remind the viewer of some of the harsh realities of rural life—the girl is rosy-cheeked but she takes her responsibilities seriously—and are calculated to arouse sympathy, perhaps reflecting Brett's desire to make the painting more "felt" than *The Val d'Aosta*, which Ruskin had criticised for its lack of emotion. In his diary entry of 31 July 1859 Brett records that "the poor old fellow who sat for the outline and was to have served as a model throughout died yesterday."[6]

Hedge laying was a traditional English rural occupation, depicted earlier by Turner in his *Liber Studiorum* (see cat. 90). The stress on solitary labour, however, in contrast to the convivial harvest scenes of his contemporaries, reflects a growing awareness of the less pleasant side of rural life, which was probably stimulated by the works of Pre-Raphaelites such as Hunt and Wallis, and looks forward to the painting of Mason, Walker and Clausen.

1. Pen and ink sketch, private collection, inscribed "a Hedger ~~and Ditcher~~." For this information, for references to the Brett diaries and correspondence and for much of the foregoing interpretation of *The Hedger* (including Ruskin's attitude towards it) I am indebted to Michael Hickox, and also to Judith Bronkhurst's (unpublished) research on the painting.

2. Joseph Arch, the farmworkers' union leader, was a skilled hedger who earned more than the average labourer: see P. Horn, *Joseph Arch* (Kineton, 1971), p. 8ff. The skills of hedge laying were highly valued by farmers: in October 1858 Arch won a prize of £1–15–0 at the Warwickshire Agricultural Society for hedging and ditching.

3. J. Lindsay, *Gustave Courbet: His Life and Art* (London, 1977), p. 59. Some of the sketches for *The Stonebreaker* suggest that Brett may have known Courbet's painting: see D. Cordingly, "'The Stonebreaker': An Examination of the Landscape in a Painting by John Brett," *Burlington Magazine*, March 1982, pp. 141–45.

4. *Athenaeum*, 19 May 1860, p. 690.

5. John Ruskin, *Academy Notes*, in *The Works of John Ruskin*, ed. E. T. Cook and A. Wedderburn (London, 1903–1912), vol. 14, p. 293; letter to Brett dated 15 July 1860 (Private collection).

6. Brett diary, 31 July 1859.

GEORGE VICAT COLE (R.A.) *1833–1893*

34

Harvest Time, 1860
Signed and dated 1860, lower left
Oil on canvas
37¼ x 59½ (94.6 x 151)
Provenance: J. Henry; . . . given to Bristol City Art Gallery by Arthur Robinson, 1909
First exhibited: Society of British Artists, 1860 (no. 106)
References: R. Chignell, *The Life and Paintings of George Vicat Cole* (London, 1898), vol. 1, p. 68; T. J. Barringer, *The Cole Family: Painters of the English Landscape, 1838–1915* (Portsmouth, 1988), no. 59

Bristol Museums and Art Gallery

George Vicat Cole was the son of an artist, George Cole, who encouraged him to study

34 (see pl. 19)

the work of Turner, Constable and Cox. Vicat Cole claimed that this painting was "painted and finished on the spot from a hut on Holmbury Hill" in Surrey. However, it is carefully composed to include as much variety as possible: the corn is being reaped, left in stooks and loaded all at the same time, although in reality it would have been left for several days or weeks to dry out before being removed from the field. A man even seems to be carrying a newly reaped sheaf straight onto a waggon. The separate details may have been painted from nature, but the composition as a whole was not.

The figures are arranged to illustrate the favourite Victorian virtues: industriousness (in the background) and happy family life (in the foreground). The woman and children, who have brought food and drink for the father of the family, are well dressed, and there is no indication that the mother has to work: indeed, her jacket shows that she has not been working (compare the rolled-up sleeves of her husband). She has the leisure to sit in the field with her baby asleep on her lap, as if she were a middle-class wife. Mid-

Victorian harvest scenes often show women resting or looking after their families, unlike late eighteenth- and early nineteenth-century paintings in which they are usually binding sheaves or gleaning.

Vicat Cole's cornfields were seen as particularly English. One reviewer wrote of *A Surrey Cornfield* (1861): "The entire tone of this picture is distinctly English, but especially the face of the country, with its green valleys and wooded uplands, and, more potent than all in impressing the eye and the sense, the golden wealth of its foreground harvest-field."[1]

Like Herring and Redgrave, Vicat Cole made the most of the contrast between the gold of the harvest field in the foreground and the dark greens of the woods and pastures in the background (compare cat. 29 and 35.)

Such paintings proved to be easily saleable. Vicat Cole's biographer and brother-in-law, R. Chignell, wrote that *Harvest Time* was very successful: "One result of this success was a demand for 'cornfield' subjects, which, however gratifying in one sense, became a positive annoyance after a few years. Everybody wanted a cornfield by Vicat Cole, and Vicat Cole did not want to spend his life in painting cornfields."[2]

1. *Art Journal*, 1 April 1861, p. 139.
2. R. Chignell, *Life and Paintings of Cole*, vol. 1, p. 68.

RICHARD REDGRAVE (R.A.) *1804–1888*

35

The Valleys Also Stand Thick with Corn, 1864
Signed in monogram and dated 1864, bottom right
Oil on canvas
28 x 38 (71.1 x 96.5)
Provenance: Mrs Richard Redgrave, by whom presented 1890
First exhibited: Royal Academy, 1865 (no. 316)
References: S. Casteras and R. Parkinson, eds., *Richard Redgrave, 1804–1888* (New Haven and London, 1988), no. 110

Birmingham Museums and Art Gallery

Richard Redgrave painted landscapes as a form of relaxation in the intervals of a busy career as an art administrator and art historian. In 1856 he bought a cottage at Abinger, in Surrey, and thereafter he spent summer holidays there, returning to London in the autumn.

The title of this painting echoes the lines from Psalm 65 inscribed on the original mount of one of Samuel Palmer's famous sepias of 1825 (see fig. 14). Redgrave was a sympathetic friend of Palmer and spent time with him in the summer of 1864; he also owned some of Palmer's Shoreham work, including *Cornfield and Church by Moonlight* (cat. 67). It is highly likely, therefore, that this painting owes its inspiration at least partly to Palmer, although the application of Psalm 65 to contemporary harvest fields was not uncommon. Like Palmer, Redgrave was sympathetic to old-fashioned aspects of agriculture: he wrote of Abinger in 1856, "As the soil is hardly worth cultivation, it may remain a few years longer unspoiled by modern agriculture."[1] In the painting, a sickle (a tool with strong biblical associations) lies in the foreground, although the

35

scythe was by now the more common tool for cutting wheat, and the stubble is so short that it looks as if it must have been mown rather than reaped.

Both landscape and figures celebrate the bounty of nature and the health and happiness of the farmworker and his family. Redgrave was personally affected by fears of revolution in the years before 1848, and he noted a change of atmosphere in the 1850s, the decade when such optimistic, celebratory harvest scenes became common. In an autobiographical sketch attached to his diary, he recalled childhood fears induced by riots and machine-breaking; he described how, as a special constable in 1848, he had "watched anxiously for the coming of the rabble"; but he noted that, in the 1850s, "the common people are much less openly brutal, the streets are much more quiet, and the suburbs and open spaces are now filled on Sundays and holidays with a much more orderly race."[2]

1. F. M. Redgrave, *Richard Redgrave: A Memoir Compiled from His Diary* (London, 1891), p. 162.
2. Ibid., pp. 6, 58

GEORGE HEMING MASON (A.R.A.) *1818– 1872*

36
Evening, Matlock, c. 1867
Oil on canvas
16½ x 18⅜ (42 x 72)
Provenance: Marquis of Westminster; . . . Alexander Henderson, 1972; Fine Art Society, 1979; Duncan MacLaren, 1982
First exhibited: Royal Academy, 1867 (no. 202)
References: R. Billingham, *George Heming Mason* (Stoke-on-Trent City Museum and Art Gallery, 1982), no. 43

George Heming Mason spent many years in Rome (1843–58), where he came under the influence of Giovanni Costa and Frederic Leighton. On his return to England he painted landscapes that often deal with typically English subject matter and concerns yet are generally Italianate in style or mood. The subject of this landscape is very En-

36

glish: a gleaner leaves the harvest field at evening carrying her sheaf. In other paintings of the same period Mason, like his contemporary Fred Walker, focuses on child labour in inhospitable landscapes.[1] Some critics saw his work as realistic: one compared him with Jean-François Millet and Walker as artists who "aimed to find beauty in rustic labour by revealing its truths completely, not by adorning or changing them."[2]

There is also, however, a strong idealising tendency in Mason's work that finds its strongest expression in *The Harvest Moon* (see fig. 24). The clothes of his figures echo classical draperies and can be compared with the paintings of Albert Moore; his subtle colouring and harmonious compositions reflect the interests of Whistler and of the Aesthetic movement. Indeed, in 1867 *Evening, Matlock* was hung near Whistler's *Symphony in White No. 1*, the first picture the latter exhibited that had a musical title. Reviewers praised the "subtle harmonies" and "perfect taste" of Mason's picture; one compared its colour to a symphony as if recognising the affinities between the two painters. The same reviewer praised the gracefulness of the gleaner and the "exquisite beauty and poetry" of the whole picture.[3]

Mason was also friendly with William Blake Richmond, son of George Richmond, a close friend of Samuel Palmer. This painting strongly suggests the influence of Palmer, especially in the moon rising as the sun sheds its last rays on the reaped field in the background. It can be compared, for example, with Palmer's *Harvest Moon* (cat. 20).

1. For example, *The Wind on the Wold* (c. 1863; Tate Gallery, London) and *The Cast Shoe* (c. 1865; Tate Gallery, London).
2. *Art Journal*, June 1873, p. 202.
3. *Athenaeum*, 18 May 1867, p. 667; *Art Journal*, 1 June 1867, p. 145.

HEYWOOD HARDY *1843–1933*
37
Corn Stooks by Bray Church, 1872
Signed and dated 1872, lower left
Oil on paper laid on board
8 x 11 (20.3 x 27.9)
Provenance: Browse and Darby; Charles Glazebrook, 1989

Yale Center for British Art, Paul Mellon Fund

Heywood Hardy is best known today for his genre scenes of people in eighteenth-century costume, often shown riding. This sensitive landscape study dates from early in his career and suggests the influence of the Pre-Raphaelites both in its subject matter and in its fine detail. A neat cornfield, with tidily stooked sheaves and regular drill lines, is shown in front of a village church, implying all the religious symbolism associated with harvest.

Hardy may also have followed Pre-Raphaelite practice in painting his landscape on the spot. The agricultural detail is consistent with this method, as the stooks have clearly been left to dry in the field before they are carried—hence the absence of labourers.

Yale only

SIR GEORGE CLAUSEN (R.A.) *1852–1944*
38
Winter Work, 1883–84
Inscribed "G. CLAUSEN. 1883–4. CHILDWICK," lower left
Oil on canvas
30½ x 36¼ (77.5 x 92)
Provenance: . . . Sotheby's, London, 3 November 1982, lot 37; Fine Art Society, from whom bought by Tate Gallery in 1983 with assistance from the Friends of the Gallery

37 (see pl. 20)

38 (see pl. 21)

First exhibited: Grosvenor Gallery, London, 1883 (no. 152)
References: Kenneth McConkey, *Sir George Clausen, R.A., 1852–1944* (Tyne and Wear and Bradford Museums, 1980), p. 39; "Figures in a Field—*Winter Work* by Sir George Clausen, R.A.," *Art at Auction: The Year at Sotheby's 1982–83* (London, 1983), pp. 72–77

Tate Gallery, London

George Clausen acknowledged the influence of Fred Walker and John Robertson Reid in the 1870s, but the most important influences on his style came from the continent. In *Winter Work* the predominant influence is that of Jules Bastien-Lepage, whose work had impressed Clausen deeply when it was shown at the Grosvenor Gallery in 1880. The choice of subject matter, however, is indebted to the English tradition and reflects the concentration of artists and writers of the 1860s and 1870s, such as Fred Walker and Richard Jefferies, on the rigours of field work in winter.

In the early 1880s Clausen produced a series of paintings at Childwick Green, near St. Albans in Hertfordshire, using photographs to help him gain authenticity in the clothing, poses and physiognomy of the labourers (see cat. 106 and 107). With their ageing figures in bulky, inelegant clothing, engaged in monotonous tasks in bleak landscapes, these paintings offer a striking contrast to the lively, sunny harvest fields of earlier and even contemporary artists. Critics and patrons, however, reacted unfavourably, and Clausen abandoned this style of extreme realism by the end of the decade.

When it was originally shown at the Grosvenor Gallery, *Winter Work* contained only three figures: the old man and woman in the foreground and the boy behind, who are pulling and trimming mangolds before putting them in the root slicer and feeding

them to sheep (cat. 81). This original composition is recorded in a drawing in the collection of the Royal Academy (McConkey, *Sir George Clausen*, p. 39). The picture remained unsold when the exhibition closed, and Clausen subsequently added the girl with a hoop on the extreme right. This addition would seem to have been an attempt to change the whole character of the painting—to make it more like the idyllic family groups in harvest scenes. The gazes of the man and woman, who had previously stared out of the picture in a stupefied and exhausted manner, now focus on the child, whose pink and blue clothing adds touches of pastel colour to what would otherwise be a very dour, earthy colour scheme. It seems, therefore, that Clausen was already becoming aware that uncompromising realism would not attract buyers and was trying to modify his work to bring it closer to established conventions.

SIR GEORGE CLAUSEN (R.A.) *1852–1944*

39

The Mowers, 1891
Signed and dated 1891, lower right
Oil on canvas
40 x 34 (97.2 x 76.2)
Provenance: Sharpley Bainbridge, 1891; Bainbridge sale, February 1922, no. 109; . . . Fine Art Society; bought by Usher Gallery, 1949
First exhibited: Royal Academy, 1892 (no. 81)
References: Kenneth McConkey, *Sir George Clausen, R.A., 1852–1944* (Tyne and Wear and Bradford Museums, 1980), no. 72, pp. 55–56

Lincolnshire County Council, Usher Gallery, Lincoln

The Mowers was painted at a stage in Clausen's career when the influence of

39 (see pl. 22)

Bastien-Lepage, so evident in the earlier *Winter Work* (cat. 38) had been replaced by that of Millet and the French Impressionists. Accordingly, he is concerned less with authentic detail than with the nobility of rural labour and the beauty of sunlight, especially in his depiction of the meadow with its quantities of wildflowers. The mower in the foreground, with his hat hiding his face, has the anonymity of Millet's peasants rather than the portrait-like detail of Clausen's earlier agricultural scenes. The agricultural detail is rather anachronistic: by the 1890s meadows would normally be cut mechanically, and the scythe would be used only to open up a field by cutting round the headland.

On the other hand, Clausen was sufficiently concerned with accuracy to defend the stance of the foreground mower in a letter to the *Magazine of Art* in 1902 (p. 279), in which he enclosed a diagram to show how the mower on the right was at the beginning of a stroke, the mower on the left at the end.[1] The inclusion in many of his paintings of older men also reflects the contemporary anxiety about the "drift from the land" in the late nineteenth century: younger men were leaving the countryside to work in the towns, and the average age of the farm labourer was rising.

1. Reproduced in McConkey, *Sir George Clausen*, no. 72.

Watercolours and Drawings

40 (see pl. 23)

THOMAS HEARNE (F.S.A.) *1744–1817*

40

Autumn (Palemon and Lavinia), c. 1783
Pen and grey ink and watercolour
10⅜ x 12½ (27 x 31.75), oval
Provenance: . . . Viscount Eccles; Thomas
Agnew and Sons, 1978; Sotheby's, 11 July
1991
First exhibited: ?Society of Artists, 1783
(no. 108)
Engraved by William Ellis for Thomson's
Seasons, published 12 August 1784
References: *Thomas Hearne 1744–1817:
Watercolours and Drawings* (Bolton Museum
and Art Gallery, 1985), no. 40; David
Morris, *Thomas Hearne and His Landscape*
(London, 1989), p. 64

Richmond Gallery, Cork Street, London

This is one of a pair of watercolours illustrating lines from James Thomson's *Seasons*;
the other, *Summertime*, is in the Whitworth
Art Gallery, University of Manchester.
Hearne's exhibits at the Society of Artists in
1783 included *A Landscape and Figures from
Thomson's* Seasons, which could be either of
these. Both were engraved by William Ellis
in 1784.

Autumn illustrates lines 203–10 from *The
Seasons*, the story of Palemon, a wealthy
landowner, who falls in love with a gleaner,
Lavinia, believing her to be a poor girl. It
turns out, however, that she is the daughter
of his old patron, and thus his social equal
and a suitable bride. The story is an updated
version of the biblical tale of Ruth and Boaz.
It was popular with artists because it gave
them an excuse to show elegant figures in an
agricultural landscape: Palemon is refined in
both his costume and his bearing, and
Lavinia, although more simply dressed, has
the delicate features of a lady. It has been
suggested that Hearne's *Summertime* influenced the first version of Stubbs's *Haymakers*

(dated 1783),[1] and there are also similarities
between this drawing and his *Reapers*. The
man reaping on the far right, for example, is
very similar to the corresponding figure in
all versions of *The Reapers*. But Hearne's watercolour is much less sensitive to actual agricultural practice than Stubbs's series is. In
the Stubbs (cat. 4) the difference between
the male and female occupations in harvesting are clearly shown: men reap, women
bind, men set up the sheaves. In Hearne's
watercolour, however, a man is binding a
sheaf, and women appear to be reaping. The
harvest field is the setting for a scene of pastoral courtship rather than a subject of interest in its own right.

---

1. J. Egerton, *George Stubbs, 1724–1806* (Tate
Gallery, London, 1984), p. 166.

JULIUS CAESAR IBBETSON *1759–1817*

41

Haymaking, c. 1792
Signed, lower centre
Pen and ink, watercolour and touches of
body colour over pencil
8¾ x 11½ (22.2 x 29.2)
Provenance: Sotheby's, 20 November 1963;
P. and D. Colnaghi, 1963

Yale Center for British Art, Paul Mellon
Collection

This watercolour was probably painted in
Wales or based on studies made in Wales.
The tall hats of the women haymakers look
Welsh, and the sledges, which are being
used instead of waggons to cart the hay, are
typical of those used in mountainous areas
such as Wales and the Lake District.

The haymakers are exceptionally elegant
and well dressed: the two women in the
foreground are reminiscent of fashion
plates, especially in the way their poses reveal both
the front and back views of their colourful

41

and picturesque dresses. Haymaking—that is, the turning and raking of hay—was a relatively light occupation, one that could be indulged in by members of the wealthier classes who wanted to play at farm work (see Introduction, p. oo). Ibbetson's female haymakers, then, look like ladies, or at least like symbols of the pastoral fantasies of the rich, rather than authentic field labourers.

Ibbetson visited Wales in 1792 with his patron, Robert Fulke Greville. The Iveagh Bequest, Kenwood, possesses a series of watercolours, the same size as this one, illustrating the customs, occupations and dress of the Welsh people; the series probably once belonged to Greville.[1] Ibbetson exhibited "Nine Views in Wales" at the Royal Academy in 1796 (no. 336).

Yale only

1. *Julius Caesar Ibbetson, 1759–1817* (Iveagh Bequest, Kenwood, 1957), no. 66.

JOSEPH MALLORD WILLIAM TURNER (R.A.) *1775–1851*

42

Autumn—Sowing of the Grain, c. 1796
Watercolour over pencil with scratching-out on wove paper
8⅝ x 12⅞ (21.8 x 32.7)
Provenance: Charles Stokes; Mrs J. Hughes (Reigate); Mrs S. V. Carey (Surrey), from whom purchased, 1970
Engraved in aquatint by John Hassell, 1813
References: A. Wilton, *The Life and Work of J. M. W. Turner* (London, 1979), catalogue of watercolours, no. 173, p. 318

Yale Center for British Art, Paul Mellon Collection

42

Andrew Wilton suggests that this water-colour and a slightly larger one entitled *Ploughing* (Henry Huntington Library and Art Gallery, San Marino, Calif.) may have been intended as a pair. It dates from early in Turner's career, when he was still working in a fairly conventional "tinted drawing" style, yet it already shows the lively interest in ordinary people that was to characterise later watercolours, especially those for the *Picturesque Views in England and Wales.*

The man on the right is broadcasting seed from a seedlip he carries on his hip, while in the background a harrow is being dragged over the ground to cover up the seed. The sower is evidently being assisted by a young boy, who has put down his seedlip next to the old woman who huddles in the fore-ground feeding her chickens. It would ap-pear that the boy is asking the sower for seed to give to the old woman; if this inter-pretation is correct, then the subject is an illustration of the virtue of charity, appro-priately set directly in front of a church.

Yale only

THOMAS ROWLANDSON *1756–1827*

43
Harvesters Resting in a Cornfield
Pen and ink, pencil and watercolour
8⅛ x 11¼ (20.6 x 28.6)
Provenance: C. F. Huth; E. R. Carter, sold Sotheby's, 19 November 1970 (no. 125); John Baskett, 1970
References: J. Baskett and D. Snelgrove, *The Drawings of Thomas Rowlandson in the Paul Mellon Collection* (London, 1977), no. 84

Yale Center for British Art, Paul Mellon Collection

Thomas Rowlandson's watercolours of rural scenes are generally light-hearted and often humorous. His women are buxom and ele-gant and would not be out of place in a rep-resentation of a society gathering. His harvest scene is a convivial occasion: workers relax and chat, and the gleaner on the right (identifiable as such because she holds her own sheaf of wheat) is apparently being welcomed by the harvesters. In con-trast to many other harvest scenes, the work

43

has stopped completely for the lunchtime
break, and the watercolour lacks the usual
emphasis on industriousness. On the other
hand, the arrangement of houses in the valley below, clearly differentiated as mansion,
farmhouse and cottage, indicates the social
hierarchy, in which the harvesters occupy a
lowly position.

Rowlandson evidently has little interest in
accurate agricultural detail: the tool shown
in the right foreground is a strange cross between a sickle and a scythe, and his harvest
field seems to be devoid of stubble. The
stooks look strange, too, although their appearance is not without foundation in contemporary practice. They have been
"hooded," that is, one sheaf has been spread
out at the top of the stook to protect the rest
from rain.

Yale only

THOMAS ROWLANDSON *1756–1827*

44

Ploughing
Pen and ink and watercolour
7⅛ x 5½ (18.1 x 14)
Provenance: P. and D. Colnaghi, 1968
References: J. Baskett and D. Snelgrove, *The
Drawings of Thomas Rowlandson in the Paul
Mellon Collection* (London, 1977), no. 80

Yale Center for British Art, Paul Mellon
Collection

Rowlandson invests what could be the rather
wooden subject of ploughing with his characteristic vigour and humour. Instead of
plodding mechanically up and down the
field, his horses rear up, and they are led by
a buxom, barefoot girl rather than the usual
ploughboy. The old-fashioned, heavy plough
is carefully delineated, but it seems to be

44

resting on the top of the soil instead of digging into it to turn it over. Later artists were more careful about such details.

The relative indifference to agricultural processes, and the emphasis on the charms of the ploughgirl (with perhaps some sexual innuendo suggested by her struggle to control the lively horses) are typical of late eighteenth-century agricultural landscape and contrast with the more documentary approach of the early nineteenth century.

Yale only

James Ward (r.a.) *1769–1859*

45

Landscape with Farm and Corn Stooks, c. 1803
Inscribed with annotations, such as "gn" (green), "potatoes," "straw colour"
Pencil
9⅛ x 14⅜ (23.2 x 36.5)
Provenance: Squire Gallery, 1946; Martin Hardie; P. and D. Colnaghi, 1961

References: C. White, *English Landscape, 1630–1850: Drawings, Prints and Books from the Paul Mellon Collection* (Yale Center for British Art, 1977), no. 107

Yale Center for British Art, Paul Mellon Collection

This is evidently a study from nature, on paper watermarked 1803. James Ward did a number of agricultural landscapes in the first decade of the nineteenth century, including *Melrose Abbey*, 1807 (National Gallery of Scotland, Edinburgh), which was commissioned by Lord Somerville, president of the Board of Agriculture. Ward was closely associated with agriculturists during this period through his paintings and drawings of livestock, and this drawing, like his other work, shows a strong and well-informed interest in agricultural practice. (See also cat. 54.)

This landscape, with its many cornfields, seems to reflect the increased production of

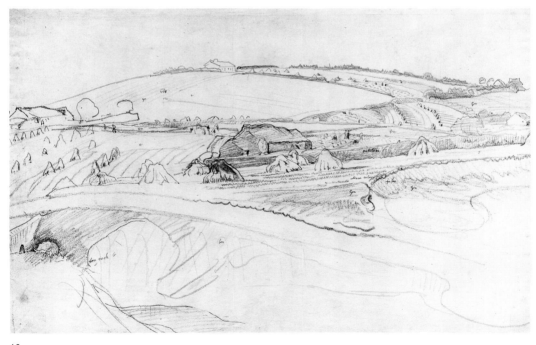

45

wheat in the years of the war against Napoleonic France. Figures are at work in the fields in the distance and middle distance, apparently cutting corn, which is then left in swathes ready for binding; in other fields, the stooks are left standing to dry before being carried. The drawing illustrates the potential variety to be found in pure agricultural landscape as a result of different crops, different stages in their harvesting, and different buildings: barns and cottages in the main part of the landscape and a farmhouse at the top of the hill, in the distance, presiding over the well-ordered countryside. Ward has utilised the drill lines in the fields for perspectival effects, and the long shadows cast by the stooks in the middle distance on the right suggest that the study was made in the early morning or late afternoon—probably the latter, as the work in the cornfields appears to have been going on for some time. The corn lying in swathes on the ground must have been cut the same day, as corn was always stooked before being left overnight.

Yale only

CORNELIUS VARLEY (O.W.S.) *1781–1873*
46
Farm Buildings with Stack Makers, c. 1805
Pencil
8¼ x 12½ (21 x 31.8)
Provenance: Squire Gallery; Martin Hardie, 1946; P. and D. Colnaghi, 1961

Yale Center for British Art, Paul Mellon Collection

Cornelius Varley, like W. H. Pyne and Robert Hills, was one of the founding members of the Society of Painters in Water-Colours in 1804. His work is characterised by meticulous study from nature: his scientific approach to art eventually led him to invent the Patent Graphic Telescope, a version of

46

the camera lucida, which enabled the artist to transcribe outlines of buildings and other objects on paper with great accuracy.

This drawing is a careful study of the activity around the farmyard at harvest time. One loaded waggon stands under a lean-to attached to the barn, another travels along the road to the right. Beyond the fence, men pitch sheaves of wheat onto a stack, which will eventually be thatched, like those on the left, to keep it dry. It could then be dismantled gradually and threshed in the autumn and winter months once the harvest was gathered in.

The barns and thatched ricks look neat and well maintained, reflecting the general interest in agricultural prosperity and improvement amongst artists of the early nineteenth century—a great contrast to the "tumbledown picturesque" that had been popularised through the writings of Uvedale Price and the paintings of George Morland in the 1790s.

Yale only

ROBERT HILLS (O.W.S.) *1769–1844*

47

Farm Labourers and Other Studies, c. 1804–10
Inscribed with various annotations in Hills's shorthand
Pencil and watercolour
11¾ x 8½ (30 x 21.5)
Provenance: Holiday; H. Wilkinson-Guillemard; T. Girtin, 1934; Tom Girtin; John Baskett, 1970
References: *Robert Hills 1769–1844* (Albany Gallery, London), 1968

Yale Center for British Art, Paul Mellon Collection

Robert Hills was one of the founding members of the Water-Colour Society in 1804; four years earlier, he, W. H. Pyne, James

Ward, J. C. Nattes and James Green had formed a Sketching Society, which met once a week for four years and took frequent sketching trips into the country. At this time, Pyne was bringing out his *Microcosm* (cat. 98), and Hills's four studies of figures engaged in rustic occupations are very close in format and conception to pages from that work. They are not copies, however: Hills evidently went out into the countryside and studied figures from nature, as Pyne was later to recommend in *Rustic Figures in Imitation of Chalk* (1817): "To become acquainted with the true rustic character, the student must go to nature, and view this class of people in their occupations" (p. ii).

These sheets of studies would have been used by Hills as records of his observations (often annotated, usually in his own shorthand), to be referred to at a later date when he was preparing finished watercolours for exhibition, such as *A Village Snow Scene* (cat. 62).

Farm Labourers and Other Studies concentrates on clothing and headgear. The men and boys wear trousers and smocks (in one case, two sets of trousers, perhaps for added warmth); the women are well covered, with bonnets to shield their faces from the sun. The woman at the top left is a gleaner, holding a sheaf in her hand as she bends to pick up loose stalks of wheat.

Yale only

ROBERT HILLS (O.W.S.) *1769–1844*

48

Woodcutter and Other Studies, c. 1804–10
Pencil and watercolour
11⅞ x 8⅝ (30.2 x 21.9)
Provenance: Thomas Agnew & Sons, 1963
References: *Robert Hills 1769–1844* (Albany Gallery, London, 1968)

Yale Center for British Art, Paul Mellon Collection

47

Here, as in *Farm Labourers and Other Studies* (cat. 47), the emphasis is on clothing rather than actual work. Hills's studies suggest that a variety of clothing was worn by rural labourers: short or long smocks (perhaps depending on what was available in the family), or waistcoats and jackets. The woodcutter, in his smart red jacket, looks more prosperous than the other labourers; he also looks posed, whereas most of the studies suggest that Hills made quick sketches while the workers went about their occupations. Occasionally one of these workers looks at the observer as if the artist

48

has aroused his curiosity, and this adds to
the impression of immediacy and authenticity.

Yale only

49 (see pl. 24)

ROBERT HILLS (O.W.S.) *1769–1844*

49

Studies of Haymakers, c. 1804–10
Inscribed at top: "about five feet in length,"
"small iron chain," "yokes leaning against a
wall," "net muzzles"; at bottom: "waistcoats,
shawls, jackets, mugs [. . .] in the bushes";
plus other annotations in Hills's shorthand.
Pencil and watercolour
11¾ x 8¾ (29.8 x 22.3)
Provenance: Thomas Agnew and Sons, 1963
References: *Robert Hills 1769–1844* (Albany
Gallery, London, 1968)

Yale Center for British Art, Paul Mellon
Collection

This sheet shows men and women raking,
tedding and pitching hay while those in the
centre appear to be having their lunchtime
break. As in cat. 47, the women are well
covered for protection against the sun, with
long sleeves and scarves under their bonnets
to shield the back of the neck. Such studies
suggest that the décolleté necklines and bare
arms of other artists' female haymakers may
reflect wishful thinking rather than current
practice, especially in an era when sun-
tanned skin was not considered to be attractive.

The carefully drawn objects in the top
lefthand corner of the sheet are yokes for
oxen. Hills did a number of studies of oxen

50

at work, such as a finished watercolour, *The Ox Team* (1810; Victoria and Albert Museum, London).

Yale only

ROBERT HILLS (O.W.S.) *1769–1844*
50
Carting Hops and Other Studies, c. 1804–10
Pencil and watercolour
11½ x 8⅞ (29.2 x 22.5)
Provenance: Mrs Lavinia Garle; Thomas Agnew and Sons, 1970
References: *Robert Hills 1769–1844* (Albany Gallery, London, 1968)

Yale Center for British Art, Paul Mellon Collection

Hills's studies often show children engaged in farm labour. In this sheet, a boy rubs down a horse at the top, then loads hops onto a cart—an unusual subject, showing the leaves of the hops being disposed of after the hop pickers have stripped them, when they would be fed to cattle. This sheet shows a scientific interest in agricultural processes and the stages in rural activities, an approach that is particularly close to that taken by Pyne in the *Microcosm*.

Yale only

51 (see pl. 25)

JOSHUA CRISTALL (P.O.W.S.) *1768–1847*
51
Hop-picking, 1807
Signed and dated 1807, bottom right
Watercolour
25½ x 38½ (64.7 x 97.7)
Provenance: Sold to Mr Boardmore, 1807;
. . . Henry J. Madgwick, 1975; Christie's, 14
November 1989, lot 102
First exhibited: Society of Painters in
Water-Colours 1807 (no. 305)
References: B. Taylor, *Joshua Cristall, 1768–
1847* (Victoria and Albert Museum,
London, 1975), no. 215

Private collection

Hop picking was never as popular a subject
for artists as the wheat harvest. Concentrated in certain areas of the country, it was
thus not widely recognised or understood by
potential art buyers.[1] It lacked the religious
connotations of the wheat harvest, and its
end product, beer, unlike bread, was a luxury. On the other hand, hop picking was relatively pleasant work, done mostly by

women and children, and the hop poles
could provide a leafy background to set off
the figures. It thus had inherent aesthetic
advantages, which are fully exploited by
Joshua Cristall in this exhibition watercolour, and also by Thales Fielding and
William Collins in later treatments of the
same theme (cat. 70 and 18).

The hop poles are being cut down by men
and then stripped of their hops, mainly by
women and children. Cristall gives his figures a neoclassical refinement (especially the
two women in the centre), and this is typical
of his work generally. On the right two
small children work, watched over benevolently by an older woman, perhaps their
grandmother. Hop picking is presented as a
healthy, peaceful activity in which whole
families can participate.

The Water-Colour Society books of
prices (Victoria and Albert Museum Library)
show that this watercolour was sold to a Mr
Boardmore for £42–0–0, a relatively high
price that reflects its size, degree of finish
and large number of figures.

52

1. See Thomas Uwins's comments, Introduction, p. oo.

DAVID COX (O.W.S.) *1783–1859*

52

A Worcestershire Farm, c. 1810
Watercolour
17½ x 25 (44.5 x 63.5)
Provenance: Presented to museum by F. J. Nettlefold in 1948
References: F. G. Roe and C. G. Grundy, *Catalogue of the Nettlefold Collection* (London, 1933), vol. 1, p. 150

Leicestershire Museums and Art Gallery

This watercolour is an early work by David Cox, with smooth washes that reflect the influence of his teacher, John Varley. The subject may have been studied on one of his trips to Wales, where he went regularly in search of sketching material from 1805 onwards. Whereas *Haymaking* (no. 53) shows work in the fields, *A Worcestershire Farm* shows the end products of agricultural labour—corn ricks and a haystack—in a village setting. The cottages and even the church echo the slightly rounded shape of the ricks, and all these elements seem to grow naturally out of their setting, surrounded as they are by foliage, suggesting a harmonious, organic community.

The old man in the foreground is a characteristic Cox type. Like similar figures in *Haymaking* and in the plate entitled *Effect, Mid-Day* in Cox's *Treatise* (no. 100), he is slightly bowlegged, presumably as a result of years of walking behind the plough, with one foot on the turf and one in the furrow.

Cox's oil sketch of 1812, *All Saints' Church, Hastings* (Birmingham Museum and Art Gallery) also juxtaposes a church tower and a haystack, and here, too, the similarities in their shapes make an important contribution to the composition.

53 (see pl. 26)

DAVID COX (o.w.s.) *1783–1859*

53

Haymaking, c. 1810
Watercolour over pencil
18⅛ x 24⅞ (46 x 63.2)
Provenance: Davis and Long, 1977
First exhibited: ?Associated Artists, 1810
(no. 78)
References: L. Hawes, *Presences of Nature:
British Landscape 1780–1830* (Yale Center
for British Art, New Haven, 1982), sec. 5,
no. 15

Yale Center for British Art, Paul Mellon
Collection

This early work by Cox depicts what was to
become one of his favourite subjects, a hayfield. It may be the *Hayfield* that is recorded
as having been exhibited at the Associated
Artists in 1810.

The heaps of cut grass, which have dried
to become hay, make pleasant curving patterns, leading the eye up to the loaded waggon on the hillside. Samuel Palmer admired

Cox in his early career, and it may be that
this drawing, or one like it, inspired Palmer's
observations of "streaked fields" and curving
furrows in his 1824 sketchbook.[1]

Cox is known to have admired Turner's
agricultural landscapes, especially his *Harvest Dinner, Kingston Bank* (1809; Tate Gallery, London).[2] This painting may have
given Cox the idea for the rather unusual
composition of *Haymaking*, with its view up
to the field from the river. In Turner's painting, the field and waggon are barely visible,
and the focus is on the river and a group of
harvesters lunching beside it. Cox has altered the viewpoint so that more of the field
(and hence of the haymaking) is seen, but
the flagon and clothes at the water's edge
imply that the haymakers have taken, or will
take, a break to eat on the edge of the river,
like Turner's harvesters.

Yale only

1. British Museum, pp. 12–13.
2. N. Neal Solly, *Memoir of the Life of David Cox*
(London, 1873), p. 29.

JAMES WARD (R.A.) *1769–1859*

54

A Wiltshire Peasant, c. 1810
Inscribed "JWD RA" and (on reverse) "A man
in Wiltshire who was in the habit of mowing
two acres of grass pr day"
Red and black chalk, heightened with white
16⅜ x 11½ (41.7 x 29.2)
Provenance: Purchased from Mrs E. M.
Ward in 1885

Trustees of the British Museum, London

In 1800 James Ward was commissioned by
the Agricultural Society and Josiah Boydell
to produce 200 portraits of different breeds
of sheep, cattle and pigs. He seems to have
approached studies of the human inhabitants
of the agricultural landscape in a similarly
documentary spirit, though not all are of
such high quality as this one.

This is a remarkably convincing study, executed in a technique that derives ultimately
from Rubens, whose work was an important
influence on Ward. The man's lined face is
observed with all the attention to characteristic detail that one might expect from a
more prestigious portrait, and yet without a
trace of caricature. The slumped pose, un-
focussed stare, slightly open mouth, shiny
temple, and wet curls clinging to the skin
are all eloquently expressive of the sweat and
exhaustion produced by a hard day's labour
in the fields.

The inscription stresses the industriousness of this labourer and also makes it clear
that he was exemplary: two acres a day was a
good average for a mower.

JOSHUA CRISTALL (P.O.W.S.) *1768–1847*

55

A Country Girl with a Sheaf, c. 1810
Pencil and watercolour
12 x 6⅙ (30.5 x 15.4)
Provenance: Mrs George Norman

References: Basil Taylor, *Joshua Cristall*,
1768–1847 (Victoria and Albert Museum,
London, 1975), no. 229

Victoria Art Gallery, Bath City Council

Joshua Cristall was recommended by W. H.
Pyne as a model to study for the depiction
of rustic figures: "Simplicity of character,
united with grandeur of style, distinguish his
designs. His cottage groups, gleaners, fisher-
men, and other subjects of the humble class
of life, are admirable specimens of the
graphic art."[1] In 1812 a critic described his
figures as "a race of healthy cottage children
that would have been chosen by the pencil
of Raphael, or described by the pen of
Virgil."[2]

Cristall's work mixes detailed observation
and classicising idealisation. The girl in this
watercolour is evidently a gleaner. She poses
like a caryatid, with an abnormally large
sheaf on her head, and her regular features
indicate Cristall's leanings towards neoclassi-
cism. On the other hand, the bulky clothing,
cheap bonnet and hole in the sleeve at the
elbow are more realistic features, suggesting
careful study from life. Cristall did many
studies of country figures between 1807 and
1818. In 1810 and 1811 he exhibited two
watercolours entitled *A Gleaner*; this drawing may be one of these, or a study for one
of them.

In 1847 Cristall re-used the pose for a watercolour entitled *A Gleaner of Herefordshire*,
which is now in the Wichita (Kans.) Art
Museum. In both drawings the emphasis is
on the abundance of wheat available for the
girl to pick up (implying the generosity of
God—or farmers—towards the poor),
rather than on her poverty or hard labour.

1. W. H. Pyne, *Etchings of Rustic Figures for the
Embellishment of Landscape* (London, 1815), p. 7.
2. R. Ackermann, *Repository of the Arts*, May 1812,
p. 304, quoted in Taylor, *Joshua Cristall*, p. 33.

54

55

56

Joshua Cristall (p.o.w.s.) *1768–1847*
56
Gleaner in a Cornfield, c. 1810
Watercolour
8¾ x 11⅜ (22.2 x 28.9)
Provenance: By descent to present owner

Private collection

This is a more finished study of a country girl than Cristall's *Country Girl with a Sheaf* (cat. 55). The young gleaner looks very similar to the girl in cat. 55 and could even be based on a study of the same model. Although this study lacks the classical overtones of cat. 55, it, too, emphasizes abundance. The girl is surrounded by top-heavy sheaves, evidence of a gloriously productive harvest, and the huge jug beside her implies that her family share in its benefits.

THOMAS UWINS (R.A.) *1782–1857*

57

A Buckinghamshire Gleaner, c. 1809
Signed and inscribed with title
Watercolour over pencil
11⅞ x 8 (30 x 20.3)
Provenance: Charles John, 5th Baron
Dimsdale; by descent to present owner

Private collection

Between 1809 and 1817 Thomas Uwins exhibited many watercolours of rural subjects
based on studies made in the counties
around London, especially Buckinghamshire, Hertfordshire and Surrey. The titles
show that Uwins had a particular interest in
gleaners, hop picking and straw plaiting, and
that these scenes often focussed on children.
In 1810 he exhibited a watercolour of a lace-
making school at Quainton, Buckinghamshire, and this study of a gleaner may have
been done at the same time as his studies of
lacemakers, in the summer of 1809.

   In this study from nature Uwins has produced a witty variation on the conventional
motif of a gleaner with a sheaf on her head.
His model has been studied from the side,
with her hat all but obscuring her face. As in
other studies from nature by Uwins, the
clothes have been meticulously delineated,
including the holes in the apron and skirt.

THOMAS UWINS (R.A.) *1782–1857*

58

A Man Leaning on a Pitchfork, c. 1811
Signed "UWINS Del" and inscribed "sketched
at . . . ham Surrey"
Watercolour over pencil
10 x 6 (25.4 x 15.2)
Provenance: Charles John, 5th Baron
Dimsdale; by descent to present owner

Private collection

This study was probably executed as part of
Uwins's preparatory work for *Haymakers at
Dinner* (cat. 59), perhaps at Farnham. It can
be compared with James Ward's *Wiltshire
Peasant* (cat. 54) for its portrait-like recording of a recognizable individual. Uwins's
studies from nature have a remarkable freshness and vitality about them, although he
himself realized that he was not always so
successful when he tried to transfer them to
more complex compositions.

57

Watercolours and Drawings

as sketched at Mart Xania Syrien

58

59 (see pl. 27)

THOMAS UWINS (R.A.) *1782–1857*

59

Haymakers at Dinner, 1812

Initialled on beer barrel: "T.U."

Watercolour

18⅞ x 27⅝ (48 x 70)

Provenance: William Smith bequest

First exhibited: Society of Painters in
Water-Colours, 1812 (no. 62)

The Board of Trustees of the Victoria and
Albert Museum, London

Uwins's letters report attempts to paint entire pictures from nature in 1809, followed
by a return to the traditional practice of
working up exhibition pictures in the studio
from sketches made previously on the spot
by 1811.[1] It is probable, therefore, that *Haymakers at Dinner* was put together from separate studies: indeed, there is a study in a
private collection of the two children bringing kegs of beer in the background on the
left, as well as a study of the man in a

smock, seated in a chair. Like Richard Westall in *A Storm in Harvest* (cat. 5), Uwins
placed his initials on the keg in the foreground, in a reference to the common practice of initialling kegs with the name of the
farmer to whom they belonged.

Andrew Hemingway quotes a review of
the 1812 exhibition which described the
man in a smock as "an epitome of the independent English yeoman" and declared that
"his labourers are such as English peasantry
should ever be—healthy, happy and neat."[2]
This reviewer showed some nostalgia for the
social harmony of an earlier time in the
countryside; and it was just four years later,
in 1816, that Southey published his lament
for the disappearance of the yeoman (see Introduction, p. 00).

In Uwins's watercolour the man in a
smock is clearly not an ordinary labourer.
He wears leather riding boots and a hat, unlike the other men, and he stands by a horse
that looks like a hunter, not a working

horse. He wears a smock, however, and holds a hay fork, implying that he has been working alongside his labourers in the field. Other farmers of the time, enriched by the increased demand for corn arising from the war with France, were criticised for having exaggerated social pretensions that distanced them from their workers. Uwins's farmer, by contrast, could be seen as setting a good example, presiding over a situation in which all the labourers look both prosperous and contented.

The watercolour is a curious mixture of artistic influences and direct observation. The farmer is a portrait of a distinct individual, the spindle-sided bow waggon is accurately observed, and the old couple on the right are convincing, but the couple in the centre look like the "drawing room rustics" of Francis Wheatley, and the woman leaning on her hay rake and the man drinking from the barrel are probably derived from paintings or prints by James Ward. The watercolour was sold to an unknown buyer on the first day of the 1812 exhibition, for £31–10–0.[3]

---

1. Sarah Uwins, *A Memoir of Thomas Uwins, R.A.* (1858; repr. London, 1978), pp. 33 and 36.
2. A. Hemingway, *Landscape Imagery and Urban Culture in Early Nineteenth Century Britain* (Cambridge, 1992), p. 153.
3. Water-Colour Society books of prices, Victoria and Albert Museum, London.

JOHN CONSTABLE (R.A.) *1776–1837*

60

Wheat Sheaves, 1815
Inscribed "15 Augst 1815, East Bergholt"
Pencil
3⅛ x 4 (7.9 x 10.2)
Provenance: Given to the Victoria and Albert Museum by Isabel Constable, the artist's daughter, 1888
References: G. Reynolds, *Catalogue of the Constable Collection at the Victoria and Albert Museum* (London, 1960), no. 140

60

This drawing is a page from a small sketchbook, now unbound, which Constable was
using in 1815. Complete sketchbooks survive from the years 1813 and 1814 (also in
the Victoria and Albert Museum) and these,
together with the drawings surviving from
the 1815 sketchbook, show that Constable
was making a systematic study of agricultural subject matter in those three summers. In 1813 and 1814 there are many
studies of ploughing, resulting in finished
paintings such as *Landscape: Ploughing Scene
in Suffolk* (cat. 16). In 1815 he moved log-
ically onto a later stage in the agricultural
year, making studies of harvest that contributed to his studies of his father's gardens and
The Wheatfield (fig. 4).

The wheat sheaves in this drawing, with
their heavy, curving tops, are reminiscent of
those in Peter DeWint's oil painting *The
Cornfield* (cat. 13), which Constable could
have seen at the Royal Academy exhibition
earlier that year. It is possible, therefore,
that DeWint's painting helped turn his attention to harvest subject matter in 1815.
Later in the same month Constable wrote to
Maria, his future wife: "I live almost wholly
in the feilds [*sic*] and see nobody but the harvest men."[1]

---

1. R. B. Beckett, ed., *John Constable's Correspondence*, vol. 2 (Ipswich, 1964), p. 149 (letter of 27
August 1815).

Joseph Mallord William Turner
(r.a.) *1775–1851*
61
Hylton Castle, County Durham, c. 1817
Watercolour
7¾ x 11 (19.8 x 28)
Provenance: Mrs Bowes, Streatham Castle;
British Rail Pension Fund
Engraved by S. Rawle for Robert Surtees's

History of Durham (London, 1816–23)
References: E. Shanes, *Turner's England:
1810–38* (London, 1990), no. 74

Private collection

This watercolour was commissioned by the
owner of the castle, the 10th Earl of Strath-
more, who took Turner to visit the castle at
the end of October 1817. Turner could not
have studied the foreground harvest scene
on this occasion, however, as it was too late
in the season.

Nevertheless, Turner seems to have considered harvesting to be a suitable motif for
this view of the castle and its chapel. As in
earlier estate portraits, such as those of Paul
Sandby and Jan Siberechts, it emphasizes
the good estate management of which the
castle was the centre and the symbol. The
couple in the foreground appear to be sharing out their gleanings (indicating that charity and benevolence are practised on this
estate); the loaded waggon and sheep on the
road below illustrate the productiveness of
the land around the house. There is an initial drawing for the watercolour in the Raby
sketchbook (T.B.CLVI-10) and an additional
colour-beginning for the composition
(T.B.CXCVII-P) in the Turner Bequest,
Tate Gallery.

Not reproduced in catalogue

Robert Hills (o.w.s.) *1769–1844*
62
A Village Snow Scene, 1819
Signed and dated 1819, bottom left
Watercolour with touches of body colour
and scraping out over pencil
12¾ x 16¾ (32.4 x 42.5)
Provenance: Meatyard; T. Girtin, 1922;
Tom Girtin; John Baskett, 1970
References: J. Bayard, *Works of Splendour and
Imagination: The Exhibition Watercolour,*

62 (see pl. 28)

1770–1870 (Yale Center for British Art, New Haven, 1981), no. 24

Yale Center for British Art, Paul Mellon Collection

Robert Hills produced at least three versions of the *Snow Scene*, all inspired by a seventeenth-century Flemish painting, *A Barn in Winter*, in the Royal Collection, which was exhibited at the British Institution in 1819.[1] At the time *A Barn in Winter* was thought to be by Rubens, although it is now attributed to the school of Rubens.

A Village Snow Scene is a finished watercolour suitable for exhibition and sale. Its figures are evidently based on earlier studies from nature, such as cat. 47–50. Varied activities are taking place in the village street. On the left, two blacksmiths are at work in their shop and horses are tethered outside; cattle are being driven down the street, followed by a covered waggon. Inside the barn, people shelter to eat and smoke, or care for

their donkeys. Hills shows complete control of the watercolour technique, using untouched paper for the large areas of snow and scraping out for the snowflakes, whose dappled effect is complemented by his characteristic use of stipple for the coloured areas.

A comparison with the seventeenth-century source, *A Barn in Winter*, is revealing. Hills's peasants are much more passive and subdued than those in the earlier painting. This may be because he is adopting a more documentary approach and thus rejecting the pastoral fantasies of earlier art, but it could also be seen as evidence of his awareness of the poverty and apathy of the farmworkers in the years of depression and unrest that followed the end of the Napoleonic Wars in 1815.

Yale only

---

1. Other versions are in the Spooner Collection, Courtauld Institute of Art, London, and in a private collection, London.

63

PETER DEWINT (O.W.S.) *1784–1849*

63

Harvesters in an Extensive Landscape in Sussex,
c. 1820

Watercolour over pencil with scratching-out
25¾ x 38⅝ (65.5 x 98.1)

Provenance: C. F. Huth; Christie's, 6 July
1895, bought by Vokins; Josiah Vavasseur, of
Kilverstone, Thetford, Norfolk; 2nd Lord
Fisher; 3rd Lord Fisher, sold Christie's, 9
November 1976; Somerville and Simpson,
1977

References: W. Armstrong, *Memoir of Peter
De Wint* (London, 1888), pl. 19; L. Hawes,
*Presences of Nature: British Landscape, 1780–
1830* (Yale Center for British Art, New
Haven, 1982), sec. 5, no. 16

Yale Center for British Art, Paul Mellon
Collection

This large, carefully finished work looks like
an exhibition watercolour, although it cannot be positively identified with any of
DeWint's recorded exhibits. It is badly
faded: the rainbow, which must once have
been an important part of the composition,
is now barely visible above the central group
of harvesters in the middle distance. The
rainbow was a symbol of God's covenant
with man, and it is significant that a distant
church spire is visible just to the right of the
rainbow. DeWint may also have been thinking of the gold that by legend is supposed to
lie at the end of the rainbow, represented in
this case by the gold-coloured and valuable
wheat crop.

Great numbers of labourers are at work in
the fields, which have no apparent boundaries and would seem, therefore, to be open
fields that have not yet been enclosed. De-
Wint liked to paint panoramic landscapes
and boundless space, a taste shared by his
admirer, the poet John Clare, who declared
himself "an advocate for open fields."[1] This

watercolour is reminiscent of John Aikin's preference for open fields as the site for the harvest scene, with its religious and social associations: "This pleasing harvest-scene is beheld in its perfection only in the open-field countries, where the sight can at once take in an uninterrupted extent of land waving with corn, and a multitude of people engaged in the various parts of the labour. It is a prospect equally delightful to the eye and the heart, and which ought to inspire every sentiment of benevolence to our fellow creatures, and gratitude to our Creator."[2] A similar open field landscape can be seen in *Haymaking in Osney Meadow* (cat. 73).

The figures grouped in the foreground (with a rake and two sickles on the ground beside them) are harvesters preparing to have lunch, and a mounted farmer or overseer, who appears to show "benevolence" towards the woman and children but also

holds a telescope to assist him in the supervision of the workers in the distance.

Yale only

---

1. Clare's Journal, 14 November 1824, cited in J. W. and A. Tibble, *The Prose of John Clare* (London, 1951), p. 122.
2. J. Aikin, *Calendar of Nature*, 2d ed. (London, 1785), p. 55.

JOSEPH MALLORD WILLIAM TURNER
(R.A.) *1775–1851*

64

Lancaster, from the Aqueduct Bridge, c. 1825
Watercolour and body colour
11 x 15½ (28 x 39.4)
Provenance: Sold by Charles Langton at Christie's, 17 May 1862, lot 104, bought by Agnew; William Leech; J. Orrock; Lord Leverhulme

64

Engraved by R. Wallis, 1827, for *Picturesque Views in England and Wales* (London, 1827–38)
References: A. Wilton, *The Life and Work of J. M. W. Turner* (London, 1979), catalogue of watercolours, no. 786; E. Shanes, *Turner's England, 1810–38* (London, 1990), no. 134

Like Carmichael's *Corby Viaduct* (cat. 21), this watercolour juxtaposes evidence of the new forms of transport contributing to industrialisation (in this case, barges on a canal) with traditional agricultural activity. Beyond the canal, reapers and gleaners are at work in a wheat field; the two women gleaning particularly attract the viewer's attention, placed as they are in the middle of the cleared part of the field, almost in the centre of the composition. The attitudes of the figures on the canal bridge indicate the great heat of the day, yet the workers in the fields below are in full sunlight—a deliberate contrast, which is further stressed by the cool water of the canal in the foreground.

PETER DeWINT (O.W.S.) *1784–1849*
65
Harvest Field, c. 1825
Watercolour, with scratching out
9¾ x 18¼ (24.8 x 43.7)
Provenance: Given by the National Art Collections Fund from the Herbert Powell Bequest

In contrast to the oil *The Cornfield* (cat. 13), this watercolour shows a more likely, less contrived combination of activities. The field is in the process of being reaped: stooks of wheat, perhaps cut the previous day, stand on the right and will stay there until they are dry. In the foreground to the left, sheaves lie on the ground: they have been bound but not stooked (an activity that usually took place at the end of the day). All the figures are depicted as hard at work, and the watercolour lacks the usual picturesque motifs of lunching groups, gleaners or loaded waggons.

The composition, too, suggests a sketch made directly from nature in the fields. All

65

the figures are on the lefthand side, and the woman on the extreme left looks out from the centre, implying that there are more harvesters to the left of her, cut off by the frame. The figures are roughly sketched, and the red of their exposed arms adds to the impression of heat.

Watercolours such as this one recall the request of the poet John Clare for "one of those rough sketches taken in the fields that breathes with the living freshness of open air & sunshine where the blending & harmony of earth air & sky are in such a happy unison of greens & greys that a flat bit of scenery on a few inches of paper appears so many miles."[1]

---

1. J. W. Tibble and A. Tibble, *The Letters of John Clare* (London, 1951), p. 239 (letter to DeWint, 19 December 1829).

JOHN LINNELL *1792–1882*
66
Mowers in the Field in Porchester Terrace, Bayswater, 1830
Inscribed "Mowers in the field in Porchester Terrace, Bayswater, June 9th 1830" and signed, lower right
Pencil and watercolour
5 13/16 x 7 3/8 (14.8 x 18.8)
Provenance: Mrs John Lucas (great-granddaughter of John Linnell); Christie's, 2 March 1971; John Baskett

Yale Center for British Art, Paul Mellon Collection

Porchester Terrace is hardly rural now, but in 1830 it was on the edge of London, an area of new building development bordering

66

on fields. Linnell moved to no. 26 Porchester Terrace in 1828, and in 1830 he moved into a house he had had built, no. 30. At this time in his career he was making a living mainly from portrait commissions, and was painting studies from nature in the fields in Bayswater and on visits to Samuel Palmer in Shoreham. Some of these studies were used for finished oil landscapes, but most seem to have been kept for future reference. This study was used many years later, as the basis for the figure group in *The Hayfield* (1864; sold at Christie's, 20 November 1964).

This is an unusually close-up study of a group of agricultural labourers at lunchtime. Only men are present—no women and children who added charm to so many painted groups of haymakers and harvesters. This makes sense, since only men would have

mown the grass, that is, cut it with the scythe; women would have come in later on, to turn it as it dried.

Yale only

SAMUEL PALMER (R.W.S.) *1805–1881*
67
Cornfield and Church by Moonlight, c. 1830
Black ink and grey wash with gum
6 x 7¼ (15.2 x 18.4)
Provenance: Richard Redgrave, R.A.; . . .
Sotheby's, 29 June 1932, bought by Thomas and Ruth Lowinsky; Justin Lowinsky, 1963
References: R. Lister, *Catalogue Raisonné of the Works of Samuel Palmer* (Cambridge, 1988), no. 119

67

Yale Center for British Art, Paul Mellon Collection

In contrast to the rich colours of *The Harvest Moon* (cat. 20), Palmer uses monochrome ink and wash in this drawing, which creates an effect of velvety moonlight. In both cases, however, the light is otherworldly and mysterious. Figures walk along a field path towards a village church, which nestles amongst leafy trees. The woman in the centre has a sheaf on her head and hence must be a gleaner, returning home after her day's labours in an occupation that evidently appealed to Palmer because of its biblical associations. One of his few historical compositions was a drawing entitled *Ruth Returned from the Gleaning*.[1] *Cornfield and Church by Moonlight* once belonged to Richard Redgrave, who may have bought it in the 1860s, when Palmer and Redgrave became friendly as a result of the close proximity of their houses at Abinger, in Surrey. (For further links between Palmer and Redgrave, see cat. 35).

Yale only

---

1. Victoria and Albert Museum; Lister, *Catalogue Raisonné*, no. 81. Palmer also did a painting of a gleaning field, Tate Gallery; Lister, *Catalogue Raisonné*, no. 164.

68

SAMUEL PALMER (R.W.S.) *1805–1881*

68

The Harvest Moon, c. 1830–31
Watercolour and body colour over pencil
4⅞ x 5⅝ (12.4 x 14.1)
Provenance: . . . A. J. Finberg, Cotswold
Gallery; Dr Gordon Bottomley, by whom
bequeathed to Carlisle Museums and Art
Gallery, 1949
References: R. Lister, *Catalogue Raisonné of
the Works of Samuel Palmer* (Cambridge,
1988), no. 128

Tullie House, City Museum and Art Gallery,
Carlisle

Geoffrey Grigson thought that this watercolour might be a study for the *Harvest
Moon* of 1833, and his suggestion is repeated
by Raymond Lister.[1] But Grigson had never
seen that *Harvest Moon* (cat. 20), and the two
compositions are entirely different from one
another. In this drawing, the valley of
Shoreham is seen from above, with a church
and cottages nestling below. Harvesters in
multicoloured dresses are visible on the edge
of the hill: it is difficult to say whether they
are binding sheaves or gleaning. A standing
figure in blue, however, holds a few stalks in
each hand, as if she is preparing to make a
straw rope to bind the sheaves, like the
woman in Stubbs's *Reapers* (cat. 4). It seems
likely, therefore, that they are binding rather
than gleaning. The agricultural activity
makes more sense than in the 1833 *Harvest
Moon*: the day's reaping has finished, but
binding and stooking continue because it is
essential that the corn be stooked before
nightfall. On the other hand, the spots and
stripes on the harvesters' colourful dresses
are rather fanciful, as is the huge size of the
haloed harvest moon, and these both contribute to the visionary effect of the scene.

1. G. Grigson, *Samuel Palmer: The Visionary Years*

(London, 1947), cited in Lister, *Catalogue Raisonné*, no. 128.

SAMUEL PALMER (R.W.S.) *1805–1881*

69

A Pastoral Scene, 1835
Brown wash
3¾ x 4⅝ (9.5 x 11.7)
Provenance: A. H. Palmer, by whom given
to Martin Hardie, c. 1912; Mrs Madeline
Hardie; P. and D. Colnaghi, 1961
References: R. Lister, *Catalogue Raisonné of
the Works of Samuel Palmer* (Cambridge,
1988), no. 213

Yale Center for British Art, Paul Mellon
Collection

This is a study for a painting, *A Pastoral
Scene* (Ashmolean Museum, Oxford), which
was based on Palmer's visit to Devon in
1833. Its composition is more open than
that of most of the Shoreham period landscapes, with a view of the sea on the left, and
yet it also contains the characteristic Shoreham features of a moon, a half-reaped cornfield and a hillside covered with lush
growth. According to his son, A. H. Palmer,
who wrote that this drawing "used to hang
among some special favourites in my room
when I was a boy," Palmer appreciated the
"heaped up richness" of the Devon landscape.[1] In the painting, Palmer reduced the
openness of the landscape, adding hills and
cottages to the valley leading to the sea, thus
obscuring the view. The loaded waggons
drawn by oxen and the man carrying sticks
(perhaps hop poles?) were replaced by sheep
and shepherds.

Yale only

1. Lister, *Catalogue Raisonné*, no. 213; A. H. Palmer, *Life and Letters of Samuel Palmer* (London,
1892), p. 55.

69

THALES FIELDING (A.O.W.S.) *1793–1837*

70

Hop-picking, 1831
Signed and dated 1831, lower left
Watercolour over pencil
7⅛ x 10⅜ (18.2 x 26.3)
Provenance: L. G. Duke; The Squire
Gallery, 1949; P. and D. Colnaghi, 1961

Yale Center for British Art, Paul Mellon
Collection

Thales Fielding was a younger brother of
the better-known Anthony Vandyke Copley
Fielding. The family ran an engraving business in Paris: Thales worked there from
1820 to 1827 and became friendly with the
French painter Delacroix, sharing a house
with him for a time.

The impressionistic handling of this watercolour would have appealed to Delacroix.
Its emphasis on the elegant dresses and bonnets of the hop pickers is reminiscent of topographical watercolours by artists of the
Bonington circle, whom Thales Fielding
would also have known; they could be fashionable ladies in a French street scene or
marine view. At the same time the viewpoint
suggests an authentic observation from nature, with the figures apparently unaware
of the presence of the artist, in contrast to
Joshua Cristall's depiction of the same subject (cat. 51), in which they seem to be posing for their picture.

There is another study of hop pickers by
Fielding in the Courtauld Institute (Witt
drawing no. 4516).

Yale only

70

71

Watercolours and Drawings

JOHN MARTIN (N.W.S.) *1789–1854*

71

Harvest Field near Pevensey, Sussex, c. 1848
Watercolour
9⅛ x 21¼ (23.2 x 54)
Provenance: George Amatt Bentlif;
bequeathed to the museum in 1897

Maidstone Museum and Art Gallery, Bentlif
Collection

John Martin is best known for his large
apocalyptic landscapes, such as *The Great
Day of His Wrath* (1852; Tate Gallery, London). In the 1840s, however, he produced a
series of harvest and pastoral landscapes that
are very different in mood, and comparable
to the subject pictures only in the use of perspective devices to create effects of vast
space. In this example, the tiny village on
the left and the windmills on the right emphasize the vast distance between foreground and background.

On close examination it is clear that the
waggon is being drawn by oxen, which were
still used in Sussex into the twentieth century. The open aspect of the landscape may
also refer to a traditional feature, the open-
field system.

The stooks are rather crudely drawn and
their number seems excessive, but these features are typical of Martin's harvest landscapes and can be compared with examples
in the National Gallery, Washington, and in
the Fitzwilliam Museum, Cambridge
(PD.14–1967).

SAMUEL PALMER (R.W.S.) *1805–1881*

72

Harvesting, c. 1851
Signed, lower right
Watercolour and body colour
15⅛ x 20¼ (38.2 x 51.4)
Provenance: A. H. Palmer; C. H. T.
Hawkins by 1904; Christie's, 20 February

72 (see pl. 29)

1928, bought by Robert Dunthorne and Son; Christie's, 26 July 1929, bought by Vicars; Royal Artillery Institution, Woolwich; Sotheby's, 27 July 1960, bought by Agnew's; Mrs Gilbert Troxell, New Haven, until 1987
References: R. Lister, *Catalogue Raisonné of the Works of Samuel Palmer* (Cambridge, 1988), no. 504

Private collection, courtesy of Agnew's, London

After widening his range of subject matter in the 1830s and 1840s following trips to Wales and Italy, Palmer returned to harvest scenes in a number of drawings of the late 1840s and early 1850s. These are very different from the harvest scenes of the Shoreham period: they are broader in handling, grander in conception, and more open in composition, lacking the enclosed feeling of the Shoreham work. As a result, they are more prosaic, less visionary, and also more conventional. They reflect the compositions of Old Masters such as Ruisdael (rather than the earlier, more "primitive" artists who had appealed to Palmer when he was at Shoreham), as well as those of Palmer's contemporaries, especially John Linnell, who was now his father-in-law.

In a memorandum of 1849 Palmer noted, "I ought to watch the operations of husbandry," and listed possible subjects to provide "Action" in his paintings, one of which was "storm in harvest."[1] At this period in his life he was making determined efforts to sell his works, and was aware that he needed to "lower the themes" and adopt "less directly poetical" subjects in order to appeal to buyers.

Despite its conventional features, this watercolour does succeed in recapturing some of the poetic spirit of the Shoreham years. The mixture of sun and storm creates an unusual effect of light, and Palmer's acuity of observation is evident in the loaded waggon, which is being covered with canvas to protect it from the coming storm. The orange of this canvas complements the gold of the corn and contrasts with the deep blues and purples of the landscape and sky.

The watercolour looks as if it was made for exhibition and sale, but it cannot be positively identified with any of Palmer's known exhibits. It evidently failed to find a buyer, since it was passed down to Palmer's son.

---

1. A. H. Palmer, *Life and Letters of Samuel Palmer* (London, 1892), p. 102–6.

WILLIAM TURNER OF OXFORD (O.W.S.)
1789–1862
73
Haymaking, Study from Nature, in Osney Meadow, near Oxford, Looking towards Iffley, 1853–54
Signed, lower left
Watercolour and body colour
10 x 14 (25.4 x 35.6)
Provenance: F. P. Morrell; Knight, Frank and Rutley, Oxford; A. P. Warren sale, Sotheby's, 24 June 1971, lot 69, bought by Thomas Agnew and Sons.
First exhibited: Society of Painters in Water-Colours, 1854 (no. 78)
References: *William Turner of Oxford (1789–1862),* (Oxfordshire County Museum, 1984), no. 79; C. Payne, "Boundless Harvests: Representations of Open Fields and Gleaning in Early Nineteenth Century England," *Turner Studies*, vol. 11, no. 1 (Summer 1991), pp. 7–15

Private collection

This watercolour illustrates how agricultural activity could enliven the flattest of panoramic landscapes, especially when land was still farmed under the open-field system, and many groups of workers could be seen in a single large field.

73 (see pl. 30)

William Turner of Oxford painted agricultural scenes throughout his career, showing a special fondness for the commons and open fields of the pre-enclosure landscape. This watercolour was probably painted while the enclosure of Osney Meadow was actually in progress (it was exhibited in 1854, but since it was "a study from nature" it must have been painted in the early summer, probably in the preceding year). The stone in the foreground may be one of the markers used under the open-field system, indicating the extent of the meadow that is to be cut, or it may show that the new post-enclosure boundaries were already being laid out as the last crop of hay was being taken from the meadow under the old system. If the latter is the correct interpretation, then the rigid lines of the new boundaries and the man on horseback in the centre act as barriers, distancing the viewer from the old world of the open fields with its bustling activity and apparent freedom.

MYLES BIRKET FOSTER (R.W.S.)
1825–1899

74

The Hay Rick, c. 1862
Monogrammed, lower right
Watercolour and body colour, with scraping out
30⅝ x 26¾ (77.7 x 68)
Provenance: G. W. Blundell, Liverpool; Christie's, 9 March 1951; L. Mortimer; P. Polak, March 1966
Engraved for *Birket Foster's Pictures of English Landscape* (London, 1863), no. 10
References: J. Bayard, *Works of Splendour and Imagination: The Exhibition Watercolour, 1770–1870*, Yale Center for British Art (New Haven, 1981), no. 90; S. Wilcox and C. Newall, *Victorian Landscape Watercolours* (New York, 1992), no. 51

Yale Center for British Art, Paul Mellon Collection

Birket Foster's early career was devoted to

74

book illustration. In 1860, however, he began to exhibit his works at the Society of Painters in Water-Colours, and he soon found that they sold so well that he was able to give up illustrating. This composition began as a book illustration. In 1859 the Dalziel brothers commissioned Birket Foster to make 50 drawings of scenes from English landscape, each to be accompanied by a verse by Tom Taylor. In the event, 30 were produced and published in the book, and this is a finished watercolour of one of them.

Men are shown loading hay from a wagon onto a rick, a subject that allowed the artist to represent labourers in heroic and active poses. In the foreground, pigs, piglets, ducks and hens rummage in the loose hay left lying on the ground in the farmyard. To the left, an assortment of objects—sticks for hurdle making, finished hurdles, a wheelbarrow and a hay rake—help frame the scene and suggest the variety of occupations of a mixed farm in the summertime. The sheep in the distance indicate the need for hurdles. This use of the foreground, with the main agricultural activity in the middle distance, suggests a return to the aesthetics of the picturesque. In the same period, the popularity of watercolours of old cottages appealed to a similar taste.

Taylor's accompanying verses make haymaking sound like a jolly occasion, a time of song and good cheer, although the last lines show his awareness of rural poverty:

> Happy, hot, hay-making time . . .
> When freely flows the farmer's beer,
> And toil shakes hands with lusty cheer . . .
> Where with song and bantering din,
> Stamping feet press down the mow . . .
> And field-born cans the ale-cups fill,
> And those who toil for once may reap
> Of the abundance that has birth
> From God's glad and generous earth.

Taylor emphasized that his verses were "meant to harmonize with and illustrate, without pretending to describe, the inventions of the painter." Nevertheless, there is no evidence of song or ale in Birket Foster's watercolour, in which, on the contrary, the labourers are concentrating soberly on their work.

Yale only

GEORGE PRICE BOYCE (R.W.S.)
1826–1897

75
Old Barn at Whitchurch, 1863
Signed and dated Aug. 63, bottom left
Watercolour, body colour, and pen and ink
8⅛ x 11½ (20.5 x 28.7)
Provenance: . . . presented by Miss Virtue-Tebbs to the Ashmolean Museum, 1944
First exhibited: Society of Painters in Water-Colours, winter 1864–65, no. 435: "Old Barn at Whitchurch, Oxon. Sketch for larger drawing"

75

References: C. Newall and J. Egerton, *George Price Boyce* (Tate Gallery, London, 1987), no. 38

The Visitors of the Ashmolean Museum, Oxford

Boyce trained as an architect, turning to painting as a career only at the end of the 1840s, partly as a result of meeting David Cox. At first his style was similar to Cox's, making use of broad washes, but he then came into contact with the Pre-Raphaelites and their circle and adopted a finely detailed manner based on painstaking study from nature. Amongst his favourite subjects were ancient buildings, especially mills and barns. He delighted in the variety of colours and textures to be found in such buildings, which made them so much more picturesque than their modern replacements.

Traditional barns, with tall doors large enough for loaded waggons to go through, were becoming obsolete now that much of the wheat crop was threshed by machine di-rectly after harvest. Like traditional harvesting itself, then, they became precious subjects for artists wishing to record them before they vanished from the countryside. Later on, in the 1870s, Boyce became a leading member of the Society for the Protection of Ancient Buildings.

RICHARD BEAVIS (R.W.S.) *1824–1896*
76

Building a Rick, 1864
Signed and dated 1864, lower right
Pencil, ink, watercolour and body colour
10 x 14⅞ (25.3 x 37.7)
Provenance: Abbott and Holder, 1966
References: J. Egerton and D. Snelgrove, *The Paul Mellon Collection: British Sporting and Animal Drawings c. 1500–1800* (London, 1978), p. 20.

Virginia Museum of Fine Arts, Richmond (Paul Mellon Collection)

Pictures of oxen at work seem to have be-

76

come popular in the 1850s and 1860s, partly as a result of the success of Rosa Bonheur's *Ploughing Scene* (1854; Walters Art Gallery, Baltimore), which was shown in London in 1857. H. Brittan Willis, for example, exhibited paintings of oxen working in Sussex, where they continued to be used throughout the nineteenth century.[1] In 1871 a critic commented on Beavis's *Autumn Ploughing: Showery Weather*: "The style, of course, recalls Rosa Bonheur: it would seem impossible for oxen to plough otherwise than in the manner made familiar by this lady."[2]

The subject of *Building a Rick*, however, had been popular with British artists for many years. Beavis's depiction of it may be compared with an aquatint after Robert Hills (cat. 99) and a near-contemporary watercolour by Myles Birket Foster (cat. 74). It is perhaps closer to the documentary approach of Hills than to the picturesque style of Birket Foster: several labourers are shown hard at work transferring the sheaves from the waggon to the new rick in the background, while in the foreground, to the left,

a completed rick is visible, resting on staddle stones to keep away vermin.

Yale only

1. For example, *Returning Home—the Day's Work Done* (1859; British Institution), reviewed in *Art Journal*, 1 March 1859, p. 83.
2. *Art Journal*, 1 July 1871, p. 174. The painting was no. 180 in the Royal Academy exhibition of that year.

DANIEL ALEXANDER WILLIAMSON
1823–1903

77
Ploughing, 1865
Signed with monogram and dated, lower left
Watercolour
7 x 10¼ (18 x 26)
Provenance: Unknown

Christopher and Jenny Newall

Daniel Alexander Williamson was a Liverpool-based painter of landscapes and

77 (see pl. 31)

genre: he was in London from c. 1847, but in 1860 he returned to Lancashire and settled near Carnforth. His work of the 1850s and 1860s shows the influence of the Pre-Raphaelites, but after about 1865 his style became increasingly free and impressionistic, reflecting his interest in the earlier watercolour tradition of J. M. W. Turner and David Cox.

This watercolour dates from a transitional period in his life. The closely observed landscape detail, especially in the foreground, is similar to the work of the Pre-Raphaelites, as is the concentration on the humble subject matter of the ploughed field. But the blurred silhouettes of man and horse and the moisture-laden sky are closer to the legacy of Cox and Turner.

The man appears to be ploughing, although the plough he is using cannot be seen owing to the low viewpoint, and the traces and plough handles are not shown in any detail. A second plough in the foreground, however, clarifies the subject mat-

ter. The watercolour is very evocative of the conditions in which ploughing was done. Williamson focuses on the bare yet rich-looking earth (with a pile of manure to the right), the birds following the plough to pick up any exposed worms and seeds, and the stark contrast between earth and sky. In short, he illustrates the atmosphere of ploughing rather than documenting its technical details.

WILLIAM DAVIS *1812–1873*
78
Ploughing, c. 1869
Signed
Watercolour
8 x 13 ½ (20 x 34.6)
Provenance: Purchased in 1964 from Mrs Sonia Rae
References: *Victorian Watercolours from the Collection of the Walker Art Gallery* (Liverpool, 1974)

Trustees of the National Museums and

78

Galleries on Merseyside. Walker Art
Gallery, Liverpool

William Davis spent most of his career in
Liverpool selling pictures to a small circle of
private collectors. In the 1850s he became
friendly with the Pre-Raphaelites Ford
Madox Brown and D. G. Rossetti, and
joined their Hogarth Club in 1858. His agricultural landscapes are very individual,
sometimes concentrating on minute details
of crops, as in *The Field of Green Corn* (cat.
32), sometimes highlighting the role of children in work on the land. His most famous
agricultural landscape was *Harrowing* (fig.
20), in which a young boy is shown alone at
work in a bleak landscape. It was rejected
by the Royal Academy, probably on the
grounds of faults in perspective, but hung
well and much admired at the International
Exhibition of 1862.[1]

This watercolour is similar to an oil in the
same collection entitled *Ploughing, Valley of
the Conway* (1869; no. 1146) and is perhaps a
reduced version of the oil. It is a careful
study of ploughing. The ploughman stands
with one foot in the furrow, one on the un-
ploughed land; the field is being ploughed in
"lands," that is, a rectangle is marked out
and the ploughman then works outwards
from the centre, going up the field on the
left and down on the right, turning the soil
over to the right each time.

Davis produced a number of oils of the
same subject, which are not always successful but are highly original. He was obviously
fascinated by the different textures of
ploughed fields and surrounding greenery,
and experimented with unconventional compositions and perspectival effects.[2]

1. F. G. Stephens, "William Davis, landscape
painter, of Liverpool," *Art Journal*, 1884, p. 328.
2. See, for example, *Ploughing*, in the Williamson
Art Gallery, Birkenhead; and a painting with the
same title sold at Christie's, 16 May 1985, lot 45.

GEORGE JOHN PINWELL (O.W.S.)
(attributed) *1842–1875*
79
Hop-picking, c. 1870
Watercolour with body colour
14⅛ x 23¼ (35.9 x 59)
Provenance: Purchased by the museum from
Spink and Co., 1972

Maidstone Museum and Art Gallery, Bentlif
Collection

The authorship of this watercolour is uncer-
tain. It has been attributed to Pinwell, and it
is evidently by him or by one of his circle,
but it is not recorded in George Williamson's biography of Pinwell, which gives a full
list of works known to be by the artist.[1] The
style of *Hop-picking* does not rule out an attribution to Pinwell: there is some fine
stippling on the faces of the main characters
that is very characteristic of his work, but
the less meticulous finish of the rest of the
watercolour suggests another artist, perhaps
Matthew White Ridley or Charles Green.

Pinwell was one of a group of artists who
came together as illustrators in the 1860s,
working for the *Graphic* and other periodi-
cals, as well as for book publishers. This
group, which also included Fred Walker and
J. W. North, took a special interest in rural
life, which they represented in a style that
was sometimes medievalising, sometimes
contemporary, ranged from the idyllic to the
more realistic and often had a wistful emphasis.

In this painting, hop picking is presented
as an idyllic occupation despite concerns expressed in the 1860s about the living conditions and habits of the pickers in Kent, who
often came from the slums of the East End
of London to take on this seasonal work.
The bonnets worn by the old women and
the young girls give this scene a country air
and tend to play down the usual urban ori-

79 (see pl. 32)

gins of the pickers. It may be, therefore, that
it is meant to be set in another hop-growing
area, such as Herefordshire, rather than in
Kent.

The baby in the cradle and the little girl
picking hops into a basket are reminiscent of
earlier treatments of the subject by Collins
and Cristall (cat. 18 and 51); the hop knife
held by the man in the left foreground is
similar to the implement lying in the foreground of Cristall's *Hop-picking*.

---

1. G. C. Williamson, *George J. Pinwell and His
Works* (London, 1900). I am very grateful to
Christopher Newall for pointing out the considerable evidence against the Pinwell attribution.
Pinwell produced an engraving entitled *Hop-
gathering*, for the periodical *Good Words* in 1868
(p. 424), but this is very different from *Hop-
picking*, although its main subject, the yearning of
a young man for a girl who seems indifferent to
him, is shared by the watercolour. In the Ashmolean Museum, Oxford, there is a watercolour
copy of the righthand side of *Hop-picking*, which
has been attributed to Pinwell at least since it was
given to the museum in 1938 by Villiers David.

GEORGE JOHN PINWELL (O.W.S.)
1842–1875
80
The Gleaners, c. 1870
On verso: sketches of figures, including a
woman bending, in pen and ink and pencil
Watercolour and body colour, with
scratching out; some outlines strengthened
in pencil
6⅝ x 6⅜ (16.8 x 16.2)
Provenance: H. Reitlinger

Private collection

This watercolour, which probably comes
from a sketchbook, presents a view of gleaning which is very different from that of earlier English artists. Whereas earlier artists
had made use of the subject as an opportunity to depict charming women and children, Pinwell's gleaners are anonymous
figures hunched uncomfortably over their
work and dressed in sombre clothing. Pinwell probably knew of Jean-François Millet's
famous *Gleaners* of 1857 (Musée du Louvre,
Paris), and this precedent may have encour-

80

aged him to treat gleaning as an illustration of rural poverty and discomfort rather than a demonstration of benevolence.

Drawings such as this one, with its expressionist outlines, may have influenced Van Gogh, who saw the work of Pinwell and Walker during his stay in England from 1873 to 1876 and referred to them in 1885 when he was painting peasants at Neunen. Van Gogh wrote that they "did in England exactly what Maris, Israëls, Mauve, have done in Holland, namely restored nature

over convention, sentiment and impression over academic platitudes and dullness. . . . I remember peasants in the field by Pinwell [and] "The Harbour of Refuge" by Walker of which one might also say, *peints avec de la terre.*"[1]

Nottingham only

---

1. R. Pickvance, *English Influences on Vincent Van Gogh* (Arts Council, London, 1974), p. 20. The last phrase, "painted with earth," comes from Alfred Sensier's description of the work of Millet.

81

SIR GEORGE CLAUSEN (R.A.) *1852–1944*
81
Feeding Sheep, 1884
Signed and dated 1884, lower left
Pastel
9 x 14⅝ (24.8 x 37.1)
Provenance: Presented by the Conference
Committee of the Unitarian and Free
Christian Churches, 1929
References: K. McConkey, *Sir George
Clausen, R.A., 1852–1944* (Tyne and Wear
and Bradford Museums, 1980), no. 36

Whitworth Art Gallery, University of
Manchester

This is one of George Clausen's earliest
works in pastel. His exploration of the me-
dium indicates a growing concern with subtle atmospheric effects, increased by his
admiration for the pastels of Millet and
Degas. It shows the destination of the mangolds being trimmed in *Winter Work* (cat.
38): they are being placed in a root slicer before being fed to the sheep.

It is interesting to compare this depiction
of children engaged in hard labour in exposed, wintry conditions with the traditional
view of the idyllic life of the shepherd boy
(see cat. 19). Clausen followed the example
of British artists such as William Davis,
Frederick Shields and Fred Walker (see figs.
20, 21 and 22), as well as Jules Bastien-
Lepage, in exposing the hardships of young
agricultural labourers.[1] Such depictions had
topical significance in this period when legislation was being enacted to limit child labour in agriculture and to establish a system
of universal primary education.

1. Compare Clausen's *Ploughing* (1889; Aberdeen
Art Gallery) and *Bird Scaring, March* (1896;
Harris Museum and Art Gallery, Preston); and
Bastien-Lepage's *Pauvre Fauvette* (1881–82;
Glasgow City Art Gallery).

82

HELEN ALLINGHAM (R.W.S.) *1848–1926*
82
Harvest Field, c. 1890
Signed, lower right
Watercolour
5 x 8 (13 x 20)
Provenance: Chris Beetles Watercolours,
from whom bought by present owner

Private collection, courtesy Chris Beetles
Ltd., St. James's, London

Helen Allingham is best known for her cottage scenes, but she also painted a few agricultural landscapes such as this one. The
presence of mother, child and (presumably)
father implies, as do so many nineteenth-
century harvest scenes, that agricultural labour can easily be combined with a happy
family life, unlike urban occupations in
which families were split up.

Allingham does not appear to have been
particularly interested in the details of agricultural practice. The crop is unusually
short, and one would expect the man to be
reaping while the woman bound the sheaves.
Nevertheless, the watercolour is very
charming and illustrates some of the most
appealing features of harvest scenes, such as
the colour contrast of golden corn and deep
green foliage, and the emphasis on attractive
women and children.

JOHN WILLIAM NORTH (A.R.A.,
R.W.S.) *1842–1924*
83
Gleaners, Coast of Somerset, 1890
Signed and dated 1890
Watercolour with body colour
26 x 36¾ (66 x 93.3)
Provenance: Chris Beetles Watercolours,
from whom bought by present owner
First exhibited: Royal Society of Painters in
Water-Colours, 1891 (no. 67)

83 (see pl. 34)

References: Herbert Alexander, R.W.S., "John William North, A.R.A., R.W.S. (1842–1924)," *Old Water-Colour Society's Club*, vol. 5 (London, 1928), pp. 35–59

Private collection, courtesy Chris Beetles Ltd., St. James's, London

North was a close friend of Fred Walker; it was while staying with North at his farmhouse in the Quantocks that Walker painted *The Plough* in 1869. Two years earlier, North, Walker and George John Pinwell had all contributed illustrations to *Wayside Posies* (1867). Walker and Pinwell died young, in 1875, but North lived on to perfect his own very individual style, which was much admired by younger artists such as Hubert Herkomer. His oils and watercolours often focus on the poetry of wintry, misty landscapes: one of these, *Winter Sun*, was bought by the Chantrey Fund in 1891.

Gleaners, however, is a summer landscape: a view of a harvest field on the edge of the Quantocks, in which the cultivated land in the foreground is contrasted with the moorland behind. Although it does not seem to be a topographically exact depiction of the area, the painting is strongly reminiscent of the view towards East Quantoxhead and the sea. Young girls are gleaning, most of them with their heads down, concentrating on their work. The one on the far left, however, holds up her gleanings as if encouraging her friend on the far right to join in.

North apparently was known for his sympathies with the grievances of agricultural labourers. He was a friend of Richard Jefferies, the writer, and when Herbert Alexander visited Somerset after North's death he records meeting an old woodman who remembered North as "a sturdy champion of the poor" who had written letters to the papers opposing the Game Laws and had stopped "the common land being taken from the poor."[1]

The subject of gleaning, therefore, probably appealed to him as a demonstration of the survival of the ancient rights of the poor, although, like Jefferies, he was aware that it was very hard work. This watercolour seems to refer to both aspects of the subject, with some figures illustrating the back-breaking labour of gleaning while others celebrate its benefits.

---

1. Alexander, "John William North," p. 36.

84

Note: Where different copies of the same print are being shown at Nottingham and Yale, the lender to the Nottingham showing is listed first.

WILLIAM BYRNE *1743–1805*
after THOMAS HEARNE (F.S.A.) *1744–1817*
84
Cornfield, 1780–85
Engraving
7¼ x 8¼ (18.3 x 21)
References: D. Morris, *Thomas Hearne and His Landscape* (London, 1989), pp. 58–63

Trustees of the British Museum

Thomas Hearne produced a set of 12 prints entitled "Rural Sports" in the early 1780s: *Cornfield* and *Ploughing* (cat. 84 and 85) both come from this series. In these prints Hearne shows more careful attention to agricultural processes than in his illustrations to James Thomson's *Seasons* (see cat. 40). Their existence suggests a growing interest in agriculture on the part of artists and patrons, perhaps as the result of the agricultural revolution.

WILLIAM BYRNE *1743–1815*
after THOMAS HEARNE (F.S.A.) *1744–1817*
85
Ploughing, 1780–85
Engraving
7¼ x 8¼ (18.3 x 21)
References: D. Morris, *Thomas Hearne and His Landscape* (London, 1989), pp. 58–63

Trustees of the British Museum

See cat. 84.

85

86

GEORGE STUBBS (A.R.A.) *1724–1806*
86

Haymakers, 1787
Stipple engraving with roulette work
19 x 26⅞ (48.3 x 68.2)
References: C. Lennox-Boyd, R. Dixon,
T. Clayton, *George Stubbs: The Complete
Engraved Works* (London, 1989), no. 89

Trustees of the British Museum
Yale Center for British Art, Paul Mellon
Collection

In 1787 Stubbs issued a pair of prints, *Haymakers* and *Reapers*, based on the paintings
with the same titles (Tate Gallery, London).
Copies of them are rare, suggesting that
they were not a popular success. Print
buyers seem to have preferred the more dramatic or sentimental depictions of rural labour by Francis Wheatley and Richard
Westall, which often feature attractive
young women and children.

87

Francesco Bartolozzi *1727–1815*
after Benjamin West (p.r.a.) *1738–1820*
87
The Reapers, 1790
Hand-coloured etching and engraving
19¾ x 24¾ (50.2 x 62.9)

Yale Center for British Art, Paul Mellon
Collection

Benjamin West's depictions of rural labour
usually present labourers as if they were figures from classical times, with Greek or Roman profiles and generalised draperies, far
removed from the workaday realities of late
eighteenth-century England.

Yale only

William Ward *1766–1826*
after James Ward (r.a.) *1769–1859*
88
Reaping, 1801
Mezzotint
18 x 23⅞ (45.7 x 60.7)

Yale Center for British Art, Paul Mellon
Collection

This print is based on an oil painting by
James Ward (untraced; in a private collection in Berkshire in the 1960s; photograph,
Paul Mellon Centre for Studies in British
Art, London). The realistic, weather-beaten
face of the labourer is reminiscent of Ward's
drawing of a mower (cat. 54).

Yale only

88

VALENTINE GREEN (A.R.A.) *1739–1813*
89
Ye Gen'rous Britons, Venerate the Plough, 1801
Coloured engraving
29½ x 21¼ (75 x 54)

Rural History Centre, University of Reading

An inscription announces that this print was dedicated "to the right honourable Lord Carrington, the Vice Presidents and the Rest of the Members of the Board of Agriculture." Its title comes from a line in James Thomson's *Seasons*.

J. C. EASLING
after J. M. W. TURNER (R.A.) *1775–1851*
90
Hedging and Ditching, 1812
Etching and mezzotint

7⅜ x 10¼ (18.7 x 26)
References: A. J. Finberg, *The History of Turner's Liber Studiorum, with a New Catalogue Raisonnée* (London, 1924), pp. 186–88

The Visitors of the Ashmolean Museum, Oxford
Yale Center for British Art, Paul Mellon Collection

This plate from the *Liber Studiorum* was based on a drawing made on Turner's journey back from Portsmouth in November 1807, after he had seen the Danish fleet, which had been captured by Britain in the war against France. Patriotic feelings may have prompted Turner at this time to see a deeper significance in humble everyday activity (compare cat. 8).

89

90

91

JOHN CHARLES VARRALL *fl. 1818–1848*
after J. M. W. TURNER (R.A.) *1775–1851*
91
Valle Crucis
Etching and engraving
6⅜ x 9¼ (16.2 x 23.5)

Trustees of the British Museum
Yale Center for British Art, Paul Mellon
Collection

This is one of the plates from Turner's *Picturesque Views in England and Wales*, based on a watercolour in the Manchester City Art Gallery (see E. Shanes, *Turner's England, 1810–38* [London, 1990], p. 176). It shows reapers and gleaners in what appears to be an open field in front of the abbey. For other representations of open fields, see cat. 63 and 73.

EDWARD CALVERT *1799–1883*
92
The Ploughman, 1827
Wood engraving
3¼ x 5⅛ (8.3 x 13)
References: R. Lister, *Samuel Palmer and "The Ancients"* (Fitzwilliam Museum, Cambridge, 1984), no. 113

The Visitors of the Ashmolean Museum, Oxford
Yale Center for British Art, Paul Mellon Collection

Calvert was a close friend of Samuel Palmer. This wood engraving represents the Christian ploughing the last furrow of life, with Christ, the good shepherd, in the top right-hand corner. It is strongly influenced by William Blake's woodcuts and, unlike Pal-

92

mer's work, has little connection with contemporary rural life. It does, however, make explicit the implicit religious meaning contained in Palmer's agricultural scenes.

EDWARD CALVERT 1799–1883

93

The Cyder Feast, 1828
Wood engraving
3 x 5⅛ (7.6 x 13)
References: R. Lister, *Samuel Palmer and "The Ancients"* (Fitzwilliam Museum, Cambridge, 1984), no. 114

The Visitors of the Ashmolean Museum, Oxford
Yale Center for British Art, Paul Mellon Collection

In this wood engraving, the mood is more pagan than Christian—indeed, it was a source of some distress to Palmer that

Calvert at this time was turning away from orthodox Christianity and feeling the attractions of the antique myths. Nevertheless, a sense of the sanctity of rural labour and the abundance of nature was common to both artists.

DAVID LUCAS 1802–1881
after JOHN CONSTABLE (R.A.) 1776–1837

94

Spring, 1830
Mezzotint
5⅛ x 9¾ (13 x 24.7)
References: A. Wilton, *Constable's "English Landscape Scenery,"* (London, 1979), pl. 4, p. 32

The Visitors of the Ashmolean Museum, Oxford
Yale Center for British Art, Paul Mellon Collection

93

94

This is one of the mezzotints from Constable's *English Landscape Scenery* (1830): it is based on an oil sketch (Victoria and Albert Museum, London) that shows the recently enclosed common being ploughed. Constable's letterpress does not, however, mention the social changes of the time, concentrating instead on the appearance of the clouds and "the joyous animation of the new season" of spring.

SAMUEL PALMER (R.W.S.) *1805–1881*
95
The Early Ploughman, begun before 1861
Etching, state VIII
5¼ x 7¾ (13.5 x 19.7)
References: R. Lister, *Samuel Palmer and His Etchings* (London, 1969), no. 9

Tullie House, City Museum and Art Gallery, Carlisle
Yale Center for British Art, Paul Mellon Collection

Palmer took up etching in the 1840s and did sets of illustrations to Milton and Virgil, in

which the implements were appropriately archaic. These to some extent recaptured the visionary qualities of his Shoreham work.

ROBERT WALKER MACBETH *1848–1910*
after FRED WALKER (A.R.A.) *1840–1875*
96
The Plough, 1887
Etching with surface tone
22½ x 33⅞ (57 x 86)

Christopher and Jenny Newall

Fred Walker's painting *The Plough* (Tate Gallery, London) was exhibited at the Royal Academy in 1870 and was much admired both at the time and after Walker's death, when the etching by Macbeth helped to spread its fame. In the late 1860s Walker had established a reputation as a painter of the harsher realities of rural life, but *The Plough* was deliberately distanced from contemporary life: the ploughman wears medieval costume. Walker read the poetry of James Thomson and Robert Bloomfield to

95

96

97

prepare himself for painting the picture, and
it was exhibited with a quotation from the
Psalms—"man goeth forth unto his work
and to his labour until the evening"—
further emphasizing its timelessness.

Robert Walker Macbeth *1848–1910*
after George Heming Mason
(a.r.a.) *1818–1872*
97
The Harvest Moon
Etching with surface tone
12 ¾ x 34 ¼ (32.5 x 86.7)

Christopher and Jenny Newall

George Heming Mason's painting *The Harvest Moon* (Tate Gallery, London) was exhibited at the Royal Academy in 1872. Like
Fred Walker, Mason was very much admired
in his lifetime and in the decades following
his death. *The Harvest Moon* was his last
painting; it is idyllic in mood, with echoes of
Samuel Palmer. Unlike other harvest scenes
of the period, it shows reapers with scythes,
reflecting current practice; evidently, however, Mason included them for the swaying
rhythm that they impart to the composition
rather than for documentary reasons.

98

WILLIAM HENRY PYNE (O.W.S.)
1769–1843

98

Microcosm; or, a Picturesque Delineation of the Arts, Agriculture, Manufactures, &c. of Great Britain, in a Series of above a Thousand Groups of Small Figures for the Embellishment of Landscape . . . the Whole Accurately Drawn from Nature and Aquatinted by J. Hill; to Which Are Added, Explanations of the Plates, and Essays Relating to Various Subjects, by C. Gray

2d ed., 2 vols., published by W. H. Pyne, printed by S. Gosnell (London, 1806)
Shown: *Gleaners*

Pyne's *Microcosm* was originally issued as a subscription series, in 30 installments of four plates. The commentary by C. Gray appears to have been added for the two-volume edition of 1806. Its twofold purpose is indicated in the title: it was intended to spread knowledge about the useful arts of the country, but its primary purpose was to act as a repertoire of figure subjects for use in landscapes. In the introduction Pyne declared that the *Microcosm* was "calculated . . . to gratify the patriot. It is devoted to the domestic, rural and commercial scenery of Great Britain, and may be considered a monument, in the rustic style, raised to her glory." A significant proportion of the plates illustrate subjects with patriotic connotations, such as military life and shipping; and there are several devoted to agriculture, including scenes of hop picking, mowing, reaping, gleaning and ploughing, which could also be seen as part of the concerted national effort against Napoleonic France.

Pyne's *Microcosm* was a great success, and

99

there are several later editions. The plates illustrating agriculture encouraged artists to paint agricultural landscapes: some artists simply copied Pyne's groups, but others went out into the countryside and made their own studies of similar scenes.

JOHN D. HASSELL *d. 1825*

99

Aqua Pictura
Printed for the author by W. Wilson
(London, 1813)
Shown: 14, *Glostershire Team of Oxen*

Trustees of the British Museum
Yale Center for British Art, Paul Mellon Collection

This publication includes aquatints based on paintings by Francis Wheatley, J. M. W.

Turner and Robert Hills. Number 17 is based on Turner's watercolour *Autumn — Sowing of the Grain* (cat. 42), and no. 14 shows "A Glostershire [*sic*] Team of Oxen" by Hills, in which the oxen wear yokes similar to those studied by Hills in a sheet of drawings made from nature (no. 49).

DAVID COX (O.W.S.) *1783–1859*

100

A Treatise on Landscape Painting and Effect in Watercolours
Printed by J. Tyler for S. and J. Fuller
(London, 1814)
Shown: Plate 4, *Effect, Mid-Day*

Trustees of the British Museum
Yale Center for British Art, Paul Mellon Collection

100

101 (see pl. 33)

Cox's *Treatise*, intended for the use of students, contains several plates of agricultural subjects, including a spacious cornfield to illustrate noon light in *Effect, Mid-Day*.

GEORGE WALKER 1781–1856
101
The Costume of Yorkshire, Illustrated by a Series of Forty Engravings, Being Fac-Similes of Original Drawings . . . with Descriptions in English and French
Printed by T. Bensley for Longman, Hurst, Rees, Orme and Brown (London, 1814)
Shown: Plate 7, *Lowkers*

Yale Center for British Art, Paul Mellon Collection

This book concentrates on activities peculiar to the county of Yorkshire (and thus omits common agricultural subjects such as wheat harvesting). Like Pyne's *Microcosm*, it was published in wartime and the introduction declares a patriotic motive: "It is hoped the British heart will be warmed by the reflection that most of the humble individuals here depicted . . . contribute essentially by their honest labours to the glory and prosperity of their country." Plate 7, *Lowkers*, depicts the women and children who weeded the corn in spring.

THE GLEANERS.

PROOF   *Published Jan.y 1, 1814 by G. Shepheard & G. M. Brighty 17 Great Ormond Street Queen Square.*

102

GEORGE SHEPHEARD *1770?–1842*

102

Vignette Designs
Etched by G. M. Brighty, published by
George Shepheard and G. M. Brighty
(London, 1814–15)
Shown: Plate 1, no. 2, *Gleaners*

Trustees of the British Museum
Yale Center for British Art, Paul Mellon
Collection

This is a more poetic, less documentary
publication than *Microcosm* and *The Costume
of Yorkshire* (cat. 98 and 101). The plates
show women and children at work in the
fields, looking healthy, well dressed and attractive. The accompanying text refers to
descriptions of rural occupations in poetry,
such as the verses of James Thomson and
Robert Bloomfield.

Photographs

103

Note: Copies of the originals are shown in the exhibition.

103
Gleaners, 1857

Hulton Deutsch Collection, London

This early photograph should be compared with artistic representations of pretty, delicate gleaners. Note especially the stout boots and layers of clothing.

104
A Threshing Machine at Work, early 1860s

Rural History Centre, University of Reading

By the 1860s the threshing machine was a common sight in the countryside, but one that artists generally ignored.

105
Farmworkers at the Sixth Annual Trade Union Demonstration in the Frying Pan, Ham Hill, Yeovil, Whit Monday, 1877

National Union of Agricultural and Allied Workers; photograph courtesy Rural History Centre, University of Reading

Joseph Arch, the farmworkers' leader, is in the centre. (On the farmworkers' union, see Introduction, p. 00.)

Sir George Clausen (R.A.)
1852–1944
106
Woman in a Mangold Field, early 1880s

Royal Photographic Society, Bath; photograph courtesy Rural History Centre, University of Reading

104

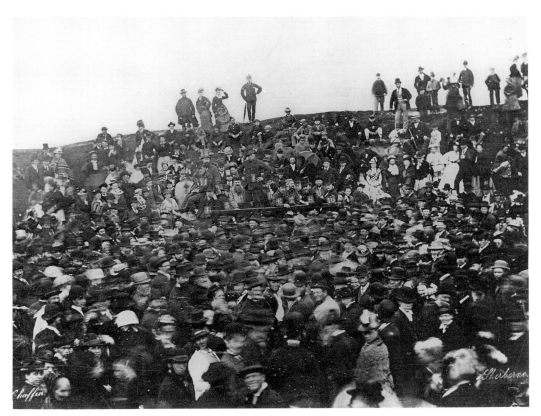

105

106

107

Clausen took his own photographs of field labourers. They are the earliest unposed photographs of farm labourers and can be considered equivalent to the sketchbook studies of earlier artists. This photograph was part of the preparation for *Winter Work* (cat. 38).

SIR GEORGE CLAUSEN (R.A.)
1852–1944
107
Labourer in a Stubble Field, early 1880s

Royal Photographic Society, Bath; photograph courtesy Rural History Centre, University of Reading

See cat. 106.

108
Hedger, 1890s

Hereford City Library; photograph courtesy Rural History Centre, University of Reading

This photograph can be compared with Brett's painting of a hedger at work (cat. 33).

109
Haymaking Scene, Garsington, 1890s

Oxford City Library

Many of the early photographs of farm-workers show groups of workers posing to-gether at the end of their labours. This photograph clearly demonstrates the in-

108

109

110

volorment of both sexes and all ages in the hay harvest.

110
Sheep-Shearing, Oxfordshire, c. 1896

Oxford City Library; photograph courtesy Rural History Centre, University of Reading

This is another posed photograph, of one of the sheep-shearing gangs who travelled round the country.

HENRY REYNOLDS
111
Labourers at Burgh, Suffolk, c. 1890

Suffolk Record Office

This shows a gang of mowers with scythes (with wooden cradles attached) who have been cutting wheat. From the mid-nineteenth century the scythe was increasingly used for the wheat harvest (scything was a quicker method of cutting), although artists preferred to show workers reaping with sickles. By the time this photograph was taken, however, even the scythe was an old-fashioned method. Photographers, like painters, tended to record the traditional practices that were disappearing, rather than the new ones involving reaping machines.

112
Women Harvesters in Norfolk, 1890s

Norwich Central Library

111

112

Like *Gleaners* (cat. 103), this photograph can be compared with the depiction of delicately pretty women workers by painters. These women are binding sheaves: a reaping machine can be seen in the background.

113
Ploughing: Ox Team, c. 1900

Oxford City Library

Oxen were still used for ploughing at the turn of the century and even later. The stunted ploughman is a reminder that not all farm labourers were robust and healthy: he appears to be no taller than the ploughboy.

114
Hop-Picking in Sussex, 1900

Rural History Centre, University of Reading

As in paintings of hop picking (cat. 18, 51, 70, and 79), this photograph shows the predominance of rather smartly dressed women and children in the hop field.

115
Harvesting with a Crook Stick and Bagging Hook, c. 1900

Hereford City Library

Many photographs from this period show elderly labourers, perhaps because they tended to continue the old practices while the younger workers took charge of the machines. The average age of the labourer was rising, too, as the young men moved to the towns in search of opportunity.

113

114

115

Glossary

Anti-Corn Law League: An organisation founded in 1839 to advocate free trade in general and the repeal of the Corn Laws in particular. It was based in Manchester and led by Richard Cobden and John Bright, who argued that the Corn Laws kept the price of bread high and benefited land-owners.

binding: The practice of tying up sheaves of corn, usually done by women.

carrying: The carting of the crop in waggons to the farmyard or rick.

commons: Lands in common ownership, that is, available for use by all the inhabitants of a parish, typically for grazing livestock and gathering fuel.

corn: A generic term covering such cereal crops as wheat, barley, and oats.

Corn Laws: Laws introduced by the British Parliament, from 1804 onwards, to impose a protective duty on foreign corn. The 1815 Corn Law permitted the import of foreign corn only when the price of wheat in England had reached 80s. a quarter. The Corn Laws were modified in 1828 and 1842 and finally repealed in 1846.

day labourer: An agricultural labourer with no security of employment, that is, employed on a day-to-day basis by a farmer and laid off without pay when there was no farm work, as at slack times of year or in bad weather.

Enclosure Acts: Acts of Parliament that allowed the common lands of a parish to be divided amongst private owners.

gleaning: The practice of picking up ears and stalks of wheat after the crop had been reaped. Poor women and children were generally allowed to do this for free.

harvest home: A feast given to workers by the farmer at the end of corn harvest.

haycock: A pile of cut grass in the process of turning into hay, left in the field to dry before being gathered onto a waggon and taken to the haystack.

mowing: Cutting grass, barley, wheat, or other grains with a scythe (or, later on, with a mowing machine).

open fields: The arable fields of a parish, farmed in long strips belonging to individual proprietors. Most of the remaining open fields were enclosed in the late eighteenth and early nineteenth centuries.

outdoor relief: Allowances, varying with the price of bread and the size of a labourer's family, paid to the poor in times of unemployment or to supplement low wages.

Poor Law: A system of providing relief for the poor and destitute of a parish, funded by the poor rates, which were levied on the better-off inhabitants.

Poor Law Amendment Act: An act of Parliament, passed in 1834; also called the New Poor Law. It ended outdoor relief for the able-bodied poor, who henceforth had to go into the workhouse to receive assistance.

reaping: Cutting wheat with a sickle.

Reform Act: In 1832, 1867 and 1884 acts of Parliament reformed the parliamentary system, correcting the representational imbalance between town and country, reducing the power of aristocratic patrons to get their nominees into Parliament and gradually extending the suffrage.

sheaf: A bundle of stalks of wheat, gathered together and bound with a straw rope.

stook: A group of sheaves placed together and left standing upright in a field to dry.

Swing riots: Outbreaks of machine breaking and arson, which affected the southern and eastern counties in the late summer and autumn of 1830 and, to a lesser extent, in 1831 and 1832; sometimes called "the last labourers' revolt."

tedding: Turning over cut grass to make hay.

Tolpuddle Martyrs: A group of six Dorset farm-workers, who were sentenced to transportation in 1834 for taking secret oaths to form a union. A public outcry secured their return from Australia in 1836.

yeoman: An independent farmer who cultivated his own land.

Select Bibliography

Additional literature on individual artists is cited in the catalogue entries.

Aikin, J. *The Calendar of Nature.* London, 1785.

Alexander, H. "John William North, A.R.A., R.W.S. (1842–1924)." *Old Water-Colour Society's Club,* vol. 5 (1928), pp. 35–59.

Art Journal. 1849–.

Athenaeum. 1830–.

Barrell, J. *The Idea of Landscape and the Sense of Place, 1730–1840: An Approach to the Poetry of John Clare.* Cambridge, 1972.

———. *The Dark Side of the Landscape: The Rural Poor in English Painting, 1730–1840.* Cambridge, 1980.

———. "Francis Wheatley's Rustic Hours." *Antique Dealer and Collector's Guide,* December 1982, pp. 39–42.

Barringer, T. *The Cole Family: Painters of the English Landscape, 1838–1915.* Exh. cat. Portsmouth, 1988.

Baskett, J., and D. Snelgrove. *The Drawings of Thomas Rowlandson in the Paul Mellon Collection.* London, 1977.

Bayard, J. *Works of Splendour and Imagination: The Exhibition Watercolour, 1770–1870.* Exh. cat. New Haven, 1981.

Beckett, O. *J. F. Herring and Sons: The Life and Works of J. F. Herring Senior and His Family.* London, 1981.

Beckett, R. B., ed. *John Constable's Correspondence.* 6 vols. Ipswich, 1962–1968.

Bermingham, A. *Landscape and Ideology: The English Rustic Tradition, 1740–1860.* Berkeley, Los Angeles, and London, 1986.

Billingham, R. *George Heming Mason.* Exh. cat. Stoke-on-Trent, 1982.

Bloomfield, R. *The Farmer's Boy.* London, 1800.

Blunt, Rev. J. J. *The Duties of the Parish Priest.* 1856.

Board of Agriculture. *The Agricultural State of the Kingdom in February, March and April 1816 . . .* London, 1816.

Bourne, G. *Change in the Village.* London, 1912.

Brettell, R. B., and C. B. Brettell. *Painters and the Peasant in the Nineteenth Century.* London, 1983.

Buck, A. *Dress in Eighteenth Century England.* London, 1979.

Butler, M. *Romantics, Rebels and Reactionaries: English Literature and Its Background, 1760–1830.* Oxford, 1981.

Butlin, M., and E. Joll. *The Paintings of J. M. W. Turner.* Rev. ed. 2 vols. New Haven and London, 1984.

Caird, J. *English Agriculture in 1850–1.* London, 1852.

Casteras, S., and R. Parkinson, eds. *Richard Redgrave, 1804–1888.* Exh. cat. New Haven and London, 1988.

Chadwick, O. *The Victorian Church.* 2 parts. London, 1971, 1972.

Chambers, J. D., and G. E. Mingay. *The Agricultural Revolution, 1750–1880.* London, 1966.

Chignell, R. *The Life and Paintings of George Vicat Cole.* 3 vols. London, 1898.

Clare, J. *The Shepherd's Calendar.* London, 1827.

Clarke, M., and N. Penny, eds. *The Arrogant Connoisseur: Richard Payne Knight, 1751–1824.* Exh. cat. Manchester, 1982.

Coats, A. W., ed. *Poverty in the Victorian Age.* Vol. 3, *Charity, 1815–70.* London, 1973.

Cobbett, W. *Rural Rides.* London, 1830.

Collins, E. J. T. *Sickle to Combine: A Review of Harvest Techniques from 1800 to the Present Day.* Reading, 1969.

Collins, Wilkie. *Memoirs of the Life of William Collins, Esq., R.A.* 2 vols. 1848. Reprint. London, 1978.

Colls, R., and P. Dodds, eds. *Englishness: Politics and Culture, 1880–1920*. London, 1986.

Cook, E. T., and A. Wedderburn, eds. *The Works of John Ruskin*. 35 vols. London, 1903–12.

Cosgrove, D., and S. Daniels, eds. *The Iconography of Landscape*. Cambridge, 1988.

Cowper, W. *The Task*. London, 1785.

Crabbe, G. *The Village*. London, 1783.

Creasey, J. *Victorian and Edwardian Country Life from Old Photographs*. London, 1977.

Crouan, K. *John Linnell: A Centennial Exhibition*. Exh. cat. Cambridge, 1982.

Disraeli, B. *Sybil, or, The Two Nations*. London, 1845.

Dunbabin, J. P., ed. *Rural Discontent in Nineteenth Century Britain*. London, 1974.

Egerton, J. *The Paul Mellon Collection: British Sporting and Animal Paintings, 1655–1867*. London, 1978.

————. *George Stubbs, 1724–1806*. Exh. cat. Tate Gallery, 1984.

Egerton, J., and D. Snelgrove. *The Paul Mellon Collection: British Sporting and Animal Drawings, c. 1500–1850*. London, 1978.

Emsley, C. *British Society and the French Wars, 1793–1815*. London, 1979.

Evans, G. E. *The Horse in the Furrow*. London, 1960.

Everett, N. "Country Justice: The Literature of Landscape Improvement and English Conservatism, with Particular Reference to the 1790s." Ph.D. diss., Cambridge University, 1977.

Fay, C. R. *The Corn Laws and Social England*. Cambridge, 1932.

Fussell, G. E., and K. R. Fussell. *The English Countryman: His Life and Work, A.D. 1500–1900*. London, 1955.

Gage, J. *A Decade of English Naturalism, 1810–20*. Exh. cat. Norwich and London, 1969.

Gash, N. *Reaction and Reconstruction in British Politics, 1832–52*. Oxford, 1965.

Glyde, J. *Suffolk in the Nineteenth Century*. London, 1856.

Gold, J. R., and J. Burgess, eds. *Valued Environments*. London, 1982.

Goldsmith, O. *The Deserted Village*. London, 1770.

Grigson, G. *Samuel Palmer: The Visionary Years*. London, 1947.

Hamerton, P. G. *Landscape*. London, 1885.

Hammond, J. L., and B. Hammond. *The Village Labourer, 1760–1832: A Study in the Government of England before the Reform Bill*. London, 1913.

Hardy, T. *The Mayor of Casterbridge*. London, 1886.

————. *Tess of the d'Urbervilles*. London, 1891.

Harington, E. *A Schizzo on the Genius of Man; in which among various subjects, the merit of Mr Thomas Barker, the celebrated young painter of Bath, is particularly considered*. Bath, 1793.

Harrison, B. "Philanthropy and the Victorians." *Victorian Studies*, vol. 9 (1966), pp. 353–74.

"Harvest." *Cornhill Magazine*, vol. 12, September 1865, pp. 358–63.

Hawes. L. *Presences of Nature: British Landscape, 1780–1830*. Exh. cat. New Haven, 1982.

Hemingway, A. "Meaning in Cotman's Norfolk Subjects." *Art History*, vol. 7, no. 1 (March 1984), pp. 57–77.

————. *Landscape Imagery and Urban Culture in Early Nineteenth Century Britain*. Cambridge, 1992.

Hobsbawm, E. J., and G. Rudé. *Captain Swing*. London, 1969.

Hone, W. *The Every-Day Book, or, Everlasting Calendar of Popular Amusements*. 2 vols. London, 1826.

Horn, P. *Joseph Arch*. Kineton, 1971.

————. *The Victorian Country Child*. Kineton, 1974.

————. *Labouring Life in the Victorian Countryside*. London, 1976.

————. *The Rural World: Social Change in the British Countryside, 1750–1850*. London, 1980.

Hoskins, W. G. *The Making of the English Landscape*. London, 1955, 1977.

Houghton, W. E. *The Victorian Frame of Mind.* London, 1957.

Howitt, M., ed. *The Pictorial Calendar of the Seasons.* London, 1854.

Howitt, W. *The Book of the Seasons; or, The Calendar of Nature.* 2d ed. London, 1833.

———. *The Year-Book of the Country; or, The Field, the Forest and the Fireside.* London, 1850.

Howkins, A. *Reshaping Rural England: A Social History, 1850–1925.* London, 1991.

Hunt, L. *The Months, Descriptive of the Successive Beauties of the Year.* London, 1821.

Inglis, K. S. *Churches and the Working Class in Victorian England.* London, 1963.

Jefferies, R. *The Life of the Fields.* London, 1884.

———. *The Toilers of the Field.* London, 1892.

———. *Landscapes and Labour.* With an introduction by J. Pearson. Bradford-on-Avon, 1979.

Keith, W. J. *The Rural Tradition.* Sussex, 1975.

King, P. "Customary Rights and Women's Earnings: The Importance of Gleaning to the Rural Labouring Poor, 1750–1850." *Economic History Review,* vol. 44, no. 3 (1991), pp. 461–76.

Kingsley, C. *Yeast.* London, 1851.

Kitson Clark, G. *Churchmen and the Condition of England: 1832–85.* London, 1973.

Kriz, K. D. "An English Arcadia Revisited and Reassessed: Holman Hunt's *The Hireling Shepherd* and the Rural Tradition." *Art History,* vol. 10, no. 4 (December 1987), pp. 475–91.

Lister, R. *Catalogue Raisonné of the Works of Samuel Palmer.* Cambridge, 1988.

Lister, R., ed. *The Letters of Samuel Palmer.* 2 vols. Oxford, 1974.

McConkey, K. "The Bouguereau of the Naturalists: Bastien-Lepage and British Art." *Art History,* vol. 1, no. 3 (September 1978), pp. 371–82.

———. *Sir George Clausen, R.A., 1852–1944.* Exh. cat. Bradford, 1980.

McCord, N. *The Anti-Corn Law League, 1838–46.* London, 1958.

Marillier, H. C. *The Liverpool School of Painters.* London, 1904.

Marks, J. G. *Life and Letters of Frederick Walker, A.R.A.* London, 1896.

Martin, E. W. *The Secret People: English Village Life after 1750.* London, 1954.

Mingay, G. E. *Rural Life in Victorian England.* London, 1977.

Mingay, G. E., ed. *The Agricultural Revolution: Changes in Agriculture, 1650–1880.* London, 1977.

———. *The Victorian Countryside.* 2 vols. London, 1981.

The Mirror of the Months. London, 1826.

Morgan, D. "Harvesting in the Nineteenth Century." M.A. thesis, University of Warwick, 1971.

Morris, D. *Thomas Hearne and His Landscape.* London, 1989.

Olmsted, J. C., ed. *Victorian Painting: Essays and Reviews.* Vol. 1, *1832–48.* London, 1980.

Owen, D. *English Philanthropy, 1660–1960.* Oxford, 1965.

Palmer, A. H. *The Life and Letters of Samuel Palmer.* London, 1892.

Parkinson, R. *Catalogue of British Oil Paintings, 1820–1860.* Victoria and Albert Museum, London, 1990.

Parris, L., and I. Fleming-Williams. *Constable.* Exh. cat. Tate Gallery, London, 1991.

Payne, C. "The Agricultural Landscape in English Painting c. 1785–1885." Ph.D. diss., University of London, 1985.

———. "Boundless Harvests: Representations of Open Fields and Gleaning in Early Nineteenth Century England." *Turner Studies,* vol. 2, no. 1 (Summer 1991), pp. 7–15.

The Pre-Raphaelites. Exh. cat. Tate Gallery, London, 1984.

Pyne, W. H. *Etchings of Rustic Figures for the Embellishment of Landscape.* 1815.

———. *Rustic Figures in Imitation of Chalk.* London, 1817.

Redgrave, F. M. *Richard Redgrave: A Memoir Compiled from His Diary.* London, 1891.

Reynolds, G. *Catalogue of the Constable Collection at the Victoria and Albert Museum.* 1960.

———. *The Later Paintings and Drawings of John Constable.* 2 vols. New Haven and London, 1984.

Robert Hills, 1769–1844. Exh. cat. Albany Gallery, London, 1968.

Roberts, M. "Sickles and Scythes: Women's Work and Men's Work at Harvest Time." *History Workshop Journal,* 1979, pp. 3–28.

Rodee, H. D. "The Dreary Landscape as a Background for Scenes of Rural Poverty in Victorian Painting." *Art Journal,* vol. 36, no. 4 (Summer 1977), pp. 307–13.

Rose, M. E. *The English Poor Law, 1780–1930.* Newton Abbot, 1971.

Rosenthal, M. *British Landscape Painting.* London, 1982.

———. *Constable: The Painter and His Landscape.* New Haven and London, 1983.

Samuel, R., ed. *Village Life and Labour.* Oxford, 1975.

Shanes, E. *Turner's England, 1810–38.* London, 1990.

Smith, H. *Peter DeWint.* London, 1982.

Snell, K. D. M. *Annals of the Labouring Poor: Social Change and Agrarian England, 1660–1900.* London, 1985.

Southey, R. *Essays, Moral and Political.* 2 vols. London, 1832.

Spargo, D., ed. *This Land Is Our Land.* Exh. cat. London, 1989.

Staley, A. *The Pre-Raphaelite Landscape.* Oxford, 1973.

Story, A. T. *The Life of John Linnell.* 2 vols. London, 1892.

Stratton, J. M., and J. H. Brown. *Agricultural Records, A.D. 220–1977.* London, 1978.

Surtees, V., ed. *The Diary of Ford Madox Brown.* New Haven and London, 1981.

Taylor, B. *Joshua Cristall, 1768–1847.* Exh. cat. Victoria and Albert Museum, London, 1975.

Thompson, D. *Change and Tradition in Rural England.* Cambridge, 1980.

Thompson, E. P. *The Making of the English Working Class.* London, 1963.

Thomson, J. *The Seasons.* Rev. ed. London, 1746.

Tibble, J. W., ed. *The Poems of John Clare.* London, 1935.

Tibble, J. W., and A. Tibble, eds. *The Prose of John Clare.* London, 1951.

———. *The Letters of John Clare.* London, 1970.

Titterington, C., and T. Wilcox. *William Turner of Oxford (1789–1862).* Exh. cat. Woodstock (Oxon.), 1984.

Turner, J. *The Politics of Landscape.* Oxford, 1979.

Turner, M. *Enclosures in History, 1750–1830.* London, 1984.

Uwins, S. *A Memoir of Thomas Uwins, R.A.* 1858. Reprint. London, 1978.

Watson, H. C. "The Agrarian Revolution and Its Relationship to British Art, 1700–1900." M.A. thesis, Royal College of Art, London, 1980.

Webster, M. *Francis Wheatley.* New Haven and London, 1970.

Wiener, M. *English Culture and the Decline of the Industrial Spirit, 1850–1980.* Cambridge, 1981.

Wilcox, S., and C. Newall. *Victorian Landscape Watercolors.* Exh. cat. New York, 1992.

Wildman, S., R. Lockett, and J. Murdoch. *David Cox, 1783–1859.* Exh. cat. Birmingham, 1983.

Williams, M. *Thomas Hardy and Rural England.* London, 1972.

Williams, R. *The Country and the City.* London, 1973.

Williamson, G. C. *George J. Pinwell and His Works.* London, 1900.

Wilton, A. *The Life and Work of J. M. W. Turner.* London, 1979.

Wordsworth, W. *Lyrical Ballads.* London, 1800.

Wrigley, C. J., ed. *Victorian Social Conscience: The Working Classes in the Victorian Age.* Vol. 4, *Rural Conditions, 1815–70.* London, 1973.

Index

Aesthetic movement, 63, 124

Agricultural Children's Act (1873), 15

Agricultural Gangs Act (1867), 63

Agricultural landscapes: in aesthetic theory, 48–49; in European landscape tradition, 48; in exhibitions, 47; patronage, 47–48, 51, 54, 73*nn*1, 2, 75*n*27, 84, 107, 142

Agricultural workers: clothing, 32, 83, 102, 130–31, 137–40, 149; diet, 10–12, 57, 87; family life, 32, 56–57, 60, 86, 116–17, 121, 142, 177; industriousness, 31–32, 52, 67*n*3, 71*n*3, 121, 145; living conditions, 7, 57, 68*n*9; piety, 32–35, 57, 72*n*26, 86; unions, 8–9, 200; virtues, 31–35, 51, 80, 86, 110; wages, 7, 16, 28–29; working conditions, 7–8

Aikin, John, 37, 39, 157

Allingham, Helen: *Harvest Field*, **cat. 82**

Allnutt, John, 98

Anti-Corn Law League, 9, 13, 41, 58, 209

Arch, Joseph, 9, 120*n*2, 200

Aristocracy. *See* Landowners

Barker, Thomas, of Bath, 45, 106; *Old Man with a Staff*, **cat. 2, pl. 1**; *Sheep Shearing*, **cat. 9, pl. 6**; *The Woodman*, **cat. 1**, 51

Barley, harvesting of, 16, 27–28

Barns, 58, 137, 170

Bartolozzi (engraver), **cat. 87**

Bastien-Lepage, Jules, 63, 126, 176; *Hay Harvest (Les Foins)* **fig. 26**, 64

Beans, cultivation of, 19, 58

Beavis, Richard: *Building a Rick*, **cat. 76**

Benevolence. *See* Charity

Bentham, Jeremy, 37; Benthamites, 58

Biblical references to agriculture, 27, 33, 37–39, 72*n*36, 122–23, 130, 192

Blake, William, 55, 102, 188

Bloomfield, Robert, 17, 18, 51, 85, 190, 197; *The Farmer's Boy*, 26, 71*n*7, 98, 101

Bonheur, Rosa: *Ploughing Scene*, 171

Boucher, François, 24, 49, 81; *Shepherd Piping to a Shepherdess*, **fig. 7**, 25

Boyce, George Price: *Old Barn at Whitchurch*, **cat. 75**, 58, 105

Breton, Jules, 61, 70*n*49

Brett, John, 58; *The Hedger*, **cat. 33, pl. 18**, 202; *The Stonebreaker*, **fig. 29**, 118–19

Theocritus, 24

Thomson, James: *The Seasons*, 24, 26, 40, 43, 56, 71*n*7, 84, 130, 182, 185, 190, 197

Threshing, 16

Threshing machines, 21, 23, 70*n*55, 200

Tolpuddle martyrs, 8, 210

Tories, 12–13, 15

Turner, Joseph Mallord William, 16, 45, 48, 52–54, 74*n*22, 121, 172; *Autumn—Sowing of the Grain*, **cat. 42**, 15, 195; *Harvest Dinner, Kingston Bank* 144; *Harvest Home*, **fig. 5**, 18–19; *Hedging and Ditching*, **cat. 90**, 120; *Hylton Castle, County Durham*, **cat. 61**; *Lancaster, from the Aqueduct Bridge*, **cat. 64**; *Picturesque Views in England and Wales*, 54, 132, 188; *Ploughing*, 132; *Ploughing Up Turnips, near Slough*, **cat. 8, pl. 5**; *Valle Crucis*, **cat. 91**

Turner, William, of Oxford, 52, 54; *Haymaking, Study from Nature, in Osney Meadow*, **cat. 73, pl. 30**, 157

Turnips, 19, 88–89, 110

Unions. *See* Agricultural workers

United States, 2, 14–15, 21, 115

Uwins, Thomas, 20, 52; *A Buckinghamshire Gleaner*, **cat. 57**; *Haymakers at Dinner*, **cat. 59, pl. 27**, 149; *A Man Leaning on a Pitchfork*, **cat. 58**

Van Gogh, Vincent, 63, 175

Varley, Cornelius, 52; *Farm Buildings with Stack Makers*, **cat. 46**

Varley, John, 52, 143

Varrall, J. C. (engraver), **cat. 91**

Vincent, George, 54; *Trowse Meadows, near Norwich*, **cat. 17, pl. 11**

Virgil, 24, 145, 190

Wages. *See* Agricultural workers

Wales, 3, 92–93, 96, 106, 130–31, 143

Walker, Fred, 26, 61–63, 75*n*45, 124, 126, 173, 175, 176; *The Plough*, **fig. 23**, **cat. 96**, 62–63, 71*n*7, 178, 190; *The Violet Field*, **fig. 22**, 61

Walker, George: *The Costume of Yorkshire*, **cat. 101, pl. 33**

Wallis, Henry: *The Stonebreaker*, **fig. 1**, 10, 58, 75*n*38, 118–19

Ward, James, 45, 52, 137, 153; *Landscape with Farm and Corn Stooks*, **cat. 45**; *Melrose Abbey*, 135; *Reaping*, **cat. 88**; *A Wiltshire Peasant*, **cat. 54**, 8, 149, 184

Ward, William (engraver), **cat. 88**

Webster, Thomas: *Good Night*, **fig. 12**, 34–35

West, Benjamin, 84; *The Reapers*, **cat. 87**

Westall, Richard, 183; *A Storm in Harvest*, **cat. 5, pl. 3**, 51, 152

Wheat, harvesting of, 15–18, 25, 27–29, 39–40, 70*n*44, 82–83

Wheatley, Francis, 51, 83, 153, 183, 195; *Evening*, **cat. 7**; *The Hay Cart*, **cat. 3**; *Noon*, **cat. 6, pl. 4**, 32

Whigs, 12, 14

Whistler, James Abbot McNeill, 124

Whitbread, Samuel, 51, 84

Wilkie, David, 3

Williamson, Daniel Alexander: *Ploughing*, **cat. 77, pl. 31**

Willis, H. Brittan, 171

Wilson, John ("Christopher North"), 27–29

Wilson, Richard, 48

Witherington, William Frederick: *Stacking Hay*, **fig. 18**, 56–57

Women in agriculture, 7, 32, 101, 106, 121, 204–6

Wordsworth, William, 26, 50, 74*n*11

Wright, Joseph, 84

Yeomen, 7, 12, 152–53, 210

Young, Arthur, 12